# Such a Good Boy

## How a Pampered Son's Greed Led to Murder

D0908711

## Lisa Hobbs Birnie

**Macmillan Canada**
**Toronto**

**Canadian Cataloguing in Publication Data**

Lisa Hobbs Birnie, date.
  Such a good boy: how a pampered son's greed led to murder

ISBN 0-7715-9153-5

1. Huenemann, Darren.   2. Murder – British Columbia – Delta.
3. Trials (Murder) – British Columbia – Delta.   4. Juvenile
homicide – British Columbia – Delta.     I. Title.

HV6535.I43B57 1992     364.1'523'092     C92-094317-9

1  2  3  4  5  FR  96  95  94  93  92

Cover design by Tania Craan

Macmillan Canada wishes to thank the Canada Council for supporting its publishing program.

Macmillan Canada
A Division of Canada Publishing Corporation
Toronto, Ontario, Canada

Printed in Canada

# Contents

**Caligula:** ...I want the moon, or happiness, or eternal life—something, in fact, that may sound crazy, but which isn't of this world.

**Helicon:** That's sound enough in theory. Only, in practice one can't carry it through to its conclusion.

**Caligula:** *[rising to his feet but still with perfect calmness]* You're wrong there. It's just because no one dares to follow up his ideas to the end that nothing is achieved. All that's needed, I should say, is to be logical right through, at all costs. ...death is not the point; it's no more than the symbol of a truth that makes the moon essential to me. ...

**Helicon:** May I ask what it is, this truth that you've discovered?

**Caligula:** Men die; and they are not happy.

Albert Camus
*Caligula*, Act 1

# DISCOVERIES

## October 5, 1990, Saanich, Vancouver Island, British Columbia

D r. Ralph Huenemann, a professor in the School of Administration and director of the Centre for Asia-Pacific Initiatives at
the University of Victoria, British Columbia, liked to keep his six-
foot-plus thin form in top physical condition. That Friday afternoon, as he did regularly, he booked a ball machine at the Oak Bay
Recreational Club for 5 p.m., practiced his tennis strokes for about
an hour, then drove to his elegant home in the Ten Mile Point
district of Saanich to await the return of his wife, Sharon, from the
mainland. The sprawling municipality of Saanich, until recently a
community of small farms and comfortable homes and now rapidly
developing as a luxury retirement area, lies generally north of
Victoria on Vancouver Island. It is partway to the ferry terminal at
Swartz Bay, where the ferries leave for Tsawwassen on the
British Columbia mainland, 24 miles away.

Darren, his eighteen-year-old stepson, whom he'd helped
raise for fourteen years, was already home. It was about 7 p.m.
Both Darren and his school friend Amanda Cousins were in the
kitchen, preparing dinner. Darren liked doing this when his
mother was late, even if he himself planned to eat out with
friends. Ralph paused at the doorway to briefly chat with the two
teenagers, then went to his bedroom, intending, as usual, to hold
dinner until his wife's return. Sometime after seven Amanda
went upstairs to watch television, and at about eight-thirty both
Amanda and Darren left the house, telling Ralph they were going

downtown. Ralph himself then went upstairs to the rec room to watch some television while he waited.

Ralph Huenemann was faintly surprised when Sharon didn't show up as usual a little after nine. Her routine was well established. Every second Wednesday she went to Tsawwassen to help her mother, Doris Leatherbarrow, with her retailing business. She drove her car to the Swartz Bay terminal, parked it, walked onto the ferry, and was met by Doris on the other side. On Friday evening she caught the seven o'clock ferry back.

This week Sharon had been quite definite about returning Friday evening. She and Ralph were seeing a real-estate agent early the next morning about selling their home and purchasing a new one. Sharon had developed a strong dislike for their three-bedroom, French provincial–style home—built to their specifications three years earlier—and after months of looking had finally found the house of her dreams. Situated in the posh Oak Bay area of Victoria, it was a Samuel Maclure–designed early nineteen-hundreds classic that had recently been designated a heritage home by the city's planning department. The chance to buy such a unique house, which exuded history and status, was too important for Sharon to pass up.

At about 10 p.m., or perhaps 10:30, Darren returned, dropping by the rec room to say good-night. He'd taken Amanda home, he said, and was going to bed. Lulled by exercise, end-of-the-week weariness, and television, Ralph Huenemann fell asleep. When he awoke the television was still on, the clock said 12:06 a.m., and Sharon still was not home.

"I phoned the ferry corporation and asked if a woman was there on the parking lot having trouble with her car," he later testified. "And there was. But it was a Volkswagen and I knew it wasn't her. I then phoned the police—the Saanich police or the RCMP, I'm not sure which. They suggested I drive the route and see if she'd had car trouble."

At around twenty minutes after midnight, still in his tennis shorts, Ralph pulled out of his double-car garage and set out for the terminal at Swartz Bay, about a twenty-minute drive on

Highway 17. As he drove, he scanned the opposite side of the road to see if by any chance Sharon's car stood there, stalled or maybe in some sort of accident.

When he reached the vast concrete parking lot at the ferry terminal, he had his answer. Sharon's 1990 Nissan Axxess sat parked, locked, wet with dew, on the well-lit deserted lot.

"I knew then that something was wrong," Huenemann said afterward in court. He drove his car across the empty lanes to one of the booths at the ferry terminal, parked it, and phoned Doris Leatherbarrow in Tsawwassen, which is part of the municipality of Delta.

"There was no answer. I let it ring. And then I called the police in Delta. By then it was about 1 a.m. or maybe 1:30. I told the police I couldn't get anyone at that number and asked them if they would go to the house and do a check. The Delta police said they were having a problem...I don't know...something to do with an unruly prisoner...and they asked for my number.

"I went home and waited. I didn't hear from them. I phoned again and said, 'Please go to the home!' I phoned them again at 3:30 a.m. and then they said that they had no news to report but that I should wait by the phone. I phoned again at 5:30 or 6:00 a.m. and they still had nothing to report, and they, whoever it was, told me to get off the line so as not to tie up the police phone number.

"I sat there for a few minutes and then the front doorbell rang. Looking out the window, I saw what I took to be an unmarked police car and two plainclothesmen standing by the door."

## October 6, about 2 a.m., Tsawwassen

Constable Darwin Drader was doing a routine patrol through the Delta area with a reserve constable, Anthony Rychkun, as his partner, when the call came to check on a private residence at 811 Forty-ninth Street in Tsawwassen. Something about a wife not having returned home and the husband unable to rouse anyone at his mother-in-law's, where his wife had been staying. It wasn't an emergency. In fact, it didn't sound like much of anything.

The town of Delta lies just inland from the coast, its sprawling suburbia surrounded by disused farmland still zoned for agriculture. The area through which Drader drove borders the empty flatlands that run down to the ferry terminal. It is marked by a large red-bricked First Baptist church, a strip of video shops, supermarkets, gas stations, restaurants, and drugstores that peter out in a wooded area that slopes up to the United States border. The homes off this main strip are well kept and prosperous. Even the more modest ranch-style bungalows have landscaped gardens front and back, and everywhere there are cedars, pines, and sometimes massive Douglas firs.

At 2:36 a.m. Drader arrived at the house on Forty-ninth Street.

"The house was partly lit," the ten-year veteran of the Delta force later testified. "I banged on the door several times. Three shelves were lit up in the kitchen. I tried the door and rang the bell. All the doors were locked except for the patio door, which was closed but slid open.

"I then returned to the police car, where Constable Rychkun said he'd found something. We returned to the house. The kitchen is adjacent to the carport and inside the house is a tiled dining area off the kitchen. Lying on the tiles, about eight feet from the door that opened onto the carport, was a body with a bloody head."

Peering through the window, the officers could just make out a second body—a smaller, younger female—also lying on her back, her head in a pool of blood. Drader returned to his car, called for a supervisor, backup, and the Identification section, and waited.

### October 6, about 4 a.m., Saanich

When the phone rang before dawn in the Saanich home of Sergeant Gordon Tregear, he and his wife, Betty, were dead asleep. Tregear reached for the receiver, muttered, listened, and hung up. He told Betty, who had also been wakened, to go back to sleep. There'd been a murder, he said; he was off to inform the family. He rolled out of bed, turned on a small sidelight, dressed quickly in the semidarkness, then drove to the Saanich police station, where Detective Murray Kilshaw was cooling his heels waiting for him.

It was cold and dark outside, the roads slick from a dew as heavy as rain. Tregear and Kilshaw knew only what the Delta police had told them. It was a double murder, and the victims were the wife and the mother-in-law of the man they were about to visit, a Ralph Huenemann, who lived on Gibson Court in the Ten Mile Point area.

This was the down side of the job—knocking on a stranger's door and announcing like some bloody angel of death that their child, or wife, or husband, or someone else they lived for was dead, done in by some creep. Both Tregear and Kilshaw had been police officers for more than twenty years, but it was still difficult to act kindly while distancing yourself from the pain that often exploded in your face, watching slyly for giveaway gestures or words. When it was murder, everyone became a suspect.

They arrived at the house at 6 a.m. First light was breaking. The slate roof, the double garage, the manicured lawn, the patterned brick driveway, and the splendid proportions of the large house were visible. They bespoke money, pride, and success. Tregear and Kilshaw parked on the street and walked across the drive to the white porticoed door.

''Where's my wife?'' The words tumbled out as Huenemann opened the door.

The officers indicated they wanted to see him inside and Huenemann let them in. The broad hall and the large room they entered were luxuriously furnished and immaculately maintained. Carpeting, drapes, couch, armchair, credenza—everything including the walls and ceiling were white or off-white.

The officers told Huenemann what they knew. At that moment, Darren Huenemann wandered into the room in his pajamas. Ralph Huenemann indicated to the police officers that the young man was his son, and taking Darren aside, he gently broke the terrible news. Darren's grief was instantaneous. Tears streaming down his face, he clutched at his stepfather, sobbing wildly.

"After the police left," Dr. Huenemann testified, "Darren and I both sat down on the kitchen floor and cried and cried and cried."

### October 6, 11 a.m., Tsawwassen

Despite the fact that they had retired, Sheila and John Kriss still got up early. Like John's sister, Doris Leatherbarrow, they had spent their lives in the retailing business, and had operated a chain of stores named Cloud 9. They were not yet sixty, had the health and money to do what they liked, and now found themselves so busy they wondered when they'd ever had time to work. This day was no different, except that it was Thanksgiving weekend and their son, Jim, his wife, Barbara, and their two children were down from Campbell River on Vancouver Island for a get-together and turkey dinner.

Sheila was making coffee, and John and Jim were sitting at the kitchen table talking, when the phone rang. John answered, and it was Ralph Huenemann.

Huenemann hesitated. "I'm really sorry," he said. "I'm really sorry...I have to tell you...Doris and Sharon have been murdered."

John stood clasping the receiver, numbed by the news. Then he said, "Ralph, are you feeling okay? What are you saying...what are you doing?"

This was not the first call that Ralph had had to make. The police had advised him to contact his relatives and friends so they would not learn about the deaths from the radio or television. His voice was calm but strained. "I'm sorry. It's true...Sharon and Doris are dead."

John turned from the phone and blurted the news to his wife. Sheila is the sort of woman everyone is at ease with. She's intelligent, straightforward, warm, feels deeply, and says little. John believes in calling the shots as he sees them. His original name was Kryciak, but after graduating in science from the University of British Columbia, he was told by his boss that a name change was a prerequisite to any advancement. "Kryciak" became "Kriss," he quit his job, graduated from McGill University with an M.B.A., and, together with Sheila, struck out on his own. This experience left him with little desire to mince words.

Now the two stood stunned, paralyzed with shock. All their lives they had been in constant touch with Doris. When they'd run the Cloud 9 chain they'd often been back and forth on the phone or in each other's stores a couple of times a day. Doris's Tsawwassen home was like a family convention center, a meeting spot where brothers and sisters and grandchildren got together to celebrate the big events of their family life.

Then they thought of Anne Ward, Doris's sister in Toronto, who seemed closer to Doris than any of them. When Doris went abroad, it was always with Anne. With anguish Sheila and John realized that Anne was all set to leave for a holiday in Paris with Doris the following Tuesday. From what Ralph had said, he had not contacted Anne. They phoned, but there was no answer. Then they called Doris's "baby" sister, Jean, and her husband, Ed Beketa, in Burnaby. But again no one was home. And then John—he later said he hardly knew what he was doing—jumped into his car and tore down the freeway to Tsawwassen.

"I wasn't rational. I don't know what I thought I could do. When I arrived there were police around, and I identified myself to someone standing in the driveway and walked toward the house. But someone shouted, 'You can't go in there,' and ordered me back.

"I said, 'What do you mean? It's my sister's house. I can't believe this. You're all out of your bloody minds. It isn't Doris and Sharon who're dead...I want to look at them...I know it's not them...' But they [the police] wouldn't let me in. They wouldn't let me near the house. I went to one neighbor's house and then another's, then noticed that two police officers were following me. I said to them, 'I'm not talking to you—go away.' But they talked some sense into me. They said they had to check me out, had to know who I was and what I was doing there. I made a statement and they drew it up, but I never signed it. Going home, I wondered why nobody had bothered to tell us, why Ralph hadn't phoned before eleven."

## October 9, Royal Columbian Hospital, New Westminster

The following Tuesday, pathologist Ruth Sellers performed autopsies on the two victims. The injuries she found later prompted prosecutor Sean Madigan to categorize the murders as "the most brutal and callous" of his lengthy career.

Dr. Sellers noted that Doris Leatherbarrow had suffered blunt-force injury to the right side of her head. Her left cheek was bruised, she had a broken right jaw, her right skull was crushed, and her ear, both fatty tissue and cartilage, was completely torn. Her throat had been cut, and the trachea totally severed. The knife had been plunged so deep it had gone into the body of vertebral column, totally severing it too.

Sharon Huenemann's throat had been slit from right to left, severing the jugular vein. There was also evidence of blunt-force injury to the head, with bruises, various lacerations, a fractured left skull, and a right skull fracture so deep it had bruised the brain.

John's demand to see and identify his sister was finally met on Thursday.

"When I went to the morgue to identify Doris, well...I really can't describe it," he said. "They had tilted Doris's head to the side. My mother, Nellie, was very tiny, very bright, sort of birdlike. I thought it was her. The shock was terrible."

# PART I

**Caligula:** What's this? None of you asks me why I've sentenced him to death? Good for you! I see you're growing quite intelligent. *[He nibbles an olive.]* It has dawned on you that a man needn't have done anything for him to die.

*Caligula*, Act 1

# DORIS

The world into which Doris Kryciak Leatherbarrow was born was one of an endless sky, roads that roll into a disappearing horizon, summer lightning that whips the burned stalks on the ground with purple fire, and winter winds that slice the dazzling, frozen fields like icy razors.

The landscape around Calder, Saskatchewan, was bitter, beautiful, and overwhelming, a battlefield between man, God, and nature since the beginning of time. Onofry Kryciak had been drawn there from his native Ukraine with the promise of a land grant from the Canadian government and the lure of a new, unknown life. He had been in his twenties—it was about 1913, his children think—and had come with all the hope and dogged energy of a man raised to believe fervently, almost equally, in God and the soil.

The land was scratch land, good for prairie dogs but useless to a farmer. It was here, however, that the 30-year-old émigré met Canadian-born Justyna Tkatchuk. Everyone called Justyna "Nellie." She was barely five feet, lively, slim, and fair haired, one of eleven surviving children in a family of thirteen. Her disposition was sunny and nonreligious; his was somber and Eastern Orthodox. When Nellie turned sixteen, she and Onofry Kryciak married.

Nellie was barely eighteen when Doris was born in December 1920. She was a sturdy child, fair haired like her mother, round faced, and contented, a first daughter destined to play the thankless role of mother's helper for as long as she lived in the farmhouse.

After giving up the grant land in disgust, Onofry took his meager savings, borrowed from the bank, and bought a small mixed farm. It was survival farming at its worst, the type of struggle that broke many families and produced a haunting pictorial history of a land peopled by hollow-eyed, grim-mouthed couples, old and gray before their time.

Onofry and Nellie, however, proved to be as tough as the land. Onofry would leave his bed before light broke, harness up the four horses, and plow until long after darkness fell. But no matter what he produced there was no market for it. He tried grain, but couldn't get rid of it. He tried potatoes, but couldn't give them away. It was the mid-1920s and the markets of the world were about to collapse.

There were six more babies in the next fifteen years—Alexander, Anne, Michael, John, Mary, and Jean. Nellie gave birth to them at home, laboring with the help of a neighbor's wife in one bedroom while the children were kept in the other. The tiny house had sawdust in the walls for insulation against subzero cold, barrels to catch the rainwater that ran from the roof's guttering, and an outdoor toilet that seemed a mile away.

The seven children slept in one bed. As they grew, Nellie set up a mattress for four on the floor, leaving three in the bed. Once a week a tub was dragged across the kitchen, filled with buckets of hot water that had been heated on the wood stove, and the children scrubbed. In the depth of winter they wore shoes, but in spring, summer, and fall they walked to the one-room schoolhouse barefooted. If the boys misbehaved, they got the strap: Onofry, blissfully ignorant of child psychology, found that even knowledge of the strap's existence worked wonders to keep the noise down and the brood in order. Nellie hadn't heard of child psychology either, but she had no need of it. Her instincts to understand and negotiate were as natural as breathing. In the Kryciak household she was the court of last resort, and it was a rare case indeed when she didn't come down on the side of the defendant.

As Doris grew, so did her responsibilities and her skills. In some of the children's memories, she was as much a little mother as a sister. Nellie taught her to knit socks, gloves, tuques, sweaters; bake the bread; wash and dry the endless diapers; clean the house; make the meals; and keep the children in order.

Doris was a good student, competent and well organized, but at fifteen she quit school. Perhaps she felt schooling was futile, perhaps she felt she was needed at home. If she was like a mother to the smaller children, she was almost like a younger sister to her own mother. In winter she'd be up and out, hitching up the horse and buggy and taking the younger ones to school. Seven hours later she'd be back at the school, stamping her feet in the cold as she waited outside, her breath fogging as she shouted to the other kids to get in the buggy or she'd be off without them. In the childhood memories of some of the Kryciak adults, Doris appeared to be everywhere.

It's conceivable that being dirt poor might have affected the Kryciak children's sense of self-esteem in adulthood. But in those days most people in Canada were poor, and took it for granted that surviving was what life was all about. Perhaps it is because of that attitude and those experiences, rather than in spite of them, that the Kryciak clan today flourishes.

Doris, eldest daughter and her mother's right hand from the time she could toddle, did not escape unmarked, however. Her experience of poverty, of being at everyone's beck and call, had a major impact on shaping her ideas of what she wanted, and didn't want, from life. Doris saw poverty as the enemy, and determined never to be subject to it again. Nor did she ever wish to be dependent, to be taken care of in exchange for having her life controlled by others. As for children and child raising—she'd had her fill.

When Doris was sixteen she met George Artemenko, the son of a local farmer. John Kriss remembers him at that time as "a natty dresser, a glitzy fellow who drove a good car." Whatever he was, he must have impressed Doris, because they married several months later. Almost immediately, they left for the West Coast.

As Doris began her metamorphosis from prairie farm girl into Vancouver businesswoman, things were also changing back on the farm. The family left Calder and moved to Kamsack, where a high-school education was available and Onofry could try his hand at something different. He moved into the livery business and the harsh edge of life began to soften considerably.

"I remember Dad going down to the Assiniboine River in winter," said John Kriss. "He'd cut out chunks of ice and haul them off on a fourteen-by-fourteen-foot horse-drawn sled. Townspeople would buy the blocks for $1 apiece, and place them in their sheds with the cows, to be used in the summer for water and cooling."

Doris, meanwhile, had fallen madly in love with British Columbia. A studio picture of her taken at this time shows a smallish, well-groomed woman in a tailored gray suit with a pin stripe. Her fair brown hair is worn in the style of the 1940s—rolled back off the face at the sides, waved across the top, with sausage curls at the back. Her eyebrows are thin and well shaped; she gazes directly into the camera through almond-shaped eyes. She looks like a woman in charge of her life and mature beyond her years.

Doris wrote her family at length and often, urging them to join her and George in Vancouver. The West Coast was nothing like the prairies, she kept repeating. There were jobs, plenty of jobs, everywhere. There were nice houses and good stores, and Vancouver was wonderful.

Anne moved out first, then Dick (Alexander), then Onofry. Nellie stayed in Kamsack until the other four children finished their school year. War in Europe was only a few months away, when she finally packed the family's things and moved with the remaining children to Vancouver.

By this time Doris and George were living on a farm in Surrey with an older couple who owned it. The Kryciaks, however, settled into a small wooden house in the 800 block on Richards Street in the heart of downtown, a five-minute walk from Eaton's, the Hudson's Bay Company, the Orpheum Theatre, and a scattering of supper clubs and Chinese restaurants. The house had no basement, and the streetcars running day and night along Richards Street shook bits of plaster off the walls. But it was heated and had running water. Within weeks of the move every family member of working age had a good-paying job in the sawmills, the shipyards, or in the downtown stores. Even Nellie took a part-time job at a nearby restaurant as a cook. Vancouver was everything Doris had said.

Doris, now pregnant, temporarily quit her job as a waitress at Estelle's restaurant on Granville Street, and stayed in her Surrey home to await the birth of her child. On March 6, 1943, Sharon Doreen was born. She never knew her father. Three months later, George Artemenko was killed in a fall at the shipyard. George's boss, concerned for the welfare of the young widow, offered her a job in the shipyards cutting steel plates for ships. Doris temporarily moved back to her parents' home where Nellie—who changed her own schedule to accommodate her daughter—could help care for Sharon.

The birth of her child, followed within weeks by the death of her handsome, 28-year-old husband, had a profound effect on Doris and on the direction her life was to take. Suddenly she found herself alone—not physically, for her family was around her—but financially, socially, and sexually. Those were times when equal opportunity for women or equal pay for equal work were unheard of. Although the war was on and women were needed in the work force, Doris knew it wouldn't last.

She knew what poverty meant, and she feared and hated it. Trained from childhood to be independent and self-sufficient, she simply accepted the fact that she alone was now responsible for her own future and that of her daughter. As she thought of that future, a longing grew—not just to avoid the poverty with which she was so intimate, but to make so much money that poverty could never touch her again. Her dreams were not only for herself: she longed to give Sharon the financial security and freedom she had never known.

When the war ended the shipyards closed down, and Doris sought a new job. After a brief stint with the Internal Revenue Department, she joined the newly created Unemployment Insurance Commission, where one minor promotion steadily followed another.

If Doris loved to work hard during the day, she also liked to play. She had never been a beautiful woman, but her hair was thick and tended to wave, her skin was clear and glowing, she was clever, and she had a lively sense of humor. There was a certain vitality about her that made her very attractive to men. She was a smart dresser, keen on fashion and aware of what looked right on her short, slightly stocky figure. She had more than beauty: she was a total package, a combination of smartness and high energy that made men proud to be seen with her.

Now a widow for two years, mature but still only 25, Doris had a feeling she was moving toward a new life. All around her, there was a sense of pleasant chaos. The social and cultural changes that followed the Second World War were beginning to turn Vancouver from a country town spread along False Creek, the Burrard Inlet, and the Fraser River into a sophisticated, if embryonic, metropolis.

She had already found that the men coming back from the war were as anxious to relax, celebrate, and recreate their lives as she was. Somewhat shy by nature, and quite reticent in conversation, she nonetheless loved to go dancing at the Palomar supper club with her girlfriends, or have an occasional drink there after work; or watch the floor show or hear a group like the Deep River Boys; or listen to some other "favorite star of radio, stage, and screen," as the club's outside billboard proclaimed. American troops were everywhere: one photo shows her with a girlfriend and a couple of U.S. Army officers at the W.K. Chop Suey House, "Vancouver's Smartest Chinese Restaurant," in the 100 block on East Pender.

The Starlit Gardens, which advertised itself as 'America's [yes, America's] Finest Outdoor Ballroom," was another favorite spot for a Saturday-night date. Situated at the time at Georgia and Denman streets, the ballroom today is just a memory buried in the soil: now a luxury condominium building sits on the site. And then there was everyone's favorite rendezvous, the Cave supper club, on Hornby Street, with "Henry Scammell and His Music," long since nothing but a memory.

Although Doris moved her residence four times in the ten years that elapsed between her becoming a widow and her ultimate remarriage, the moves were essentially within the same general area. For the first four months after George

Artemenko's death, she stayed with her parents but when Nellie extended her working hours at the restaurant that stood at the corner of Robson and Richards streets, Doris decided to board with a family in North Burnaby called Beckwith. Mrs. Beckwith was home all day and available to look after Sharon while Doris was at work. The arrangement was so convenient that when the Beckwiths moved to South Vancouver, Doris and Sharon moved with them. Finally, when Onofry and Nellie Kryciak left their Richards Street house for one on Twelfth Avenue near Semlin, Doris and Sharon returned home. There was a complete suite in the basement, and a school nearby for Sharon, who was now in Grade 2. Either Onofry, now about 60, or a neighbor across the street were on hand to care for Sharon when she returned from school. Doris was anxious to be a good mother, but her choices were few. She was satisfied with this arrangement.

All through these years, Doris had held on to her dream of securing a comfortable future for herself and Sharon. In the late 1940s, the idea came to her that she should buy and run her own dress shop. At first it had seemed a wild and improbable fancy, but the years of balancing her own checkbook, her success at work, even the few social flings that she'd had, convinced her that she had what it took. Trained from childhood to respect frugality, to take satisfaction in finding alternative, cheaper ways to get things done, Doris started to trim her already-modest expenditures, depositing every possible penny into the bank. It was about this time, 1948, that Doris met Rene Leatherbarrow.

Rene was a handsome man of medium build, but with a certain solid masculinity. He appreciated the good things of life, set a high price on manners and courtesy, and had a rare ability to listen well. And he owned a '42 Chev, the only fellow in his wide circle of friends with a car. Faced with his easy charm, Doris fell like the proverbial ton of bricks.

It was not until June 1953, five years after she'd met Rene, that Doris Artemenko became Doris Leatherbarrow, floating down the aisle of Chown Memorial Church on Cambie Street wearing a bridal gown that was the quintessential wedding outfit of those times: an ankle-length, tulle-over-georgette strapless dress (to do double duty as a party dress later) and a lace, three-quarter-sleeved jacket with a Peter Pan collar. In her gloved hands she held a bouquet of orchids and satin ribbons. A little bar of lace, tulle, and flowers sat on her tightly set curled brown hair. Pictures show her glowing with happiness. Sitting nearby at the long banquet table, dressed in a pretty party dress and surrounded by adults, is ten-year old Sharon.

The five-year delay in getting married was the result of federal-government policy that, in 1953, still forbade the employment of married women! Doris knew that the moment that she wed, she'd be fired from her job with the UIC. So for nearly five years the couple planned and saved. They bought a block on Fifty-ninth Street near Frazer in South Vancouver, slowly built their own house, landscaped it, and furnished it. Nine months before their marriage, they moved into it, taking Sharon with them.

Doris's longing to have her own dress shop still dominated her dreams. She now had Rene to help her. Fired, as anticipated, by the UIC, Doris took another job, and she and Rene started to look for a store to buy. They could find nothing that was either affordable or that suited the customer market they had in mind. Finally they dropped the idea of buying an established store and decided to start from scratch. Six years passed before they found the location they wanted, in a strip of new shops on Scott Road in Surrey. With a loan of $2,500 from the Royal Bank, Rene's Ladies Apparel was under way.

"Neither of us knew anything about the fashion retailing business," Rene Leatherbarrow recalled. "There was no Merchandise Mart—a building where suppliers show their samples and retailers put in their orders—in 1959. Suppliers hired rooms at the Hotel Vancouver and showed their goods there. I remember Doris and I wandering along the corridors of the Hotel Vancouver in a state of near terror, bewildered and confused as to how and what to buy for the next season ahead."

Finally, a representative of several fashion lines took them under his wing. "Trust me," he said, "let me do the buying for you." Innocent of the dog-eat-dog world they had joined, they let him. Although their act of trust could have spelled disaster, the unknown sales rep's choices were inspired. Each item proved to be a winner. It's indicative of Rene's personality that for years he fretted over not being able to recall the merchant's name so that he could thank him.

As the business grew, Rene and Doris began to have difficulties. Doris was a hard worker with plain ideas. Rene, still employed at B.C. Tel, had more flash and imagination, and saw the possibilities in the rapidly growing Vancouver area. When he found the right place for a second store in Surrey, Doris was panic-stricken. He felt they should hire an accountant; she felt they were just as well off doing the books themselves.

"In those days much of our business was done by keeping monthly accounts. People didn't use credit cards. We would give the customers the goods and simply bill them at the end of every month. We had over 1,500 customers and I handled the lot of it, keeping the books, billings, receipts. It was time consuming."

Rene also did the maintenance work for the stores and, for a while, did all the cleaning. Doris was totally immersed in selecting, buying, and selling the fashions, running daily from the wholesalers to store to store with an intensive hands-on approach that seemed to mark the business as hers alone.

By the time they had two stores, Rene felt strongly that their so-called equal partnership was equal in name only. He also felt that the time for him to quit B.C. Tel was past due. But Doris disagreed. She enjoyed his salary in addition to the store profits, and argued that his job provided security in case the shops hit a down market. It was clear to Rene that his salary was a touch of gravy that Doris didn't want to do without.

"If I'd insisted on quitting, Doris would simply have said all right, all right, and that would have been the end of it. She wasn't argumentative in that sense," said Rene.

What had become depressingly clear to him was Doris's deeply rooted resistance to sharing her business with anyone. She was a one-woman show: teamwork wasn't in her character. "Doris felt nobody could do things as well as she could," he said.

A close friend described the situation at that time: ''Rene felt used. He was to be husband, escort, lover, bookkeeper, and general handyman, but never a 50 percent business partner.''

But there was another problem, which sprang from the same source and which couldn't be shunted to the side or glossed over in the hope that it would go away. All her life Doris had been careful with money. When she entertained family—and she often had the whole family over for dinner including all the children— her table groaned with food and her liquor cabinet was packed. However, that was the exception. Frugality was the rule. Family members would chuckle about her tightness: sometimes at Christmas she would give as gifts sweaters or blouses that she had not been able to sell in her stores. But the family accepted it, understanding that although being poor as kids hadn't made them phobic over money, it had affected their big sister differently. At times her closefistedness was infuriating, but mostly her parsimony was seen as a regrettable, almost endearing, trait in an otherwise substantial and unique woman.

Living with such thriftiness day in and day out was another matter. Rene was fully aware that Doris's penny-pinching had helped build a thriving business. But why squeeze every nickel now that money was rolling in? In Rene's books life wasn't a dress rehearsal: he liked having money and he liked spending it.

Rene denies he was extravagant, says he simply couldn't see any reason for Doris and him to go to second-rate hotels or restaurants. He liked to tip well, to buy gifts of the same quality he himself liked to receive. He would rather have dropped dead than get into a shouting match with a cabdriver over the size of a tip. Good standards were not only a matter of pride and self-esteem for him but a lifelong habit. What else was money for? Whittling costs to hoard money simply wasn't his style.

Sharon, by now in her late teens, was working for her mother and living at home, home being the comfortable, custom-built house in Tsawwassen they'd moved to in 1961. On the surface they appeared to be a contented threesome, but it seemed that the more money Doris made the tighter she became.

Rene wasn't the only one to notice it. Sharon commented on her mother's penuriousness to a close friend, and Doris's own family observed the trend, at first with jokes, and then with regret. Slowly, the making and keeping of money appeared less a pleasurable objective than a powerful obsession. All other interests—and they'd been limited to start with—were neglected for business. Doris started to get home later, work on Sundays, talk of little else but the deals she made. All her life she'd loved to garden: now she did the minimum. She quit playing golf— except for fund-raising games occasionally staged by the Merchants' Association—never had time for a movie, rarely watched television, or if she did, would work at three or four other projects at the same time. As the Leatherbarrows' income grew and they holidayed in Mexico, Hawaii, and the Cayman Islands, the question of how much everything was setting them back and how much everyone was profiting from them became a frequent topic of conversation. This did not make for relaxed vacations.

"Doris," said Rene Leatherbarrow, "is a very hard woman to explain. There was something very deep and very good about her. When we were married, I have to say that despite everything, she was a very good wife. She'd do things for you that no husband would expect. It hurts me to think about it. One night, for instance, I was just sitting watching television, wondering where she was, and there she was in the kitchen. She'd taken out all my shoes and polished them. Can you imagine that? Polished my shoes. She did old-fashioned things like that. But it was also part of her not being able to sit still and relax."

Was she good to her employees? "Not really" Rene said after a long silence. "She paid poorly. That's simply a matter of record. Hundreds of people in Vancouver know that—I'm not giving away any secrets. A hundred times I told her that the store managers and clerks were making the money for us. They were our representatives. But she wouldn't budge. I could see the best employees come, stay awhile, get some experience, and then move on. When I'd point this out to her she'd brush it off with 'Anyone could do what they were doing.' She was a substantial woman with real integrity, but she simply didn't appreciate other people. She'd been brought up to survive, not to be a person who could enjoy their life.''

''Doris's tightness was well known among all of us who worked for her,'' said a former store manager. ''I'd look out across the mall and see her hurrying along with a pile of blouses and dresses over one arm, and I'd say to the other assistant, 'Look out, here she comes!' In one way we dreaded her visits— she was so intense and fussy, driving you crazy with the way she fretted over details. And nothing got thrown out. She'd save rubber bands, paper clips, old hangers, envelopes. The drawers would be jammed with them. As for her employees, she paid the lowest wages she could. She didn't value good employees. We were forever having farewell lunches. She'd rather lose a top saleswoman than pay a few cents extra an hour.

''What's just as true is the fact that we all deeply respected her. She was a businesswoman to the core, tough, a survivor. But there was also about her a deep sense of goodness, a certain generosity of spirit, even a tenderness, and it was so deep that her tightness and pigheadedness seemed somehow forgivable, unimportant. You felt she was as much a victim of these traits as the rest of us. I knew her for years, knew Sharon, knew Darren, had been in their homes. And all I can say is there's simply no way of describing Doris, because there just wasn't one Doris. There were many Dorises.''

After sixteen years, the marriage of Doris and Rene Leather-barrow broke up. There are several versions why, but when they're all boiled down, what seems to be true is that Rene finally tired of spending his life alone while Doris followed her bliss. Doris and Rene had been pulling in different directions for a number of years—Doris to build an ever-increasing fortune, Rene to sit back and spend it. According to friends who knew the couple at that time, Rene finally found a young lady in one of Doris's stores who expressed something more than a sympathetic interest in his situation. Tongues wagged and soon the news reached Doris.

She was devastated, and told Rene to get out of the house. She accused him of infidelity; Rene denied it; Doris relented. But in the meantime some hard truths had been voiced, wounding truths that cut like razors and left marks for a lifetime. Before packing his bags, Rene spelled out his dissatisfaction with their life, citing her willingness to sacrifice everything and everyone for their business, her tightness with money. Although it was Doris who told Rene to get out, after she relented she never forgave him for leaving.

When Rene did become seriously involved with his sympathetic shop assistant, Doris longed for him to return. Now 49 years old, she felt humiliated and abandoned. Her brothers and sisters advised her to forget it, reminded her that she had a beautiful home, her own business, and plenty of money. What did she need Rene Leatherbarrow for? After Doris's death, when the family went through her personal possessions, they found several books on "how to be a good wife and mistress." A sales slip in one of them indicated they had been purchased shortly after Rene's departure; apparently at that time she had nursed the hope that one day he'd come back.

Rene, however, had had enough. He and Doris were divorced in September 1969, and Doris bought him out, borrowing from the bank to pay off the $75,000 share in the business due him.

It looked like game over. But there were two chapters yet to be written in the ongoing saga. It took little time for the flames of Rene's new love to fizzle, and for Rene to discover he wanted to negotiate a return to his true love, Doris. By then Doris had completely recovered, and couldn't imagine anything she wanted less in her life than Rene Leatherbarrow. Now it was his turn to be devastated.

Once Rene was no longer involved in Doris's business, he became a real-estate broker. During those years, he and Doris maintained a relationship, sometimes lunching together or meeting for coffee. They discussed their private lives, their past together; would sometimes flirt around the prospect of their getting together again.

On one occasion, about three or four years after their divorce, Doris drove out to his real-estate office, deeply sad and weeping. She asked him to return, said that she needed him. But Rene had

developed another relationship, and he refused. Doris never
forgave him for this humiliation, though they continued to main-
tain their friendship. But when Rene's second relationship broke
up, leaving him vulnerable and profoundly hurt, Doris's deep and
unresolved anger toward him surged to the surface.

"She was totally unforgiving and merciless," someone close
to the situation said. "The depth of her need for revenge, the
harsh words with which she rejected him, astounded even her
own family. Of course, she'd gone through sheer hell when he'd
taken off, and there was something between them that never
quite died."

Nonetheless it surprised a lot of people when in 1981 Rene and
Doris, together with Doris's sister Jean and her husband, Ed
Beketa, went off to Mexico to see if they could work something
out. This trip—eleven years after their divorce, when they were
both in their sixties—testifies to the extraordinary vitality of the
ties between Doris and Rene Leatherbarrow. Doris by that time
had been living on her own for more than a decade. She was
independently wealthy, traveled abroad once or twice a year with
her sister Anne, and had marvelous fun. Her daughter, Sharon,
by then had a child of her own, a beautiful grandson and heir for
Doris named Darren. Doris wasn't at all sure that she needed
anyone underfoot, let alone someone to share her life and fortune.

Rene didn't have a fortune, but he had done well in real estate.
However, he had his own doubts. He felt certain that Doris
wanted him back—but entirely on her terms. For his part, he
would return only as a full partner financially and emotionally. But
that wasn't on Doris's agenda. He could see that Doris feared the
move could cost her money and power, and that, said Doris's
sister Jean, was precisely what was uppermost in her thinking.
Rene feared that unless Doris agreed to a full partnership, she'd
soon have him back playing his old role of escort and fix-it man.
He couldn't accept that.

The Mexican holiday turned into a standoff. A few days before
the vacation ended, nature intervened and brought the faltering
negotiations to a close. Rene, 61 years of age, had a moderately

severe stroke. Doris, who according to some members of her family was often uncomfortable, even impatient, with illness, flew off to Vancouver and left him there. Rene made arrangements to be met by someone else on his return to Vancouver— someone whom, when he had completely recovered, he later married and from whom he was later divorced. After Doris's death, Rene Leatherbarrow would say, ''I never ceased loving her. But I couldn't live with her.''

During these decades in which Doris was making her fortune and working out her love life, her only child, Sharon, was dealing with problems of her own.

# SHARON

Sharon Artemenko was born into a world that her mother as a child could only imagine. It was a world of early springs and snowless winters, of restaurants, movie theaters, streetcars that rattled and clanged late into the night, of multistoried shops filled with endlessly tempting, pretty things, all within walking distance of the Richards Street home in which she briefly lived with her mother and grandparents. Nearby was a Catholic cathedral named Holy Rosary, whose bells rang day and night, and at the bottom of the street was a deep blue harbor filled with great ships and rimmed by snow-tipped mountains.

Unlike her mother, young Sharon was servant to no one. There were no siblings born after her to draw attention from her needs. Her grandparents, uncles, aunts, and cousins surrounded her. She was the reigning princess in a large adult household, and the apple of her young mother's eye.

Unlike Doris, Sharon had no father. All she knew of him was the gray-and-white picture of a handsome young man dressed in a suit and staring into the camera, a man with an open expression, regular features, and thick dark hair slicked straight back. But there was not a single memory. She had a grandfather, Onofry, but Onofry didn't speak a word of English.

Ask friends and relatives today what Sharon was like as a child, and they pause before replying as they search back through more than forty years. In the end, they come up with little. Sharon, it seems, was unexceptional. "Very sweet," an aunt will say, or "well mannered." "A dear little thing" was the consensus.

While some details about Sharon's upbringing are less vague than impressions of her personality, family and friends strongly disagree about just how much hands-on mothering Doris actually did.

"From what Sharon told me, she felt that she was essentially raised by her grandmother, Nellie, who was a wonderful woman," said Nancy Poirier, a friend of Sharon's since high-school days. Nancy is a high-energy businesswoman who owns and runs a hairdressing shop in Tsawwassen and a small manufacturing business that produces miniature dolls. "Nellie certainly didn't baby-sit her all the time, because Sharon and Doris lived elsewhere. But Sharon always felt it was from Nellie that she learned her ordinary day-to-day living habits. Nellie lived into her nineties, lively, spry, interested in everything. She cleaned her own house, did her own cooking. Finally, when Nellie slowed down, Sharon would go and do some of those things for her. Sharon loved her deeply. Maybe that's why she felt she'd been essentially raised by her. Her feelings toward Nellie were simple and straightforward."

Rene Leatherbarrow, who first met Sharon when she was only four, quietly but forcibly disagrees with Sharon's assessment of her upbringing. "When Doris was widowed she was getting $70 a month in widow's aid. She had no choice but to go out to work every day and leave Sharon. It wasn't Nellie who raised Sharon. It was Doris who was ultimately responsible. And *if* there was anyone who had more input in raising her than Doris, it was the Beckwiths, with whom Doris and Sharon boarded in Burnaby. Mrs. Beckwith had Sharon daily for over two years."

"It wasn't that Doris neglected her, because she didn't," said Sheila Kriss. "But she didn't give Sharon what Sharon wanted, which was her presence. How could she? She was a single mother, and desperate to secure her own, and Sharon's, future. But there was another element beyond that. She was capable and ambitious. She didn't want to settle for a marginal existence. She felt the effort and the absences were for Sharon's benefit, too."

"Of course Doris loved Sharon," said Anne McDonald, another smartly turned-out matron of the Tkatchuk-Kryciak clan.

Anne was Doris's aunt but, as one of Nellie's younger siblings, was younger than Doris by several years. "But Doris hadn't been raised to show affection in a hugging sort of way. She was very interested in Sharon, but always at a bit of a distance."

It's possible that Sharon for whatever reason—being father-less, or her own personality, or never living in a home that was really her own until her tenth year—needed an inordinate amount of her mother's attention, and that need was so demanding that few women could have filled it, let alone Doris with her particular history and priorities. Sharon as a small child knew nothing of her mother's experiences and dread of poverty, and even if she had, could scarcely have been expected to understand.

Sharon was in high school before Doris and Rene found, in Surrey, the site they wanted for building their first store. By then Sharon had been living with Doris and Rene in the house on Fifty-ninth Avenue for six years.

By late 1959—Sharon was now sixteen—Doris was beginning to hit her entrepreneurial stride. The business was surpassing her and Rene's most optimistic expectations, and there was a potential for a second store. All Doris's and Rene's energies were concentrated on consolidating their success. The business ate up weeks at a time, and next to its challenges, it would be understandable if Sharon's schoolgirl problems, and even her triumphs, were less than riveting to Doris. Then, too, compared with Doris's life at sixteen, Sharon was living on easy street.

During that time Rene or Doris, sometimes both, often worked at night. "If I wasn't home Sharon would wait at her gran's or with a neighbor, and then we'd all go home together, tired out," said Rene Leatherbarrow. "Maybe we'd order dinner in, a Chinese dinner or something like that. It wasn't what I wanted, not my idea of living."

"I think it was about then that Sharon started making a lot of extravagant demands on Doris," a school friend of Sharon's said. "It was as if she were trying to get her own back—I don't know what for. Sharon knew how to press her mother's buttons to get what she wanted. She had an extravagant wardrobe for a teenage girl."

Sharon's wardrobes overflowed with the newest fashions. At one stage three huge drawers were filled with new sweaters. Doris, so tight with everyone else, couldn't give her daughter enough.

"The truth," said outspoken John Kriss, "was that Doris doted on Sharon from the time she was a child. But she had a guilt complex to her dying day that the way she brought Sharon up was incorrect. It wasn't a hugging family. There was a deep affection or, better put, deep ties, but it wasn't a warm family necessarily. The things everyone says about Doris being tight—they are true. She'd give the government $50,000 without worrying but would not give a girl in her shop a raise in pay. There was something about Doris that wasn't likable that way.

"But she did love Sharon. She just made a mess of it. Quite innocently, of course. When Sharon was a teenager she was overdressed, overclothed. Doris didn't have any influence over her, and why should she? From what I remember Sharon spent a lot of her time being baby-sat by one person or another. Doris felt very guilty because she really wanted to do her best by Sharon. But there was this terrible drive to succeed in business, and she kept acting against her better judgment. Sharon kept demanding, and to make up for it, Doris kept on giving in to her."

Other members of the immediate family strongly disagree with this opinion. "It is ridiculous and unfair to say that Doris felt guilty. She had nothing whatsoever to feel guilty about," one sister said in response to her brother's statement. "Sharon was the most important thing in Doris's life."

The truth is likely all of this—that Doris loved her child, worried about her future, indulged her, made the best child-care arrangements possible for her. It's also a fact that Doris had needs of her own. She was capable, young, ambitious. If she felt guilty because she sometimes attended to her own needs before those of her child it is a feeling that most mothers have experienced. In Doris's case, however, the need to succeed in business was so evidently all-consuming that it later became the dominant feature of both her personality and her life-style. It is possible therefore that Sharon, as a child, *did* experience strong feelings of being of secondary importance in her mother's life. Not appreciating the origin of her mother's needs, she might well have perceived this as a form of neglect.

Later, when referring to her school days, Sharon would claim to have been a perfectionist, never satisfied with anything less than straight A's. Her mum expected the best of her and wouldn't take anything less, she said.

But Rene Leatherbarrow's memories are different. He couldn't remember Sharon regularly getting A's; nor did he have any memory of Doris pressuring Sharon to perform well. He remembers that Sharon cruised through life pleasantly and somewhat effortlessly, a sweet young girl but unremarkable.

Whatever Sharon's grades, the pictures in the John Oliver High yearbook show her looking like a superfeminine young lady in a highly traditional way—crisp, prim, neat, and pretty. No matter whether she was all dressed up or coming from the gym after a compulsory (and disliked) workout, she appeared well turned out. Her hair was always neat and shiny, her clothes just right. Her nickname at this stage was "Mutt."

"As a future nurse, will be one of the best," the school yearbook for 1961 said. "An outstanding person with keen sense of humor, Mutt was often heard to say 'Not well adjusted, are you?' We wonder if she was referring to Eric." Eric was Eric Wieser, Sharon's romantic interest at the time. The description of Eric in the yearbook is revealing, since it suggests that even then Sharon was intensely interested in the image "her man" projected; it also gives a glimpse into how Sharon's contemporaries perceived her: "Whether or not Sharon has had any influence remains to be seen, but he is one of the best dressed males of the senior school."

Although Sharon projected the image of a happy, carefree teenager, she was, like many otherwise-sweet girls of her age, insensitive to the realities of her mother's life. She resented Doris's strong work ethic and serious approach to life, poked fun at her frugality, and seemed somehow ashamed of her mother, who with the passage of time had become plump and unfashionable. "I hate the way she's always trying to save money!"

Sharon exploded once to a friend. "It's so embarrassing. It makes us look so cheap."

An incident that occurred some years later typifies how different the attitudes of the two women were. Doris needed a better washer and dryer but was hanging on to her old equipment. Sharon was selling a perfectly good set to upgrade, but she refused even to consider giving her set to her mother. "Let her buy her own," she told a friend. "She can afford it. But she prefers to use junk. Mum's always been like that."

Despite this, teenaged Sharon was to all intents and purposes a conforming young woman and a most dutiful daughter. She did not drink, never used vulgar language, always dressed like a lady. Doris made no secret of the fact that she wanted Sharon in the business; that had been understood for years. After all, it would one day be hers.

With her trim little figure, blue eyes, fair hair, delicate features, Sharon appeared tailor-made for a career in the retail fashion business. More than that, she had a natural eye for fashion, was always on top of the latest style, and made decisions quickly and shrewdly. When she had helped out in the stores over Christmas and the holidays, her charm and abilities had impressed all the regular staff members.

She left high school and drifted into her mother's business. She had spoken of becoming a nurse, but made no attempt to follow through. Doris put her on the payroll, and Sharon's career in merchandizing began.

A life devoted to buying and selling women's fashions was not on Sharon's agenda, however. She was anxious to marry—and not because she wanted to keep house, but because she wanted the status of being a wife, of having a fine home, good furnishings. Even, perhaps, a couple of children. Time would show that these things were less important to Sharon for their intrinsic value than for the way they reflected on her and validated her worth.

When she was nineteen, Sharon went on a bus tour of Southern California with her best friend, Molly Dieno. There she met Brent Weinberger, a tall, slim medical student who was interning at a Los Angeles hospital. They fell in love, and against all objections—they had known each other only weeks and Brent was the son of a devoted, and widowed, Jewish mother—they married.

"It created quite a stir," said Great-aunt Anne McDonald.

The "stir" reached its finale with a wedding in Doris and Rene's home in Tsawwassen. The house's architecture had been Rene's idea—a modern, subtly Japanese style with a shoji screen in the entrance, heavy beams in the family room, dining room, and foyer, but none in the living room, with its sixteen-foot-high ceiling. All the bedrooms had walls that reached the ceiling, but in the other rooms the walls stopped at about six feet. Every room had a different type of wood paneling. There was gunstock walnut in the living room, Polynesian walnut for the cabinets in the kitchen, cherrywood in Sharon's bedroom, and teak paneling on one wall in the master bedroom.

Mrs. Weinberger stayed with Doris and Rene for three days before the wedding while Sharon, determined to be a perfect wife, rushed back and forth to a rabbi in Bellingham, a nearby town on the U.S. side of the border, for instruction in the Jewish faith. Meanwhile, Doris and Rene dashed off to work during the day, and tried to entertain their inconsolable guest in the evening.

Doris, among her other talents, was gifted with a green thumb, and although she had sacrificed all other extraneous activities to her business, she still did some work on the garden surrounding her large backyard pool. By the end of spring it was usually lush with blossoms. But that year, despite Sharon's and Doris's ferocious determination that the at-home wedding would be so perfect it would stun Mrs. Weinberger into an acceptance of the unwanted union, there wasn't a bud in sight. And so the day before the big event, the Leatherbarrows brought in a gardener from a greenhouse in Delta to plant a couple of hundred dollars' worth of instant garden. On the day of the wedding the backyard was bursting with blooms.

"When we bade Sharon goodbye at the airport, both Doris and I shed a few tears," Rene recalled.

Immediately after the wedding, Sharon returned with her husband to Los Angeles and continued her studies in Judaism. Six months after the wedding Doris and Rene received a weepy call from her. Come on down, she pleaded. They flew to Los Angeles and found that the love between Sharon and Brent had already vanished into the smog. Sharon complained bitterly about interference from her mother-in-law, and was so unhappy with Brent she wanted to leave him.

On the other hand, Sharon explained, she didn't want to return to Tsawwassen at once. She wanted to buy a car while in California and bring it back into Canada duty free. But this required a year's residency in the States. When Doris and Rene returned to Tsawwassen, they sent Sharon money to get her own apartment in Los Angeles. She found a job at Sears as a salesperson in the jewelry department, and stayed another six months. One year and one day after leaving Tsawwassen as a bride, Sharon pulled into Doris and Rene's driveway behind the wheel of a pale blue Mustang convertible, looking prettier and sharper than ever. Her marriage with Brent Weinberger was over.

A few days later, Sharon was back on the payroll and working in one of the three stores that now constituted Rene's Ladies Apparel.

Sharon was a successful retailer, well liked and admired. But her unappeased desire for home and husband was as powerful as ever. One day while driving in Tsawwassen she broke the speed limit and was pulled over to the curb by a policeman. The officer was Charles (Chuck) Gowan. A few days later, he was on the phone to her. She was very taken with him: he projected the image that she favored—tall, meticulously groomed, with razor-sharp creases in his trousers; methodical; seemingly well organized. In his uniform, she told a friend, he was a "knockout."

Doris was less knocked out, but following the wedding of Sharon and Chuck at Saint Stephen's United Church on Granville Street, she gave the couple $20,000 toward the purchase of a new Spanish-style house on Gilchrist Drive, a few minutes' drive from Doris's own Tsawwassen home.

Those who knew the Gowans during this time say that Sharon worked hard at being the perfect wife, creating a gorgeous home and becoming a gourmet cook. She'd make intricate desserts from recipes three pages long, would prepare her own pizza dough. She was generous with her recipes, and gave out the best of them to those who'd admired a special dish, attaching little notes that read "Watch this very carefully—tends to burn easily."

In addition she continued to work at her mother's stores. She was a chic, high-energy woman, a supreme perfectionist. "Not compulsive," a friend insisted, "just a perfectionist." Nothing was too much trouble once she had made up her mind to do it. And now she poured all her energy into her husband and home. Soon, she would pour it into her child.

On September 19, 1972, Sharon gave birth to a son, Darren Charles. She made no secret of the fact that she was thrilled the child was male, and told close friends she wasn't interested in female children. Darren was a beautiful boy, strong, healthy, and bright. "He's going to be," Sharon told her friends and family, "a perfect little gentleman."

By the time Darren was born to Sharon and Chuck, Doris had been divorced three years. She and Rene had reached a financial settlement, and she was attempting to manage entirely on her own. At about this same time, Chuck Gowan was denied a promotion he felt he deserved, and he quit the Delta police force. Seeing a place for him in her mother's business, Sharon talked a reluctant Doris into hiring him. It didn't work. Doris—whose perception of her sons-in-law seems to have been soured by the fact that she contributed substantially to the homes they lived in—took it into her head, rightly or wrongly, that Chuck Gowan was acting like the boss in her office, throwing his weight around and usurping her role. She reacted to her suspicions by promptly firing him.

Sharon was furious. On a couple of earlier occasions when she'd been angry with Doris, she had punished her mother by refusing to let her see Darren. Doris, who adored her grandson, had been deeply wounded by her daughter's spitefulness. Now Sharon showed how well she understood her own power. For months— during mid- and late 1973—Sharon denied Doris all access to Darren. Doris begged her, wept, but Sharon was unrelenting.

"It broke Doris's heart," said a close friend of the family. "But Sharon didn't like being thwarted and she simply decided to teach Doris a lesson. Sharon had nice manners, but in fact she was a very domineering and aggressive woman."

Sharon's anger with her mother for having fired Gowan appeared at first to be the healthy reaction of a loyal wife, as well it might have been. But there was another issue, one that assumed increasing importance as the months went by. That was the question of Gowan's future. He'd long been out of his natty police uniform, and now he was out of a job. Sharon was, from all available evidence, captivated by strong images, particularly where the men in her life were concerned.

In late 1974, Sharon decided she wanted to divorce Gowan. There appears to have been no negotiating or compromising once she made up her mind. She simply had divorce papers served on her devastated husband.

"She had an extraordinary ability to be strong, determined, and in control," a close friend said. "Chuck didn't want to leave. He loved Sharon—and his son. And the divorce was bitter and combative as a result. But Sharon got her own way. She got the house, kept Darren, and got rid of Chuck. Sharon simply decided that Chuck wasn't going to have the sort of brilliant future she wanted her husband to have. After leaving Doris's business, he became a truck driver. Sharon's image of the husband she wanted was a little different."

Soon after her breakup with Chuck, the Gilchrist Drive home was sold. The $20,000 Doris had given Chuck and Sharon to help buy the home was never returned to her. Family members claim that this hurt and angered Doris for years; furthermore, it made her cautious and suspicious about contributing any sums to Sharon's later marriage.

Despite the fact that Sharon had wanted a child, she had returned to work soon after Darren's birth in the fall of 1972, leaving the baby with a solid Scotswoman named Jean Symonds, who lived nearby. Mrs. Symonds's husband, Raymond, had died and her own children were grown. Now, with the Gilchrist Drive home sold, Sharon went to live in Jean Symonds's basement—after having it completely renovated to suit her tastes.

"Jean was the answer to Sharon's prayers," said Mildred Kjar, a neighbor of Mrs. Symonds. A short, vivacious woman in her late fifties, Mrs. Kjar raised five children of her own and was herself widowed in 1987. She lived across the street from Mrs. Symonds for about twenty years and, because Sharon was living there, got to know both her and Darren well.

"Jean had been strict with her own kids, and with neighborhood kids. So the way she behaved with Darren was totally out of character, because she took all the nonsense he dished out. I assume that Sharon laid out all the ground rules from the time of his birth, and that Jean didn't have much say. He was stamping his little foot by the time he was two, and by the time he was three and four he'd say, 'You listen to me, do you hear me, Jeannie? I'm talking to you.' He demanded attention and would scream or holler until he got it.

"Whatever Darren wanted Darren got. He was surrounded by women—by Sharon, by Doris, by Jean—and they were amused at everything he did. Nobody nipped the bud of his precocity. Funnily enough, he did become a real little Prince Charming. As he grew, his mother insisted on good manners. That meant a lot to her. She said she wanted a perfect little gentleman."

Sharon's insistence that young Darren be perfectly mannered led her from the beginning to impose excessive control over the child. Many people close to her were bothered by her obsessive need to supervise and plan for him.

"He was an extremely protected child," said Jean Beketa, Sharon's aunt, but also her contemporary in age. "It was so bad that when he was small all the arranging to play was done by appointment."

A former neighbor agreed. "Sharon would not allow any casual playing around. She made phone calls and arrangements for any play Darren was involved in. I know because I was involved in some of the arrangements. Darren didn't have many friends. Usually he would be the one to do the inviting over to his house—once Sharon had approved, of course! There was never any playing around in the streets, or hanging around with the kids in the neighborhood."

Darren's birthday was in September, so Sharon held him back a year in starting school. As her son, it was essential that he do well, and she saw this as a way of ensuring that. She put so much pressure on Darren to perform that he would cry in elementary school if he got an answer wrong. Jean Beketa said that some teachers were sorry for Darren when he was a younger child, for "he was always striving to be perfect. Sharon seemed to think everything Darren said or did was a reflection on her."

As Nancy Poirier watched Darren grow, she felt uneasy. A mother herself, she thought Sharon far too controlling of her only child. "She wasn't wise about some of the things she did, but she really adored him. Sharon had a controlling nature, and it's true she monitored and supervised the child all the time. But she was also well liked, vivacious, and charming. There was another side to her—she could be really mean and quite aggressive—but I like to remember the good things. She wanted her son to have perfect manners—she took great pride in that. After all, she herself was a perfectionist."

Why was it so important to Sharon that Darren be perfect?

"Sharon was very smart. Not intellectual, but smart. I wouldn't say she was ambitious. Result oriented, maybe. She wanted gorgeous homes, fine furniture. Everything had to be just so. Darren was part of that picture. She wanted to produce the perfect man like she produced the perfect meal, the perfect home."

Darren was three and well on the way to becoming the perfect gentleman of his mother's dreams when Sharon met Ralph Huenemann. The timing couldn't have been better. Attractive, divorced, heir to a modest but growing fortune, Sharon was ready to embark on the next chapter of her life.

Huenemann was an American widower with two young school-aged children, who lived opposite Jean Symonds. Shortly after Sharon had separated from Chuck Gowan, Jo Anne Huenemann, Ralph's North Dakota–born wife, had committed suicide in Manning Park. The suicide was perhaps accidental. Jo Anne, who had been a schoolteacher, had taken alcohol and tranquilizers, fallen unconscious on a park bench, and died of hypothermia. The date was May 30, 1975.

After Ralph met Sharon, they started to date. He had a B.A. from Oberlin College, Ohio; an M.A. from Harvard University; and an intense interest in music. He and his late wife had spent some time living abroad, and now he had a grant while he worked on a part of his Ph.D. thesis that did not require being in a university city. He was the type of man Sharon had in mind as husband for herself and father for her son. Sharon undoubtedly saw him as having a future, perhaps a brilliant future, which she would take a role in molding. And he was tall, slim, fit. In short he was "absolutely marvelous, so intelligent, he knows every-thing," she told Mildred Kjar.

Mildred Kjar lived next door to Ralph Huenemann for three years and remembers him as essentially a noncommunicative sort of man who never expressed his emotions, at least not to her or her late husband, Cal. On better acquaintance, she liked and respected him, despite what she felt was his extraordinary inabil-ity to show any feeling.

However, she observed, "Ralph did a lot about the house. He was home all the time, of course, endlessly working on his Ph.D., which, by the way, he would never have finished if Sharon hadn't driven him on. She was very ambitious for him. She could see herself being pulled up by his star. Even so, he was helpful with everything and looked after the children a lot. I remember once he took his son and my son, Rick, on a camping trip. Rick was used to camping with his dad, but apparently Ralph didn't have the slightest clue what to do. Camping just wasn't his thing. But he tried. He really wanted to do the right thing with his boy."

On August 13, 1976, Ralph Huenemann and Sharon Gowan were married. This time Sharon decided against wearing the traditional white bridal gown, but chose instead a long, peasant-style, pale blue dress. With her shoulder-length hair, now bleached several shades fairer than her normal light brown, she looked bewitchingly pretty.

As Darren grew, it became commonplace for Sharon to praise him aloud to others. Some people thought her boastfulness about her son was an astounding breach of good taste. "I found it absolutely impossible to say anything about my own children to her," a former neighbor in Victoria noted. "It was Darren this and Darren that all the time, that she never had any trouble with him, etc., etc., etc. Later on, I saw him occasionally with Sharon, and often at Mount Douglas [high school], and he seemed to me a harassed, nagged, and browbeaten young boy—to the point where he didn't seem fully masculine in the ordinary use of that word. There was a certain delicacy, a softness, about him."

"Sharon was the type of mother I always backed off from," said a neighbor of Doris. "I've never bragged about my kids or flaunted their abilities. Sharon spoke as if Darren was going to be the greatest of the greatest. He had this potential that was going to amount to brilliance. I am not talking about years ago, but on her last visit here, two days before she died. Sharon sat in the living room and talked about Darren and his brilliance to the point where I wondered, 'Is she doing this to convince herself that he is special, or am I interpreting it wrongly?' "

As the years passed, it seemed that Sharon had achieved the glittering status, wealth, beauty, and success that she'd discreetly craved. Happily married to Dr. Ralph Huenemann for fifteen years, she was the wife of a respected academic at a respected university, mother of a charming, well-mannered young gentleman, heir to a substantial inheritance, and owner of a superb home.

But Sharon still lacked a deep sense of well-being and contentment. Her addiction to perfection was as powerful as ever, yet the flawless image that she tenaciously pursued still eluded her.

For one thing, there was the house. From the day she, Ralph, and Darren had moved into the house on Gibson Court—Ralph's two children had already left home—she had slowly become possessed by a desire to move elsewhere. The problem really had to do with image, money, and power, but on the face of it, it was about carpeting. The protagonists in what became a Victorian soap opera were Sharon and a local contractor by the name of Norman Porter.

Porter had built the French–provincial style, three-bedroom house in 1987. He is a member of a respected Victoria family, and his nonmanipulative, straightforward good manners and speech reflect a substantial background. His father, the late Monty Porter, who made a fortune in industrial manufacturing, was liked and highly regarded by the local community, for whom breeding and background are paramount, while money, if considered at all, comes in a poor and undistinguished third. Son Norman, while having the reputation of being a creative builder, meticulous and extremely clever, has strong ideas about what's right in a house, and this characteristic, combined with a litigious streak, has resulted in his spending an inordinate amount of time in civil court quarreling with former customers. Given these facts, Norman Porter and Sharon Huenemann were fated to collide.

Porter claims that Sharon was one of the most aggressive women he has ever dealt with. The row they had was not the result of Sharon's being a perfectionist and demanding down to the last penny exactly what she had contracted for, said Porter, because he himself is a perfectionist and customers are entitled to get what they pay for. The trouble was that Sharon had much higher expectations than what she was willing to pay for.

"They first looked at the house when it was ready for drywalling in July 1987. They didn't want all the gingerbread and they wanted more elaborate kitchen cabinets. They ordered $6,000 worth of extras. I say 'they,' but it was Sharon. Ralph showed no interest whatsoever. He sat outside and seemed to be bored with the search for a new house. A lot of people are like that. They see something in a magazine, want it, but won't pay for it. But when Sharon didn't get what she wanted she turned threatening, intimidating, and ruthless," said Porter.

Sharon chose an off-white Berber carpeting for the living room, but somewhere an error was made and a slightly different carpet, with a tinge of beige, was laid in its place. Porter said he was upset about it himself, but "Sharon flipped." Until the moment Sharon opened the front door of her new home and saw in one glance what had happened, Porter and the Huenemanns had gotten on splendidly.

"She used to come back from Vancouver with all sorts of presents, a soapbox car, robots for my children, and sweaters she'd picked up at Rene's. She was always arriving with some well-chosen, thoughtful little gift,'' said Porter. ''I really liked her. But after the carpet business the change was shocking. I was there a day or two later, and Ralph took me into his study. 'We're going to have to talk about finances, as there is a substantial amount of money due,' he said. Ralph spoke in a very calm, methodical sort of way. He said that the structural integrity of the building wasn't right, and produced a copy of the National Building Code. Well, I was a building inspector for seven years, and I challenged him on that. He became as arrogant as hell. Ironically, his name didn't occur on the title at all, just Sharon's and her mother's. There's no doubt Sharon wore the pants in that family as far as finances went. I was owed about $75,000 and got a garnishee [*sic*] on their bank account. Sharon worked herself into a frenzy and slammed the door in my face. In November 1989, the matter was finally settled out of court and they paid approximately $20,000.''

In the interim, however, Porter alleges that he was systematically harassed. ''My phone started ringing in the night. Sharon phoned a lot of people I knew and really bad-mouthed me. I had an office downtown and had a partner, named Barry Lehna, sharing the building. Barry's company, Alarm Guard Security, provided the security for the Huenemann house. They had an elaborate security system. Sharon threatened to cancel Lehna's contract because we shared the building.''

Lehna said he didn't have any dealings with the Huenemanns other than wiring the house. ''There were a lot of accusations about substandard work, and Sharon and Norm Porter got into litigation. When she found out that Norm and I were linked in some property, she contacted me and was really upset. She'd gotten it into her head that I might aid Norm in penetrating her house—that I might fix the security system so that he could do a break-and-enter.''

Was the system elaborate? Lehna said no. ''Just perimeter openings, some interior traps. There was a sort of small wine cellar in the basement, and a nanny's room or rec room upstairs, but all the bedrooms were on the main floor. The alarms were set on the windows and sliding doors to go off if they were open more than six inches. And there was a sensor that comes on when you're away. Some of the wardrobes were fixed, too. Just a regular package.''

Lehna told Sharon he wasn't about to fix the system, nor was Porter about to break into the house. ''But she went on building a case against him, and she made a point of seeking out other clients that Norm Porter had dealt with. It's fair to say that Mrs. Huenemann was quite an aggressive woman.''

Sharon's list of things that she insisted be redone included Verathaning the kitchen floor again because she had found a small piece of hair varnished into the hardwood. It appeared to be a nasal hair from one of the original workers, but Sharon insisted that it was a pubic hair, and demanded that the entire floor be stripped and redone. When the new crew arrived, they found the area with the offending hair circled off.

Despite the quality and beauty of her home, its small deficiencies were sufficient not only to spoil Sharon's pleasure in the house, but to release an anger that surged with a stunning power for months.

What was the source of this anger, of her need to be so controlling, of her capacity to be so spiteful to Doris and so aggressive toward others when crossed? Why did everything have to be so absolutely perfect? Her upbringing would scarcely explain such a profound vulnerability with its consequent rage: imperfect though it might have been, there's ample evidence of love and concern. Yet something had festered deep within her since childhood that fueled her social ambitions, her need for perfection, and her determination to control her life. This something, another impediment to her happiness, was shame about her roots, about her family. Whether the shame was essentially of her own family with its individual members or of her Ukrainian heritage is unknown.

Sharon was raised at a time when human rights and multiculturalism were only gleams in the eye of God as far as Canada was concerned. Jokes about Ukrainians—about anyone who wasn't white, British Isles stock, for that matter—were not unusual. Demeaning attitudes—as evidenced by the boss who told her uncle John Kriss to change his family name of Kryciak—were an unchallenged, integral part of many institutions. Sharon's grandfather spoke not a word of English. Her own solidly Ukrainian name of Artemenko perhaps exposed her to the cruel barbs of other children.

It is not known whether prevailing societal attitudes were the cause of Sharon's deep sense of humiliation. Experts say that a child can usually weather racism when parents are not only unashamed, but proud, of their cultural roots. Sharon's sense of shame could have developed from her own experiences, or been inherited from other family members who were ashamed of either their own family history or their ethnic heritage. If this shame was a theme within the family, it would have been that much stronger.

Whatever the cause, Sharon wanted to distance herself from her origins. She hated the stories of her immigrant family's struggles and the poverty in which her mother grew up. They embarrassed her. She loved Doris's money, but disrespected Doris. Perhaps all the talk about Doris's mothering has the picture inverted, and the problem was not Doris as a mother but Sharon as a child, who because of some deep shame cut herself off from the nurturing that Doris offered.

The facts are that as a child Sharon was demeaning to her mother, and as an adult manipulated her for whatever she wanted. Even when physically present and socially agreeable, she remained ultimately distant, essentially a stranger with most of her relatives, and over the years whittled down her attendance at the big family parties that Doris occasionally threw. She discouraged Ralph from going, and when he accompanied her they both left early.

"Sharon knew what she wanted to do with her money, how she wanted to use it," said Norma Cockroft, Doris's closest friend. "Sharon had no education—that had been denied her. Her first marriage to a doctor was to give her prestige, then Chuck Gowan provided the image, and Ralph was the one she was happiest with. I always liked Ralph. Sharon was enormously proud of him. He took forever, twice the normal time to get his doctorate, but she stood by him. It was terribly important to her that he complete it. It was part of her plan. Left alone, Ralph, in my opinion, would never have completed it.

"It was Sharon who didn't want Ralph to get involved with her family. She wanted to protect him from it. She was quite ashamed of her family. She hated the stories of Doris going to school barefoot, the sod floors, the poverty. She wanted to wipe it all out. Much of her life, her energies, were spent trying to wipe it all out. Being married to Ralph helped."

A school friend of Sharon said, "I used to visit Sharon when she and Doris and Rene lived on Fifty-ninth. I was a child, but I used to feel uncomfortable with the way Sharon treated her mum, who I thought was great. Sharon would put her down. She'd say, 'Oh, Mum!' in a sort of scornful way, as if Doris didn't know how to do things properly, as if she wished she'd had another mother. Sharon particularly disliked her uncles. She said they were always teasing her. They probably did. Sharon didn't put on any airs, but there was something about her, as if she felt a cut or two above them."

The house on Gibson Court and the unchangeable reality of her family roots were two problems—one solvable and one insolvable—that stood between Sharon and perfect happiness in the summer of 1990. But there was something else, an allegation made by Doris against Darren. Doris had said that Darren had "acted strangely" with her. When Sharon had demanded to know what on earth she was talking about, Doris, weeping, said that on several occasions Darren had tried to fondle her while they were in the pool together. It was accidental, Sharon curtly replied. Everyone knew Darren tended to play roughly in the pool, like a kid. But Doris was adamant. It was no accident. Darren had problems, Doris told Sharon, and she should get psychiatric help for him at once.

Later, when Ralph Huenemann testified in court, the memories presented of his home life and of his stepson, Darren, were those of a contented man, memories untainted by even the slightest wisp of anything amiss or disagreeable. His remembrance of Darren at the time of his marriage to Sharon was particularly touching.

"He was a friendly, talkative little tot," he said. "He always called me 'Mr. Huenemann.' One day after the marriage he asked me with great solemnity if he could call me 'Dad.' We really *were* one big happy family."

# DARREN

The Huenemann family gave every appearance of being the "one big happy family" described by Dr. Huenemann. Images of a loving, trusting, well-heeled Canadian family spill out of bulging photo albums and a score of carefully framed photographs taken over the span of Darren's childhood. The five brightly smiling people are doing those things that families at the end of the twentieth century like to see recorded—they wave at the camera as they lick ice-cream cones, play in motel swimming pools, ride on miniature trains at a carnival. There are scenes of family parties at Doris's Tsawwassen home, turkey dinners at Thanksgiving, Christmases with presents scattered across carpeting already a foot deep in wrapping paper. The homes are all well furnished, polished; they exude warmth, comfort, orderliness, good taste, and the relaxed air that goes with the absence of a second mortgage.

As Darren grows there are fewer pictures of his stepsister and stepbrother at the ritual festivities. Because many of the relatives of the Huenemann children resided in the United States and they themselves were older than he was—particularly Ralph Huenemann's son—Darren was frequently an "only" child during the summer and other school holidays. Soon after he entered his teens, he had Sharon, Ralph, and the house, entirely to himself. Family members say that although the relationship between Sharon and her stepchildren was congenial, no significant bonds, let alone deep bonds of warmth and commitment, were apparent. "As soon as they could manage on their own, they were out of the house," a source close to the family said. The relationship between Ralph and his children, however, remained supportive and loving.

Darren's growth can be traced in a hundred pictures, from the time he was an infant lying on his stomach, chubby, bright eyed, his raised head covered in a reddish fuzz as he beams trustfully into the camera. There's Darren at two in jeans and a checkered shirt, with four rabbity baby teeth and an enormous grin; Darren at four on the merry-go-round at a carnival, proudly clutching the handles of a motorcycle. There are pictures of Darren taken in California, where they all lived for two years while Ralph taught at a Santa Cruz college and did research for his Ph.D. In the Santa Cruz pictures Darren, about five, is dressed as a snowball in a Christmas parade: "Marching past the judges in the parade," Sharon proudly noted on the back of the photograph. "He loved it and they all loved him." There's a solemn Darren at six in a chef's hat, playing at getting dinner; at twelve, thoughtfully unwrapping a Christmas gift; at fourteen, sitting imperiously in a plush captain's chair at a restaurant; at seventeen in blazer, shirt, and striped tie, his hair now thick and brown with only a hint of red, his teeth even and his smile perfect, most of his baby fat gone.

The photographs recording every stage of his life also caught moments in the lives of his mother and his "beloved gran." There are pictures of a serene young Sharon, Darren cuddled in her lap; pictures of a brown-haired, plump but shapely Gran kneeling by the fireplace, as she holds her four-year-old treasure close to her with unmistakable pride. There are pictures of Doris and Darren at the beach; of Ralph smiling as he holds up a platter of Thanksgiving turkey; of Doris, Sharon, and Darren skiing; of a heavier-set, gray-haired Gran swimming in her pool with her teenaged heir, beaming at him as she had for fourteen years.

These are the images of their lives that Sharon and Doris recorded for posterity, images of loving and caring and joyful family times together, and the pictures were no more staged than most family pictures. There *were* happy Christmases, memorable Thanksgivings. Sharon *was* adoring; Doris *was* infatuated with Darren; and Darren *was* quite beautiful. There is no hint that anything could be wrong. If there was aberrant behavior, nobody identifies or understands it. We see only an attractive family that seems to have everything. And at the center of it was Darren.

"Things were more balanced when he was at home with his dad, Chuck Gowan, but once Chuck was out of the picture Darren spent almost all his time with Jean Symonds and his mum and gran," said Mildred Kjar. "He was a smart kid and learned very quickly how to act, how to please and manipulate and get exactly what he wanted. It used to annoy me to see what he got away with. But, then, I was prejudiced, because Sharon was not a person I liked. I couldn't feel close to a woman who brings a baby into the world and dumps him onto someone else straight away so she can go back to work, when there's absolutely no reason for it. As soon as he was born she plunked him with Jean."

By the time Darren was in the third grade he had the rules of his relationship with his mother—and the rest of the world—down pat. He had to be clean, polished, polite, under control, understanding, and always very nice to other people.

Earlier experiences had already taught Darren that if he expressed himself in disapproved ways—if he got dirty or lazy or wanted to swear like other kids—he would lose his mother's love. Not only lose her love, but make her angry. And when Sharon became angry with her son, she became spiteful and humiliating, comparing him with other children and asking, "Why aren't you like that?" On the other hand, Darren had learned that if *he* became angry he must not show it. He must keep those feelings down, pretend they weren't there, deny them, or substitute other feelings.

In one of their many old-buddy times together after their tumultuous divorce, Rene Leatherbarrow was over at Doris's Tsawwassen home—their former home together—when Darren wandered over from his nearby home. It was a weekend, but Darren wasn't off playing soccer or football with the kids. Unlike many young boys he was never involved in any physical sports. No activity with a potential for becoming either hurt or dirty was allowed him.

Rene was outside using a chain saw on some branches that had come too close to the house. Darren was about eight years old, spick-and-span as usual. For a while he hung around Rene, watching him work. When Rene invited him to help with the chain sawing, Darren was ecstatic. In Rene's memories, Darren was "a really nice young boy, just laughing and relaxed and easy to kid around with, chattering away like crazy and making jokes. There wasn't anything uptight about him—just a normal kid." This incident stuck with him because he usually saw Darren only in the company of Sharon and Doris. "And then he was different." How different? "Quieter, uptight, superpolite."

It used to bother Great-aunt Sheila Kriss to see what a little goody-goody Darren was. She didn't think it was normal for a child to be so polite. "It was more than being polite—you'd have to say smooth. I never felt comfortable with the way he was. It was unnatural—so solicitous of adults, so thoughtful, complimentary. Always saying the right thing, doing the right thing. It wasn't real." Darren showed another surprising characteristic: whereas it was normal to see some of the other children or grandchildren in the large extended family being a bit cheeky or defiant, Darren and his mother never, never argued. He obeyed cheerfully and at once.

Another woman was less kind. "I always thought of him as a fink, a real kiss-ass, if you'll pardon the expression. It made me sick how every second sentence of Sharon's was how perfect Darren was. And as he got older he'd say things like 'That dress looks just beautiful,' or 'You're looking lovely tonight!' He was like an older person—I hate to use the expression because it puts women down—but he was like an old woman. I found it creepy."

To all intents and purposes, Darren had become the perfect little prince of his mother's dreams. Just as Sharon as a teenager was unfailingly well groomed, never vulgar in speech or manner, and gave every appearance of being a loving and dutiful child, so now was her son, Darren. Whether the larger issues of Darren's character development were ever understood or addressed by Sharon is not known, but there certainly is no evidence of it at that time.

Psychoanalyst Alice Miller has a great deal to say about the effects of this type of upbringing—in which children develop the art of not expressing their feelings—in a book entitled *Prisoners of Childhood: The Drama of the Gifted Child.* Her perceptive comments could well apply to what went on in the Huenemann household.

"Accommodation to parental needs often leads to an 'as if' personality or a 'false self,' " she states. "This person develops in such a way that he reveals only what is expected of him, and fuses so completely with what he reveals that one could scarcely have guessed how much more there is to him behind this 'masked view' of himself. He cannot develop and differentiate his true self because he is unable to live it."

Dr. Miller speaks of parents who sometimes use their children not only to confirm their own existence, but to affirm their own worth. Such a mother "finds in her child's 'false self' the confirmation she was looking for." She loves her child excessively, "though not in the manner that he needs, and always on the condition that he present his 'false self.' "

The picture painted by those who knew Darren as a small child is that of a bright, normal youngster molded under constant monitoring into the shape his mother desired for her own psychological needs. When this happens, according to experts, there is a partial killing of everything that is alive and spontaneous in the child's unique core. He becomes empty, impoverished, a sort of mirror of his mother's needs. His own intellect supports the new "false self" simply in order to survive, and to avoid being driven mad.

Dr. Miller's vivid and compassionate description of the small and lonely child who is hidden behind the charm and achievements upon which his mother has insisted—upon which, in fact, she has made her love contingent—brings to mind the tears that Darren shed as a child when his school results were not perfect.

When such a child goes into analysis as an adult, Dr. Miller says, he or she wakes up and ask: "What would have happened if I had appeared before you, bad, ugly, angry, jealous, lazy, dirty, smelly? Where would your love have been then? And I was all those things, as well. Does that mean that it was not really me whom you loved but only what I pretended to be? The well-behaved, reliable, empathic, understanding, and convenient child, who, in fact, was never a child at all?''

Because the true child has to protect itself, Dr. Miller says, it keeps itself in a ''state of noncommunication.'' The child develops a ''false self'' and learns to live behind a mask. Such a child ''has never had to hide anything so thoroughly, so deeply, and for so long a time as he has hidden his true self.''

While there is compelling evidence of the powerful role played by Sharon in her son's life, the influence that Chuck Gowan and Ralph Huenemann had on Darren is unknown. No psychiatric or psychological reports are publicly available to answer the critical questions about their roles. Therefore their influence remains a large and perplexing question mark.

Some facts, however, are known. When he was small Darren would regularly spend weekends with his father, Chuck Gowan. As he grew, he would occasionally accompany his father on trucking trips to towns in the interior of the province, ''dressed with such spit and polish,'' one family member said, ''you'd think the poor kid was going off to church.'' Although Sharon initiated the divorce from Chuck, she appears to have supported the two of them spending time together. As Darren got older, these visits became less frequent, but the two kept in regular touch by telephone, as well.

Throughout these years Chuck Gowan, according to everyone who knows him, remained deeply in love with Sharon, even obsessed by her to the point that he wept whenever he spoke of her. However, this fixation did not prevent him from marrying again. In fact, he married three times after Sharon divorced him, which seemed to amuse Sharon: ''He's now on his third Vietnamese wife,'' she told a number of people.

Adolescent boys identify with their natural fathers (if they are around) as they form their own identities. Sharon had dumped Chuck, who had felt very possessive about her. ''I've been in the house when he'd order Sharon 'Make the tea,' '' a source close to both families said. ''Sharon would do so. He would watch her, and as she poured water into the teapot, he'd set his stopwatch so that the tea would be precisely steeped so. He tried to be, well, masterful.''

Had Chuck Gowan wanted a more passive, docile, conforming wife? What effect did Sharon's independence and her ability to take control of her life have on Chuck? What did it do to his ego? And, as a result, what did Darren—shunted regularly as a child between his natural father and his mother—make of it all?

What did cosseted Darren think, if anything, of Chuck's work as a truck driver for a department store? What did he think of Chuck's marriages, and his various other enthusiasms—his weight lifting, his flirtation with wine tasting and collecting, his Harley Davidson motorbike, his venture into the used-car business, activities likely inconceivable to the stepfather with whom he actually lived?

Could Darren, living in his very proper and predictable Saanich home, develop a satisfying emotional bond with a man who appeared to make up his life as he went along? Psychiatrists say yes, a young boy could become quite emotionally attached to such an interesting father figure. The extent to which he would identify with him or be influenced by him could depend on other factors.

Ralph Huenemann lived with Darren from the time Darren was four until past his eighteenth birthday. Yet there is little information available about the true nature of their relationship, and it is impossible to gauge in any way how he influenced Darren's development, or if, in fact, he really influenced it at all.

Though Ralph Huenemann is liked and highly respected by most people acquainted with him, few people seem to know him well. The son of a gentle and retiring clergyman and his strong and extroverted wife, Ralph is an intensely private person with an enormous control over his emotions and an astounding ability to hide his feelings. Police who investigated the murder of his wife were impressed with this extraordinary control, just as Mildred Kjar had been when his first wife died.

"One day he came over and said, 'I've got bad news. Jo's dead,' " Mildred recalled. "He didn't say how or why. He was completely expressionless. My husband and I immediately said, 'Can we do anything?' And he said something like, 'As a matter of fact you can, you can drive me to Princeton.' [Princeton is a small town east of Vancouver.] That's where Jo's body was then, but we didn't know it. Ralph didn't give out any information.

"The next day Cal, my husband, drove him to Princeton. Jo's car was there. Cal and Ralph went straight to the police station. Jo's purse was open on the counter and there were so many pills spilled out it looked like a pharmacy. When Cal got home he told me, 'What made me so mad, so terribly angry, was that Ralph then turned to me and said, "I can handle it from here, Cal." He just dismissed me, not even a thank-you.' " She concluded, "I liked Ralph, but if ever there was a stone-faced Indian, he was it."

Mildred Kjar's uninhibited opinions contain elements common to many people's impressions of Ralph Huenemann. He is generally seen as self-contained, noncommunicative, emotionally flat but nonetheless sincere, courteous in speech but prone to making inappropriate remarks. Several people who've known him over the years say that he was essentially nonambitious. He was deeply interested in Asian studies and loved music, but had no driving force to finish his doctorate, and probably would not have done so without Sharon's ambition—and lavish financial support—to fuel his energies.

While Ralph Huenemann enjoyed the kind of life Sharon's money afforded, all the talk about money and possessions that went with it certainly wasn't his style, and he likely would have been just as happy with a simpler existence devoid of such talk. Nonetheless, he had bought into that situation when he was well into his thirties, so it is fair to assume there was a willingness to accept, or at least go along with, Sharon's standards and her search for prestige. Close friends believe that Sharon's emphasis on money and possessions embarrassed and discomforted him, but there is no evidence to indicate that he and Sharon fought over fundamental principles in raising Darren, although this could well have been the case. He did counsel Darren not to talk about money—an indication that the boy talked about it too much for his stepfather's taste.

"I have always admired and liked Ralph," said Norma Cockroft, Doris's neighbor, "and if he arrived at my door at any time I would welcome him in. He was a good man. Sharon was the happiest with him."

Sharon's demand for total compliance and perfection were the core of her relationship with Darren. Did Ralph try to modify her demands? Was he passive, taking, in domestic matters, a silent back seat to the family comptroller? Did Darren resent Ralph's inability to protect him from Sharon's dominance? And what about Ralph's own children? Both were extremely bright. Did Darren feel overshadowed by their academic abilities?

In trying to understand Darren, it is tempting to ignore these questions or minimize their importance. They raise perplexing and troubling issues for which there are no simple explanations. Nonetheless, they remain of critical importance. All that can be said with any certitude about Darren's upbringing is that looking good and being nice seem to have been the predominant lessons.

The product of these lessons, the polite and smiling child Darren, is what the world saw. Norma Cockroft described him as "a proud boy, a real charmer, for he had learned how to behave, and how women liked him to behave."

Into Darren's mid-teens, the Huenemanns continued to live in Tsawwassen. Darren dropped by his gran's frequently during the week, and always on Sundays. With her grandson, Doris had always been tender, loving, and maternal, as if all her softness, denied for years and set aside in her mad rush to make money, was now allowed full play. Doris, not up on movies or rock 'n' roll, or any of the phantasmagoric elements of the teenaged world, chatted on about the only thing she knew inside out—the retailing business. For hours the grandmother in her sixties and the boy barely in his teens discussed business and money. He went with her to her stores, or wandered around the Merchandise Mart, where she proudly introduced him to everyone. Innocently she told him, "One day it will be all yours. You'll be a very rich young man."

When Darren's sixteenth birthday neared, Doris, without consulting either Sharon or Ralph, decided to give Darren a new car, an air-conditioned Honda Accord. Ralph was taken aback; Sharon was furious that her mother had acted without consulting her. Darren, no doubt observing the flack caused by his grandmother's offer, decided he wasn't ready for a car. He politely refused it, saying he had to wait until he was "older, and more responsible." Doris was embarrassed, feeling that she'd overplayed her grandmother's role and had been put in her place. But Sharon saw Darren's refusal as proof positive that all her efforts had succeeded. This, she boasted, just went to show how special, how different from other teenagers, Darren was!

Actually, Darren looked as if he had it made. In the late summer of 1987, he and his family moved to Victoria, where Dr. Huenemann, having left the University of British Columbia, had joined the faculty of the University of Victoria. Sixteen going on seventeen, Darren was a moderately good-looking boy with regular features, gold-rimmed glasses that lent a slightly academic air, clear skin, white teeth that flashed a great smile when he laughed, which was often. He was physically fit, a reasonably good student who liked good movies, had been exposed to good music, enjoyed fine food but wasn't fussy about it, lived in a beautiful home, and had a room as meticulously kept and luxuriously furnished as a world-class hotel. He also had his own transportation, having accepted, after some months' delay, Gran's gift of a Honda. His wardrobe was filled with casual, fashionable clothes, and his bank account was filled with money— some $40,000, as Gran had put him on the payroll of Rene's Ladies Apparel. Like a first-class passenger on a luxury cruise, he was moving through life cared for, pampered, and amused.

Among his friends he was considered a witty fellow, at times extremely amusing, irreverent, and iconoclastic. His favorite course was drama, and he prided himself on his acting abilities, believing he could fool anyone if he chose to. Although he had never been given the freedom to work for anything, he had everything. From his conversations and activities, there is no evidence of any strong beliefs, convictions, or values, but that didn't matter in his circle: pleasing and being pleased seemed to be what life was all about.

# Part II

**Caligula:** I've learned the truth about love; it's nothing, nothing! That fellow was quite right—you heard what he said, didn't you?—it's only the Treasury that counts. The fountainhead of all. Ah, now at last I'm going to live, really *live*.

*Caligula*, Act 1

# THE WILLS

Although Doris had been a multimillionaire for several years, and was getting richer by the minute, she had never bothered to make a will. Sharon, acutely aware of the mess that results when a wealthy person dies intestate, had been at her mother for years to get her affairs in order, but Doris kept putting her off. She said she was too busy; she'd do it soon, soon. Finally Sharon settled on a different strategy. She made an appointment for herself with a lawyer, met her mother that day for lunch, then hauled Doris off to the lawyer with her on the pretense that Doris could act as a witness. It worked. Doris was pleased with the lawyer and started talking about her own affairs.

On May 25, 1989, Doris and Sharon both made wills. Under the terms of hers, Doris left half her fortune to her daughter, Sharon, and half to her grandson, Darren. It was a simple testament, with a modest sum bequeathed to each of her brothers and sisters, nothing to her son-in-law, nothing to any of her employees. Sharon left a couple of Registered Retirement Savings Plans; shares in D. D. & S. [Doris, Darren and Sharon] Holdings Ltd., which was the warehouse; two automobiles; and some cash to her husband, but her share of the fortune to be inherited from Doris was bequeathed entirely to Darren or, in the event of his death, to his children.

No one close to the family believes that Sharon's exclusion of her husband from her real fortune reflected on her relationship with Ralph Huenemann: on this point all members of the family are unanimous. A will excluding Ralph would have been drawn up—if not at Doris's insistence—at least in consideration of Doris's wishes, for she was adamant that not one penny of her money get out of the hands of her immediate family. Sharon, knowing that she would live long beyond her mother, could well have felt that she had years ahead in which to draw up another will that reflected *her* wishes, not her mother's. Simply to ensure that her aging mother got her affairs in order and did not die intestate, Sharon expediently agreed to the will that Doris wanted. Even so, it is a measure of the relationship between mother and daughter that even in making her own will, Sharon could not act separately and independently.

Doris was pleased and relieved that she had finally taken a step that had been overdue by years. She told her brothers and sisters that she had finally gotten herself organized. Sharon was satisfied, too. She could see her mother slowing slightly, losing her edge a little in swift decision making and depending more on Sharon when she made her twice-monthly marketing visits. Both women felt a powerful need to let Darren in on the good news about the wills. They'd never made any secrets that he'd inherit, but now the need to talk about the specifics was irresistible.

"I've heard both Doris and Sharon half a dozen times on separate occasions tell Darren what a rich young man he was going to be when they died," a friend of Doris recalled. "Maybe it made them feel more powerful or loving. But Sharon did it once in front of my granddaughter. 'Do you know Darren's going to be very rich one day?' she said. My granddaughter felt sorry for Darren, saying that in front of him. It was humiliating, as if that was the most important thing he had going for him."

There was, in fact, considerable exposure to talk about money in Darren Huenemann's life. Many children, exposed to the money talk of adults, experience no effect. But money to Doris Leatherbarrow and Sharon Huenemann wasn't simply currency, a convenient artifact to provide goods and services. In Doris's mind it was survival, security, warmth, freedom, and victory over incredible odds; in Sharon's it was the most powerful expression of approval, love, retribution, revenge, authority, and superiority that she understood. Of all their emotional associations with money, the one Doris and Sharon had in common was the perception of it as power—Doris's power to give, Sharon's power to *make* her mother give. This association was central to Sharon's anger and shame, central to her *fear* of not having control over her life, as well as her ability to gain control over her life. The means by which Sharon expressed her anger as well as her power was in her strong and unequivocal sense of entitlement to her mother's fortune. And as John Kriss observed of their earlier relationship, "The more Doris gave in the more Sharon demanded."

For whatever reason, the possession of the perfect home, perfectly furnished, in the perfect neighborhood, was central to Sharon's longings and fantasies as an adult. Yet—despite her convoluted relationship with Doris—nowhere is her inability to separate psychologically from her mother seen more clearly than in the matter of housing, where the ties of dependency were so strong that Doris bankrolled every house that Sharon lived in. The manipulating went both ways. Sharon, middle-aged, did not mind that Doris owned her home. On the other hand, Doris never made an outright gift of the money that Sharon required (although when Sharon sold the first house, she pocketed the cash); Doris was haunted by a fear that her daughter's husbands might get hold of it.

A member of Doris's family said, "She never reclaimed the $20,000 that she lent Sharon and Chuck Gowan for their Gilchrist Drive home. And although she knew Rene was entitled to his fair share, she felt burned and resentful at having to pay out $75,000 to him at the time of their divorce. She fretted that someone outside the family would get her money, and as a result was determined to keep Sharon's houses in her name."

This obsessive fear was a reflection of Doris's phobia more than any reality. There is no evidence—nor has any family member suggested—that any of Sharon's husbands were interested in gaining monetarily through marriage to Sharon.

What Darren learned about life, power, and money from his father, Chuck Gowan, or from his stepfather, Ralph Huenemann, is not known. Darren's later testimony indicated that Ralph had no taste at all for the emphasis on money, and he stated that his dad (Ralph Huenemann) "always said it would do no good to talk about money in front of people." Lacking any evidence to the contrary, it would appear that the most powerful influences in Darren's life came from his mother and grandmother. He was not only a witness to the attitudes and actions of these two powerful women—he was also a recipient of their affection and attention, the focal point of a supercharged triangle.

By the time he was seventeen, Darren had not only picked up his mother's and grandmother's attitudes toward money and power, but had likely picked up on the tension that ran like a dangerous undertow between the two women. Darren's attitudes and actions—as revealed later in testimony—show that he, too, had come to regard money in many ways other than currency: as a form of freedom; a weapon to manipulate and control others; a means of gaining status; the perfect channel through which to send out messages of hostility and love. And most of all he saw it as power, the power to create his own kingdom on earth. Neither Sharon nor Doris had any way of knowing that Darren's deepest thoughts and desires were detached from reality and heavy with grandiose fantasies—that, as testimony would later reveal, he thought himself a fit subject for a bronze statue at Mount Douglas High, that he wanted to be referred to as "His Celestial Highness," or that he fancied himself a sword-carrying duke or emperor, absolute ruler of an exotic Eastern land.

By the time he was seventeen, Darren had also picked up on Sharon's powerful sense of entitlement to Doris's millions, and, because he was constantly reminded that one day it would all be his, had probably extended this sense of entitlement to himself. By now his "true self" was hidden so thoroughly and deeply he was no longer in touch with it. He had accepted the life others had created for him, had fused so deeply with it that what he appeared to be—devoted, obedient—was, for all intents and purposes, what he really was.

Sometime in the fall of 1989, Doris and Sharon told Darren of the contents of their wills, that on their deaths he would be sole heir to a fortune of about $4 million. They had no way of knowing that inside the charming young man who listened intently there was a second, unsuspected personality with a cruel heart and a distorted mind. They would have been astonished that their words were flowing into Darren's mind like a powerful toxin, that they carried a promise of freedom to construct his own identity, rid himself forever of those who now controlled him, and create a world according to his richest fantasies.

Sometime in the late fall of that year, Darren Huenemann decided to kill both his grandmother and mother. Believing that his stepfather, Ralph, would be the executor of their wills, he decided to kill him, too.

# DUNGEONS AND DRAGONS

Two months after Doris and Sharon had made out their wills Darren noticed an advertisement in a local Victoria newspaper inviting experienced Dungeons and Dragons players to join a group that met on Friday nights in downtown Victoria. Sharon had given Darren the game when he was fifteen; he found the intricate problem solving challenging and the fantasy and role playing far more satisfying than the science fiction that he occasionally read. In July 1989, Darren joined the downtown group. Colin Newall, a thin-faced, serious-looking young man who earned his living as a grocery clerk, was dungeon master. It had been difficult to find skillful players, and he was pleased to have the keen, well-mannered sixteen-year-old join the group.

Dungeons and Dragons is a game that demands intense concentration, but Darren was soon acting as if the Friday-night get-togethers were mainly a chance to let loose. The other players, most of whom were at university, were friendly, accepting, and older by at least two years. Sharon or Ralph at first chauffeured Darren there and back, but once he had his own car he was free to offer rides home or drive the gang around after the game for a bite to eat. Feeling at ease and among friends, immersed in fantasy and role-playing, he felt increasingly free to voice the taboo ideas that were beginning to possess him. Later, his defense counsel, Christopher Considine, would suggest that his words were meaningless idle talk, a carryover from the game, maybe part of the game. Experience with Dungeons and Dragons indicates that this could not have been the case.

Unlike a science-fiction story, where the lives of the characters are created by the author, Dungeons and Dragons players create their own characters as well as the setting and style of their adventures. The object of the game is straightforward: the players, acting out their character roles, set out to make their way through an imaginary dungeon to reach an imaginary treasure, or an enchanted object, or a throne, or whatever else has been designated the purpose of their campaign.

The dungeon master is the person who constructs the dungeons, which can be any passageway that confounds those working their way through it—a medieval castle with subterranean passages, or a maze, or a series of intricate corridors with many entrances and exits. It can even extend simultaneously into different dimensions of existence, so that demons and gods and other-worldly powers can be appealed to. The master peoples this world with characters of his own choosing—monsters, dwarfs, goblins, demons—and he can design the campaign, the threats and booby traps, any way that strikes his fancy. The player's goal is to get his character through the dungeons, meet all the challenges thrown at him, stay alive, and achieve his objective.

Glen Doucette, in an article entitled "Violent Role Playing in Dungeons & Dragons: The Prelude to Real Violence," published by B.A.D.D. (Bothered About Dungeons and Dragons), a citizens' group founded in Richmond, Virginia, describes the way in which a player acquires a character by rolling a special dice. "This process determines the six basic abilities of the character—his strength, intelligence, wisdom, dexterity, constitution, and charisma, with the scale of ability ranging from 3 (low) to 18 (high). This initial dice roll constitutes the given for each player and is the basis on which he must decide what class of character he will become. There are several character classes (cleric, fighter, magic-user, thief, monk) and several character races (dwarven, elven, gnome, half-elven, halfling, half-orc, human).

"The next step is choosing an alignment for one's character. The alignment of a character refers essentially to *how* a player will use the talents and abilities that were bestowed upon his character in the initial dice throw. The basic alignments are:

chaotic evil, chaotic good, chaotic neutral, lawful evil, lawful good, lawful neutral, neutral evil, neutral good, true neutral. Characters of the alignment 'lawful good' are 'strict in their prosecution of law and order...and...follow these precepts to improve the commonweal...truth is of highest value and life and beauty of great importance.' On the other hand characters of the alignment 'chaotic evil' disdain 'law and order, kindness and good deeds...By promoting chaos and evil, those of this alignment hope to bring themselves to positions of power, glory, and prestige, in a system ruled by individual caprice and their own whims.' "

Once all the players have acquired characters, named them, and chosen alignments, the campaign begins, with the master acting simultaneously as the creator, narrator, guide, referee, and participant. He will tell them what they are seeing, smelling, and hearing to help them visualize their surroundings and whatever threats come their way, and, because of his in-depth knowledge of all the intricate rules of the game, will adjudicate all questions and disputes.

This role playing demands great concentration and personal involvement, as each player has to make decisions for his or her own character, act them out in a strange and magical world, and face the consequences. A single game can last months, even years, with players accumulating power by killing monsters and enemies. In order to reach the throne, or treasure, the player has to kill the person who possesses it.

Colin Newall had been delighted with Darren when he'd first joined the group. The character Darren had then was that of a good priest (cleric), and he'd proven to be quick, clever, and imaginative, just the type of player Newall had been looking for. But after a few weeks, Newall's opinion soured. Darren, bored with a role he found dull and confining, decided to spice it up by acting out a priest who was drunken and blasphemous. He seemed to delight in disrupting things; worse, he was often genuinely funny, breaking up all the guys and completely ruining the atmosphere of total immersion essential to the game.

And then there was Darren's idiotic chatter about having a Throne of Hell in the game. This really bugged Newall. All his games were based on good and evil, but he'd never put a Throne of Hell in any of them. Yet Darren insisted on talking as if there were one, and saying that his grandmother was sitting on the Throne of Hell and that he'd go up to her and snap her neck. He'd go on and on about snapping his grandma's neck and then someone snapping his neck. Then he'd start dragging another player, Andy Thomas, into the grandma fantasy, saying, "Now you'll snap my neck."

Andy Thomas, a 22-year-old student at the University of Victoria, liked Darren, found him genuinely amusing, if a bit off the wall. Darren dominated Friday nights with his chatter and antics, acting up around the game, and talking about his rich grandmother who gave him money for everything he could possibly want and how she paid him for getting good grades and if he wanted a new shirt she'd give him six silk ones. It went on interminably—during the game, before and after the game, and during the breaks. It seemed to Andy to be getting worse: by spring Darren was positively ranting about her and how he was going to snap her neck. However, when Darren turned to him one night and offered him $10,000 to act as a hit man and do Gran in, Andy didn't believe him. He figured that Darren was simply trying to get under player Peter Tyrrell's skin because Peter was religious. Needling Peter, who was a Baptist, about killing your own grandmother was exactly the sort of thing Darren would do. Nobody, thought Andy, could take an offer like that seriously, because nobody would actually do a thing like that.

Peter Tyrrell, a student majoring in education, didn't take the offer of $10,000 in contract money seriously, either. Darren and Andy both liked to ham it up. It was obvious Darren's grandmother doted on him: you just had to look at his new car, his sharp clothes, the money he had, to know that. He was always saying that if she died, he'd get her money. But he didn't need any money because he had everything he could want. It wasn't as if he said, "I'm going to do it tonight!" although one time when Darren announced to the group, "I had a chance this week to push Granny down the stairs," it stuck in Peter's mind.

Bjorn Friedmann, a 21-year-old university student who was also a Friday-night player, didn't hear Darren make the offer to Andy, but he wouldn't have taken any notice, anyway. Darren had been ranting for so long about killing his grandmother Bjorn had long since dismissed anything he said.

Darren reveled in the Friday-night get-togethers. They were a place where, under the guise of black humor and horseplay, he could let his thoughts flow without cleaning them up, act out his feelings, and give glimpses of his hidden fantasy life, without fear of any consequences.

As winter 1989 became the spring of 1990, Darren continued to talk openly about his insistent and powerful fantasies. Even at school he felt no obligation to shut up. In the small family-management class of six students, he boasted of his grandmother's wealth and her line of clothing stores. To seventeen-year-old classmate Toby Hicks, Darren confided, ''If I kill Granny I'll get half of the money, but if I kill my mother I'll get it all—about $4, maybe $5, million.'' Toby thought it was a crock and responded with the equivalent of ''Oh, yeah.'' It is likely the more Darren talked about his grandmother's murder the more reasonable such an act seemed, so that in the end it is impossible to say exactly when his thoughts emerged from the realm of fantasy and became a clear determination to kill. It is probable that he decided on killing his mother and stepfather soon after voicing his plans to kill his grandmother, as it must have become obvious that Gran was just one obstacle blocking him from the fortune and freedom he now saw within his grasp. But he realized he'd have to plan things carefully. He'd need help to kill three people without getting caught, because no way was he going to do it himself.

The mother of another high-school student, who saw Darren frequently, noticed a change in him about this time. ''He seemed to come into his own. He was somehow freer, more definite, and certainly more cheerful. I remarked on it to a couple of people because it was striking. He'd always seemed to be a demasculinized boy, soft, undefined, unformed. He was seventeen years old, but he seemed more like fourteen. But, then, he'd been kept as a perpetual adolescent. But now it was as if a burden had been lifted. I noted it at the time, but it didn't mean anything to me. But after the murders it came back, and I realized it was about nine months or so before Sharon's and Doris's deaths.''

During the 1989–90 Christmas holidays Darren had invited a couple of Mount Doug students, Derik Lord and David Muir, to his Gibson Court home for a game of Dungeons and Dragons. David Muir had been in class with Derik Lord in Grade 10, but they'd never struck up any particular friendship. Darren, however, was friendly with Derik, and Derik was anxious to introduce Darren to David.

They seemed an unlikely trio. David Muir, fifteen, was a tall, powerfully built boy with a somewhat pudgy face, a trace of truculence around his mouth, black close-cropped curly hair, and rosy cheeks. By nature he was introverted, a loner who got straight A's, read constantly—mainly science fiction—and played the flute in the school band. The eldest child, and only son, in a family of three children, he had never given his parents, John and Vivien Muir, the slightest trouble. He had not been in any difficulty with the police or school authorities, nor had he ever used drugs or alcohol. John Muir had a Ph.D. in biological science and worked with the provincial department of forestry. Viven, who had an M.A. in plant pathology, was a homemaker. She had recently enrolled at Mount Doug Secondary to pursue her interest in photography and woodworking. Like everyone else who knew David, John and Vivien Muir thought their son absolutely trustworthy, responsible, and straightforward.

Derik Lord, a pale-faced sixteen-year-old, wasn't as gifted as David, yet he was an intelligent and capable boy. His big problem was his non-compliant and rather sullen attitude. The Mount Doug faculty assured his parents that he'd do well if he'd only put some effort into his studies, but he disliked teachers and didn't give a damn about school. He *was* interested in judo, a fact reflected in his wiry body and fighting forces–style, crew cut. He didn't drink or use drugs, and he held down a part-time job in a local Kmart. Although he'd crossed swords a few times with the school authorities, he had never been in any trouble with the police. Derik was the middle child, and only son, of Elouise and David Lord. His mother had a bachelor's degree in science and taught at a private school in Victoria. His father, an electrician with B.C. Hydro, was often away on work projects.

Neither David nor Derik had a girlfriend. They were both shy and socially awkward—not unusual at their age—but these two felt out of it even with their peers. They had hardly any friends of their own, although David had one close friend, whom he'd known since his early school days, the son of friends of his parents. Derik in particular was an anxious boy: he found it hard to express his feelings and impossible to share them, and one result of this—and his nasty, hell-raising attitude at school—was that unlike David, he didn't get on well at home.

At first David thought Darren was a bit weird. He told a lot of stories about violence and sex that were all mixed up with fantasy. One day he said that there was a mine under the school and semen was mined there. Darren also liked to tease. He suggested to one student that he'd been raped by his father, teased another because his father was the priest at the local church, and needled David because of the photography and woodworking classes his mother was taking at Mount Douglas. Still, Darren was *somebody*. Both David and Derik felt you only had to see the way Darren operated to know he had it made. It' was awesome to think that they were the two guys he'd picked to be his best friends!

Both the Muirs and the Lords owned their own homes, which were comfortable, but modest in comparison with the Huenemanns' place. Although all three houses were located within a twenty-minute drive of each other, none of the parents knew one another.

Despite their differences, David Muir and Derik Lord had in common a passionate interest in weapons, knives in particular. Both the Muirs and the Lords were aware of this interest, but they were totally unaware of its extent and intensity. They simply saw it as a normal, legitimate hobby, not at all unusual in young boys, and certainly of no cause for concern. The Muirs had given

David a Swiss Army knife when he was a Cub, and later a fine hunting knife. A relative of the Muirs was a crack marksman, and Vivien and John had discussed the possibility of David's joining a rifle club with a neighbor who was a member. Derik had been interested in knives since he was eleven, and had a collection of various types—a couple of poor-quality combat knives, a couple of boot knives, and a lock-blade knife. He also owned a BB gun.

David had never played Dungeons and Dragons, and when he arrived with Derik at Darren's home that Christmas in 1989 he found Darren in the middle of a game that had been going on for nearly two years. Darren was the dungeon master and David was assigned the role of magician.

Neither David nor Derik cared all that much for Dungeons and Dragons, but soon the closeness of the clique and all the freewheeling talk and—more than anything—having your own gang to mess around with became addictive. It was hard for Derik and David to imagine what they'd done in their spare time before knowing Darren, and the thought of annoying him and getting kicked out was scary. Soon Derik and David were going to the Huenemann house or cruising around town with Darren all the time.

In late January David bought a BB gun without a word to his parents. Whenever he could—he still had a part-time job in a muffin shop and chores at home such as washing the dishes and mowing the lawn—he'd take it from its hiding place and he and Derik would target-practice with bottles down on the wintry, deserted beach. By now he was meeting Darren every day before school and at noon. For hours the trio would browse through weapons magazines. In early spring, without informing any of their parents, they wrote to a U.S. weapons mail-order house and ordered a Damascus steel dagger. Darren announced that when he was emperor of Brunei (a part of Borneo) he would wear it.

Later that spring, David went with the Mount Douglas Secondary School Band to Hawaii. While Vivien and John Muir were at home, proud of their fine-looking son's achievements, David was in Hawaii using his time off to tour gun and weapon shops. On his return to Vancouver, he smuggled in several prohibited knives, a

Chinese throwing-star martial-arts weapon, and a butterfly knife. The butterfly knife is particularly vicious, with a handle molded to fit into the hand and fingers and a button on the back that springs the eight-inch blade. It's possible to punch with the knife firmly held in the palm, then spring the blade in making body contact.

The Muirs did not particularly care for David's friendship with Darren. Darren never came into the house but always sat in his car and waited for David outside, and whenever Darren phoned, David seemed to comply with anything Darren suggested. At school David continued to pursue his athletics and his music and to excel academically, but Derik's school problems worsened. Tossed out of a class for acting up, he climbed up onto a beam at the second-floor level and refused to come down. Sent to the school counselor, he threatened to blow up the staff room. What counseling he received is not known. While Derik's problems were close to the surface, and David's were not, it's a fact that neither the Lords nor the Muirs had the slightest suspicion of the direction that their sons' lives were taking. The Muirs, in particular, supervised their teenaged son as closely as is possible in today's society.

By now David had found another way of getting his fellow students to pay some attention to him. He brought some of his smuggled weapons to Mount Douglas Secondary and offered them for sale. The prohibited knives, capable of killing, were an immediate hit. David knew that if he could somehow get weapons into Canada without paying the usual 15 percent duty, the threesome would have a thriving business.

Early that summer, Darren said he had the solution. The parents of a friend of his, Martin Lankau, had a summer home in the American resort town of Point Roberts, situated on a bluff that juts into the Georgia Strait close to the Tsawwassen area. Darren said he would ask Martin to set up a post-office box for them in Point Roberts, receive the goods there, then bring them back into Canada hidden in his parents' car. Martin, saying nothing to his parents, agreed to do it. The trio decided to name the scam Operation Free Trade.

# THE PLOT

In June Darren quit the downtown Dungeons and Dragons game. He had a big puzzle on his mind and didn't seem able to solve it. How could he wipe out his family, when Doris, Sharon, and Ralph were rarely all together? He laid out the problem to David and Derik: would they be willing to help him get his hands on the money if he paid them? He promised to reward them well. He would buy David 100 acres with a cabin in the wilderness, maybe at Sooke, because real-estate values were going up there. Derik could live with Darren, and act as his bodyguard to get an allowance. Or maybe he'd buy Derik his own apartment and give him some land. But shit! said one of the boys. What if they were caught? They could go to prison forever. No way they'd be caught, Darren assured them. In any case, if they were, they were juveniles and would come under the Young Offenders Act. The very most they could get would be three years and it would be a cruise. At the end he'd be there waiting for them with the payoff.

For hours the three boys would drive around town, or drink Cokes at Uncle Willy's restaurant, or sit in the Huenemann home, kicking around the rewards of the venture. Finally it was agreed by all that if David and Derik would kill Darren's grandmother, mother, and stepfather, David would get a new car and some money, and Derik would get some land and an allowance.

But how would they do it? Darren had first thought of going to his grandmother's house in Tsawwassen while his mother was there, opening the gas pipes, and blowing the house up. But this wouldn't solve the problem of Ralph, who, as the executor of both wills, would control Darren's money. A second plan was drawn up. Derik knew a lot about explosives, so why not somehow get Gran over to Saanich for a night, and blow up the Huenemann house while Sharon and Ralph were in it? Darren liked the idea, until he realized he'd lose all his parents' art. Perhaps he could have his gran over for the day, tamper with the brakes of her car, get Sharon and Ralph into the car with her, and fix it so they'd all go rolling down the hill together into the main flow of traffic. That wouldn't work: you can tell when brakes are tampered with, and besides, they might all get just injured and not killed. But if you fixed the car up with explosives so they blew up when the ignition was turned—how about that? Could Derik do that? Sure he could. But wouldn't it be suspicious, a car blowing up like that? God, it was a problem to get them all at once! Hey—how about getting Gran over and attacking them all while they were sleeping? David and Derik could beat up on Darren, chloroform him, and make it look like a break-and-enter turned into murder? Slowly the outline of the actual plan that would rob Doris and Sharon of their lives was emerging.

For weeks murderous out-of-this-world ideas slithered around in their heads like snakes at the bottom of a pit. Darren had other problems to solve as well as the actual wipeout. He needed an alibi. At the end of June he phoned a fellow student named Amanda Cousins. He'd never spoken to Amanda, but he saw her daily, as her locker was two down from his. She was a neat-looking girl, straight blond hair to her shoulders, no makeup, looked in fact more like twelve than sixteen. They knew of each other because they had a mutual friend, a student named Cynthia.

Amanda was surprised to hear from Darren. They talked for a while about school and the various teachers, and Amanda explained that she'd be making several trips out of town that summer because she was involved in a school softball tournament; then, in the second week of August, she was going to hike the West Coast Trail. The following day, in fact, she'd be leaving for a game in Nanaimo. Darren said he'd be in touch. When she returned a week later, he sent her a rose, a small bottle of essential oil, and some incense. After that, although they had never met and it would be seven weeks before they did, he called almost daily, long calls that soon became another outlet for his infested ideas.

At first they continued to talk about school and other students and teachers they knew, but soon Darren started testing the waters with Amanda, the self-contained young woman whom he likely assessed as just tough and rebellious enough to provide him with the alibi he had to have. He told her about his grandmother, mother, and stepfather—not their names; just "Gran" and "Mum" and "my stepfather"—but he did say his grandmother was very wealthy and if she died half her money would go to his mother and half to him. Then if his mum died he'd get the lot. Yes, Gran was a very successful businesswoman, he boasted. "If I got the lot I'd get about $4 to $6 million." Darren didn't need to tell Amanda these details to get her to go out with him, but by doing so he staked out a role for her.

About the middle of July Darren said he'd like to do away with his family, whom he now freely referred to by their names. In fact, he confided, he already had a couple of friends who were willing to help him, Derik Lord and David Muir. Amanda vaguely remembered David Muir: she'd met him once when they were both at Arbutus School. But Derik Lord she'd never heard of. Did they know Doris and Sharon? Amanda asked. Why would they kill them? Darren said there'd be a big payoff for both of them— David Muir would get money and Derik would get property. Maybe he'd hire Derik as his bodyguard. Every time Darren called Amanda the payoffs kept changing, but the main puzzle of how to wipe out his family when they were rarely all together remained.

Amanda listened and said little. How much she believed, whether she thought Darren was giving her a line to make himself more interesting, whether she thought it was a joke, is hard to assess. She was sixteen, probably detached from certain aspects of reality in a way that many teenagers are, living in her own world where nothing much other than herself and her own needs existed. And Darren had been right when he'd perceived her as self-reliant, maybe a little tough. She was a good athlete, and there was a certain coolness, a detachment, about her. She'd been bruised by her parents' divorce six years earlier and upset when her mother moved the family from Nanaimo to Victoria three years later. Her mother, Sara, finding herself divorced with two teenaged girls to raise, had returned to university to acquire a degree in education. Amanda had found it tough going into classes at junior high where she didn't know anyone and many of the kids had been together for years. She didn't like school much, anyway, and frequently skipped classes, so she had few close friends.

Darren's spacy talk didn't bother her: it was probably all a joke. She'd never met him, but she knew from Cynthia that he was a good student, and when she got back from her trips it was pleasant to get phone calls from a fellow who could be an excellent conversationalist—at least, he always asked about her life and seemed interested in what she'd been doing—and was sometimes quite witty. And his manners were wonderful.

Throughout the summer the phone calls continued. Darren just didn't seem able to make up his mind whether to blow his parents up with dynamite or blow up his gran's house with gas. He worried that if he blew up Sharon's car with them all in it, it would look like an "assassination." Maybe the best thing would be for Dave and Derik to pose as robbers and kill the three of them with lead pipes and crowbars. They could gas Darren, who'd then give vague, inaccurate descriptions of the robbers so they wouldn't get caught. Amanda asked why they would use lead pipes. Darren said because they were "typical robber weapons."

On August 15, Amanda returned from a six-day hike over the tough 72-kilometer West Coast Trail, which runs from Port Renfrew in the south of Vancouver Island to Bamfield at the beginning of Pacific Rim National Park. Darren continued to phone almost daily, then on August 22, he proposed that they go out on a date. Nothing special, maybe go downtown and shop around a bit. He called for her the following day and for the first time they met. Darren opened the car door and ushered her into his polished, meticulously kept, air-conditioned black Honda. Amanda sometimes had the use of her mother's old car, but this was impressive stuff. Darren actually *owned* the car! They cruised around town, strolled through the malls, and chatted. On the following night, August 24, he called for her again and took her to a play.

Sometime in this period Darren told Amanda that he wouldn't have to kill his stepfather after all. He'd found out how his mother's will was set up and learned that his great-aunt, Mary Matheson, would be executor, not Ralph. There'd be no problem getting money out of her: it would be his money and he'd be able to control it all. He'd only have to kill his mother and Gran, and this made it a lot easier, because they were often together. Darren could now see a way: he started to talk about it incessantly. Slowly, Amanda began to worry. Maybe, just maybe, he meant to do it.

The summer of 1990, hotter and drier than any the province had experienced in years, flew by. Despite the length and frequency of Darren's calls, it drew to a close with Amanda having gone out with him only twice. Athletics had consumed a large part of her summer, while Darren had spent most of his time huddled with Derik and David, whom Amanda had still not met apart from her casual brush with David Muir a year or two earlier.

Darren, David, and Derik were by now up to their necks plotting the murder. The plan to kill Sharon and Doris had been worked over a dozen times, and it was just a matter of ironing out a few wrinkles. Darren, having decided that the perfect time would be during one of his mother's visits to Gran in Tsawwassen, had already been to the Capital Iron store in downtown Victoria and bought two crowbars for the boys to use. He was pleased with his purchase, he said, as he'd gotten them cheap. He had thought a lot about the knives they'd need to do the job properly, but decided the prudent course would be to use Gran's own steak knives, as any other knives would be traceable. "Cut their throats!" he told the boys. "Make sure they're dead."

By this time, they'd launched their first Operation Free Trade scam by placing an order with a U.S. weapons house for several types of prohibited knives, and were awaiting delivery.

On September 2, Amanda celebrated her seventeenth birthday with a small party for a few friends, including Darren, at her home. They all went down to the local beach later in the evening and then Darren drove Amanda back home. Alone in the car, she asked him if he was serious, if he really meant to kill his mother and grandmother. Yes, he said, he did.

"What will happen if I go to the police?" Amanda demanded.

"Well, then I'd stop it from happening," Darren replied. "Amanda, you must tell me first if you decide to go to the police so I can stop it. You see, I don't want anyone getting caught."

Darren then pointed out, as he had to Derik and David, that the boys were juveniles in any case, and would only get three years under the Young Offenders Act even if they were caught, which was unlikely. If he himself was caught, he'd act insane. He felt he could pull it off so that any jury would be convinced. But if it looked like a first-degree conviction "I'd fall on my sword."

Darren glanced at Amanda sharply: she hadn't told anyone, had she? Amanda said no. "Good," he said, "and I hope you don't, because if you do talk to Cynthia or to your sister, you'll be putting their lives in danger." Amanda retorted that there was nothing to stop her from going to the police and telling them everything. Darren found the thought amusing. "The police would never believe you," he calmly replied. "You've got no proof. They'd think you were crazy." And then he added thoughtfully, "Of course, if you did try anything like that I'd have to stuff you. Then I'd keep you around the house, sitting in one of the chairs."

A few days later they all returned to Mount Douglas High.

# CALIGULA

Darren, according to his own declaration, was "a very good actor." He relished his drama class and, during the summer, had explored several books of plays, seeking the one work that might best show off his talents. When he read Albert Camus's nihilistic, existentialist *Caligula*, he knew that he'd found it.

According to Don Neumann, principal at Mount Douglas Secondary, the idea of staging *Caligula* was Ralph Huenemann's, not the school's. Dr. Huenemann had seen *Caligula* performed at the University of British Columbia, had been impressed, and had recommended it to Darren as a possibility.

When Darren returned to school in the fall he suggested to his drama teacher that the senior class put on *Caligula* as that year's major production. He assured his teacher he was willing to do the work involved, and even suggested he would fund the play if it was beyond the school's budget. It was. Darren promised that he would come up with the money.

Darren's enthusiasm for the project was contagious. He had free time on his hands, since he had quit the downtown Dungeons and Dragons group early in the summer, and had the capacity to memorize the 60 or so pages of dialogue. Nobody was surprised when he was given the leading role. He'd initiated the project, and seemed a natural for it.

The coming together at this time of Albert Camus's *Caligula* with the apparently detached, grandiose mind of Darren Huenemann was an ominous coincidence. *Caligula* is considered by scholars and playgoers to be one of the most powerful and disturbing works of modern times. The play is brutal in its portrayal of a world that is futile and absurd, a world of suffering that has no meaning. Because the world is meaningless, Camus's main character reasoned, nothing can be forbidden because everything is devoid of significance. Evil, virtue, life, death, fidelity, betrayal—all are on an equal footing.

The power of Camus's writing is heightened by the fact that his central figure has a historical basis—the third of the twelve Caesars, as described by the Roman historian Suetonius. John Cruickshank, author of *Albert Camus and the Literature of Revolt*, quotes a *Le Figaro* interview of September 1945, in which Camus states he "invented nothing, added nothing" but accepted the account of Caligula given by Suetonius—*"un journaliste qui savait voir."*

According to Suetonius, Caius Caesar Caligula came to power in A.D. 37 at the age of 25. Involved in an obsessive, incestuous relationship with his sister, Drusilla, Caligula nevertheless managed a reign that was stable, progressive, and orderly. Following her sudden death, however, he became the epitome of vice and cruelty.

Camus begins his play after Drusilla's death, when a distraught Caligula returns to the imperial palace. The patricians around him assume his grief springs from his loss, but in fact Drusilla's death was merely a catalyst for a greater revelation—Caligula has "discovered" the truth of human existence, a truth "that is difficult to discover and heavy to bear...men die; and they are not happy."

The death and despair of human beings sum up the absurdity of life for the emperor. But while he accepts this inevitable absurdity of life, he rebels against it. "Really, this world of ours...is quite intolerable," he tells the patrician Helicon. "That's why I want the moon, or happiness, or eternal life—something, in fact, that may sound crazy, but which isn't of this world."

When told that such a goal cannot be realized, Caligula argues that "It's just because no one dares to follow up his ideas to the end that nothing is achieved." If one is logical to the utmost limits, the seemingly impossible is obtainable. In the context of the absurd, this means the destruction of all traditional values, and the reduction of everything to the same level of importance— or unimportance. "Everything's on an equal footing—the grandeur of Rome and your attacks of arthritis," Caligula tells his mistress Caesonia.

To prove his point to his fellow citizens, Caligula begins to use his power as caesar to turn society on its head: he orders all parents to disinherit their children and leave their money to the state. He has a simple plan: "As the need arises, we shall have these people die. A list will be drawn up by us, fixing the order of their deaths. And then we will step into their money." To those who protest, he proclaims, "If the Treasury has paramount importance, human life has none. People who think like you are bound to admit the logic of my edict, and since money is the only thing that counts, should set no value on their lives or anyone else's."

Caligula arbitrarily closes the public granaries and decrees famine, orders torture and execution, insists that the prize for civic virtue go to the citizen who has made the most visits to the state-owned national brothel, rewards a thief with the gift of a fortune, orders the torture and death of an aide who has been faithful. Camus's Caligula is determined to remove all limits to his liberty and "give the impossible a chance." He sets out to become equal to the gods once he realizes "it is enough to be as cruel as they are."

While the cosmic cruelty of the young emperor makes for highly dramatic and spectacular theater, it is Caligula's philosophy, with its absolute logic, that gives the play such stunning impact. This philosophy touches on a universal fear—that man counts for nothing, that existence has no meaning—and because the play focuses on Caligula and is dominated by him, it carries an immense emotional and intellectual charge.

Few people knew that for some months Darren had been seeing a psychiatrist regularly in Victoria. Doris knew—she was the one who had pleaded with Sharon to get Darren help—as did one or two other members of the extended family. To them Sharon admitted that there was a minor problem, an excess of virtue, as it were, that Darren was "too neat, compulsively neat." (In fact, he showered up to five times a day.) The family reasoned that it wasn't surprising: Darren had been dominated all his life by Sharon's addiction to perfection and her fascination with appearance. What Darren and his psychiatrist discussed and what conclusions the therapist drew remain confidential. The psychiatrist did not testify at Darren's trial and doctor/patient confidentiality has remained absolute.

Although few adults knew of Darren's psychiatric sessions—and certainly none knew he was in the thick of plotting assassinations of his own design—it seems unfortunate in retrospect that nobody saw fit to question the wisdom of Darren's delving into the challenging, and despairing, territory of *Caligula*.

In court Dr. Ralph Huenemann was asked whether he knew Darren was trying to put on a school play. Dr. Huenemann said yes.

"It was something you were fully aware of?" defense lawyer Chris Considine asked.

"Oh, yes!" said Dr. Huenemann. "The only difficulty is that it is an intense play, powerful and moving, a statement against fascism."

"Darren understood what Camus's message was?" Considine asked.

"Absolutely," retorted Dr. Huenemann.

It is a fact that when *Caligula* had its premiere in Paris in 1945—it was written in 1938—it was received by many as a political morality play, with comparisons inevitably made by the newly freed French between the actions and personality of the emperor on stage and that of Hitler. However, considering Darren's love of money, possessions, and personal power, and the fact that he was up to his neck in plotting murder, it seems unlikely that his fascination with *Caligula* arose from an abhorrence of fascism or a love of abstract philosophy. What is more likely is that *Caligula* provided Darren with a bridge between the dark world of his own psyche and the real world out in the light of day, onstage, where all could see.

As the lead, Darren could proclaim, "I live, I kill. I enjoy the rapturous power of the destroyer, compared with which the power of a creator is merest child's play." Obsessed with a need to be ruthlessly faithful to his own truths, Darren/Caligula could sneer at those around him who, convinced that he must be stopped, are too fearful to act on their own truths. "Oh, Caesonia! Just look at them! The game is up; honor, respectability, the wisdom of the nations, gone with the wind. The wind of fear has blown them away."

*Caligula*, quite clearly, did not lead Darren to kill. Long before Darren had heard of Camus, he'd set his heart on killing whoever stood in the way of his fortune. Now, standing centerstage, ordering executions, torturing on whim, grandiosely giving rewards, philosophizing over the world and his own insatiable need for order and happiness, Darren seemed soaked, infatuated, with the character he portrayed, impervious to any outside influence.

Later evidence leaves little doubt that playing emperor reinforced Darren's already-existing fantasies of grandeur and power, and strengthened the imperial self-image that he had long entertained and that gave him so much pleasure. Surely, with his own heart so loaded with dark secrets, Darren felt a surge of recognition at Caligula's sardonic quip "It's always nice to see a face that hides the secrets of the heart."

Within days of reading the play, Darren identified so strongly with the central character that he was referring to himself as Caligula and "emperor." Weeks later, after David Muir questioned his judgment and suggested Darren had made a mistake, Darren began speaking of murdering David in punishment for his comment.

"That remark is treasonous," an angry Darren told Amanda Cousins, referring to what Muir had said. These identical words are used in the video *Caligula*, made by *Penthouse* magazine publisher, Bob Guccione. This Italian film, a variation on the *Caligula* story, is so bloody and pornographic it was cut three times before it gained distribution rights in the United States. It remains outlawed in Canada, but there are copies around. Darren's use of the film Caligula's very words suggests that his fascination with the role might have been sufficiently strong for him to have searched out a copy.

When Amanda admits to being uncomfortable in Sharon's presence, knowing "the fate that awaits her," Darren calmly speaks of his mother's impending murder as an absolute inevitability: "Don't worry. It has to be done." Sharon's fate seemed set in stone: there was no possibility of escape because some Caligula-type logic had determined it.

Each day Amanda stood on the sidelines, listening to his plans and watching him rehearse the play, hearing him tell Caesonia, "I feel a curious stirring within me, as if undreamed of things were forcing their way up into the light—and I'm helpless against them."

Amanda had hoped to play Caesonia, a woman who, like herself, had uneasily gone along with her "emperor," not understanding but accepting. But the role had been given to a fellow classmate, and to Amanda's annoyance she was relegated to helping out with the props. However, Darren's need for her as an audience, a listener, remained. One day he enthusiastically confided to her, "I'll be able to play Caligula so much better after I've killed Mum and my grandmother." He then added an afterthought, "And I'll have the money to make the production more elaborate."

There seems little doubt that Darren's dark forces were drawn to the tyrant emperor as if by a magnet. His words attest to the fact that at least part of his own identity, already dwarfed, had so merged with that of Caligula that he viewed the murders of his mother and grandmother as a grand learning opportunity, as a hands-on experience that would enhance the quality of his stage performance. His impatient anticipation of these murders, offering freedom as well as money, could well have been heightened by the sheer pleasure of playing onstage a role that allowed him to freely express, in public and with total impunity, the poison of his own hatreds and contempts. He could announce his plans to the world.

Darren's casual exposure of his heart in his declaration to Amanda makes it reasonable to wonder if *Caligula* might well have given him the final affirmation, the final validation, to proceed with his plans.

Perhaps he had not yet memorized, or understood, Caligula's words to his friend Scipio: ''Those we have killed are always with us. But they are no great trouble. It's those we have loved, those who have loved us and whom we did not love: regrets, desires, bitterness and sweetness, whores and gods, the celestial gang! Always, always with us!''

Perhaps he simply thought that there would be time enough to deal with that.

Doris and her first husband, George Artemenko. Three months after their daughter Sharon was born, George was killed in an accident.

After her husband's death, Doris had to go to work to make ends meet. As post-war Vancouver opened up, Doris managed to find time to relax with friends at some of the popular supper clubs.

In 1953, Doris married Rene Leatherbarrow. The couple was determined to realize Doris's dream of owning her own dress shop and life with Sharon was filled by long hours and hard work.

*Courtesy L. Hobbs Birnie*

Shortly after she graduated from high school, Sharon married a doctor, Brent Weinberger, despite his family's opposition, and moved to California. A year later, Sharon was back home.

*Courtesy L. Hobbs Birnie*

Sharon settled into a job in her mother's business and married Chuck Gowan, a local police officer she met when he pulled her over for speeding.

Darren was his mother's dream and she took charge of every aspect of his upbringing. Sharon and Darren's father, Chuck Gowan, were divorced when Darren was two years old.

In 1976, Sharon married Ralph Huenemann. Although Darren continued to see his father Chuck, he called Ralph Huenemann "Dad." Ralph, Sharon, Darren and Ralph's two children from a previous marriage were "one big happy family."

Darren spent many happy times with Doris, his adoring Gran. Swimming lessons, birthday parties and family get-togethers were held at her home.

As Doris's business grew, she began to spend her money a little more freely. She gave Darren a $30,000 Honda Accord for his 16th birthday and treated herself to holiday trips. At the time of her death, her estate was worth $4 million.

The teenaged Darren continued to play the perfect gentleman even as he was hiring his underage school friends David Muir and Derik Lord to murder his mother and his grandmother.

David Muir gave the police a full confession during negotiations for crown witness status. The deal fell through and David instead faced trial by jury, his confession inadmissible as evidence.

Derik Lord (above, right) attended court accompanied by his father and other family members. Derik's mother, Elouise, (right) provided the boys with an alibi on the day of the murders, insisting that they were at home with her.

Officers Bill Jackson (left) and Gord Tregear (right) headed up the complicated investigation into the brutal murders that had yielded virtually no clues at the scene and few suspects.

Crown Prosecutor Sean Madigan (right) and his assistant Fran Maclean (left) battled through a series of hearings and trials to remove Lord and Muir from the protection of the Young Offenders Act and to seek justice for Doris and Sharon's families.

# REPRIEVE

Dolores and Norman Davis are a genial, handsome couple whose agency at Vancouver's Merchandise Mart represents some of Canada's top fashion producers in the medium-price range. They've been in the business for more than three decades and in a certain sense fulfill the West Coast dream: they give great parties, own a 37-foot sailboat, and live in a small, secluded home that overhangs a deep-water cove whose surrounding slopes are covered in lush green undergrowth. Now in their late, glossy fifties, they are a popular and respected couple, who knew both Sharon and Doris for decades. They remembered Sharon when she was pregnant with Darren, down at the mart, even then helping Doris to make the right fashion decisions.

On this particular day in the late summer of 1990, Darren accompanied Doris and Sharon on their regular visit to the mart. He wanted a new leather jacket and Doris had suggested that he graze through the offerings at the mart and she'd pick up the tab. Because of a remark Darren made, they were never to forget this particular visit. In fact, the whole conversation was unforgettable.

When Sharon and Doris arrived at the Davises' they set to browsing through the racks of spring samples while Dolores sat with Darren and showed him pictures of their boat. Dolores hadn't seen Darren for a while and was struck by his appearance. He looked more like fourteen than eighteen, and was as smooth as oil. Without knowing it was an expression that Sharon herself had hit on years earlier, Dolores told Sharon that her son was "a perfect gentleman."

"All my neighbours say, 'Aren't you lucky to have such a perfect son!' " Sharon responded. Darren, sitting in the corner flipping through a yachting magazine, said nothing.

The braggadocio of the response struck Dolores Davis as amusing, as well as excessive.

"But…I liked Sharon very much," said Dolores. "She always had the time for conversation and she was good company, warm, energetic, and more giving than Doris. She was very interested in gardening—I'd imagine exotic potted plants rather than grubbing around in the soil—and she would give me little notes about various plants that she thought I'd like to grow myself. There'd be instructions on them like 'Do *not* let it flower first season. If flower pod forms, pick it off.' She was very generous that way. And she had great style, always meticulously dressed but never overdressed. Very clear-cut look. Usually the only jewelry she wore, apart from her wedding ring, was a large emerald-and-diamond ring that Doris had bought for her. They made quite a couple—Sharon with her shiny brown hair, bright eyes, petite figure, and so much style, and Doris short, a bit heavy, lacking any real style, with pink tinted glasses and an almost-unbeaten record for being late for her appointments. Sharon kept her mother on track. 'Look, Mum, you said you'd be there,' she'd say, and drag her mother off to another appointment. Doris was a very good retailer. If there was a sale to be had she'd get it. One dress meant a $50 profit to her and she'd hound you till she got it. A half-dozen times a day she'd be on the phone—'Have you got that repeat yet? Have you heard from the factory yet?'

"But in the last two years she was having trouble making up her mind," said Dolores. "If Sharon was here, all their decisions would be made faster, cleaner, more decisively. Sharon would say, 'Mum, you've covered this look and that look, but you haven't covered this look. You have enough skirts but not enough blouses.' I think Sharon was very fond of her mum."

Was there any particular reason to think that?

"Well, it was obvious in her manner toward her. On this particular day they chatted all the time about the old stately home that Sharon wanted to buy. She didn't say that Ralph wanted to buy it. In fact, she never spoke of Ralph. Never. All women refer to their husbands sooner or later—they did this together, they did that—but not once did Sharon ever refer to him. It was as if they did nothing together.

"Sharon had decided she hated the house and the neighborhood where she was living—she particularly hated the carpeting in the house. She told her mother, 'I can get $500,000 for the house we're in. All you have to do is give me the $150,000 for the balance and about another couple of hundred thousand to fix it.' At that Doris protested, 'But that's nearly a million dollars!' 'We will enjoy it while we're all together,' cajoled Sharon. 'I'm going to get it [the money], anyway.' "

Norman Davis commented, "Sharon made absolutely no bones about the fact that she felt her mother's money was hers. Then Doris said abruptly, 'Well, I'm not dead yet!' Darren was there and he was listening to it all. Yet when they spoke directly to him, they really talked down to him, as if he were a child. He went on turning the pages of the magazine and suddenly looked up and asked, 'Mum, how many generations does it take for money to be considered "old money"?' I don't remember what Sharon said, if anything. I was taken aback with an eighteen-year-old asking a question like that. Later on, I couldn't get that remark out of my mind."

It's also unlikely that the remark went unnoticed by Doris. Although she had loved Darren since birth, all joy was now gone from that loving, replaced by a deep and heavy sense of apprehension. There was something unhealthy about the boy: he was unnaturally physical with her, kissing and cuddling excessively, touching with the same lack of inhibition as a three-year-old child. There was an edge of something else in those excessive attentions, something that Doris couldn't name but that disturbed her deeply. Almost a challenge, almost a loathing. She remembered an incident on a boat, as far back as a year earlier, when she had sat huddled with him under a blanket and there had been an unmistakable wandering of his hands. Worried sick, she had afterward mentioned it to members of her family, but, although they voiced the opinion that his actions were "disgusting," they were, like her, too upset to look for any deeper meanings. And that had seemed to be the end of it.

Darren's physical mauling of Doris had continued. When she would push him away, saying sharply, "Oh, Darren!" he would laugh and turn the tables by saying, "Gran, what's the matter with you!" Doris wondered if she was exaggerating, imagining, being too sensitive. Darren's touches were subtle, seemingly accidental, as if they sprang from an exuberance of affection when he and his grandmother met, or parted, or swam in the pool. Then in the pool it became worse: on several occasions Darren sought to squeeze her breasts, touch her private parts. For Doris there was no longer any doubt. Her plain, rational mind, unused to psychological or psychiatric terms, now knew with a hard certainty that something was terribly wrong with the grandson on whom, despite everything, she still doted. When she at last confided her worries to Sharon and suggested that Darren be given psychiatric help, Sharon reacted with anger. Darren was simply being childish and silly, Sharon stated, while Doris on her side was exaggerating, finding problems where none existed.

Doris had been grievously troubled about Darren for a couple of years when two horrifying incidents occurred. Doris was convinced that twice in the summer of 1990 Darren had tried to drown her.

From the time he was a child, Darren had loved to play in Doris's large, oblong pool, surrounded by the well-kept lawn and pots spilling over with colorful flowers, and tall forest trees rimming the high fence. He played games that other family members thought were weird, physical games in which he had to involve Doris, jumping on her, grabbing her legs, and rough-and-tumbling her. It used to annoy Doris, but she tolerated it.

Darren was a good swimmer—he had taken private lessons in Doris's pool—but Doris had allowed herself no such luxury. She could not swim. She would get into the pool and go through the motions, sometimes venturing in a little over her head by holding on to the side. But, although Darren often tried to entice her into the deep end, she was always cautious, for she panicked easily in the water. Darren teased her about that, and would become like an aggressive child, pretending he was going to shove her under. And then one day he did.

Norma Cockroft's house was a minute away from Doris's, and for years the two women would meet after work and keep each other company on a brisk walk along the gently winding, tree-lined streets. Norma, a pharmacist several years Doris's junior, had raised her own family, and over the years a warm friendship had developed between the two women. Occasionally it included sharing confidences and discussing problems that could be aired unhindered because of the loyalty and trust that the years had built. For this reason, Mrs. Cockroft was deeply hesitant to reveal any of the content of their discussions, and finally spoke of the drowning incidents solely in the hope they would contribute to an ultimate understanding of the tragedy. Furthermore, the confidentiality of these discussions had been already breached because the police, and others, had learned of their content from other sources.

"During the summer I had taken to picking up Doris at the door of her home," Mrs. Cockroft said. "She had been quite troubled about Darren for the last couple of years—she felt very troubled about his attitude toward money, and she had become aware of other obsessions. Her own obsession with money was apparent, but she would never flaunt it, or anything else. Doris was in manner very humble. If there was any hostility, any anger, she would take the side of the underdog. She was a strong woman, a survivor, with a very basic logic to her. Since we were walking on a regular basis, it became apparent that she had started to question many things. Several times she said, 'There's something wrong with Darren.'

"One day when I went to her door, she was doing up her shoelaces, getting ready to come with me. She was trembling and I could see that she had been crying. She was so upset I asked, 'Would you rather not go for a walk?' But Doris was a person who would never let you down. 'No, I'll go,' she said, but she was deeply troubled, and couldn't wait to dump her feelings. 'Darren tried to drown me,' she said. She said it had happened twice. Darren had held her head under water until she had almost choked, and when she had struggled up out of his grasp and cried at Darren, 'Don't you see I was almost choking?' he'd laughed and ridiculed her fears. 'Oh Gran, you just got a little water in your mouth.' ''

Doris told Norma that when it had happened the first time she had talked herself into explaining and excusing it, but the second time there was no mistaking Darren's firm grasp, the pressure of his hands on her head as he held her under. This time Doris felt, too, his intent and his hate. The knowledge of his hate filled her with more pain than she could bear.

''I think, ultimately, she felt Darren would never be able to drown her himself,'' Norma Cockroft said. ''I believe that to be true myself—that Darren himself could not do it. It was a love-hate relationship, a mixture of both when he played in the pool like an aggressive child, but when he was apart from Doris the hate for her festered. The thought of him doing anything else, well, it never occurred to me. And I don't think it really did to Doris. Not really. *That* was beyond imagining.''

Nonetheless, after the second incident Doris could not deny a gut sense of things hideously awry. She had a codicil put on her will, stating that if she died Darren was to inherit nothing of the bulk of the fortune except money for education and living expenses until the age of 25. And she told family members she had removed the key to her house from its hiding place under a false ''key stone'' by the kitchen door.

To most members of her family, and certainly to her employees, Doris seemed to be her old self. She was ''a deeply hurt woman,'' in Norma Cockroft's words, but she was also a survivor. As the summer of 1990 came to an end, Doris went ahead making plans for her life, several times intimating that she was thinking of buying a retirement home, a town house, or a condominium somewhere on the lower mainland. Obviously she couldn't stay on forever in her own home alone—she'd be 70 in December—but her health was fine and she'd been talking on and off about a retirement home for at least two years. Sometimes she'd browse through the housing sections of the local newspapers, and a couple of times she and Sheila Kriss had visited a new retirement development and gone through all the plans and facilities. But that had been the end of it.

Doris's anxiety-ridden attitude toward money still dominated those intermittent forays into the world of retirement housing. She had always dithered about making large decisions, especially those involving a substantial cash outlay—except, of course, for Sharon. This was no exception, even though selling the Tsawwassen home would blunt the edge of any cash output.

To the mingled dismay and amusement of her family, she kept hoping that a perfect condominium would be found for about $250,000. This in a market where a patched-up, ill-situated old house could cost $200,000 and a new tract home on a handkerchief-sized lot elbow to elbow with neighbors could cost about $375,000.

Sheila Kriss, who had a special spot in her heart for Doris, was saddened and irritated by Doris's frugal and unrealistic attitude. Sheila knew from her experience of running her own retailing business how her sister-in-law had slaved to become as successful as she was. Doris had earned the right to the best and the family wanted her to have it. They hated to think of Doris, who had underwritten Sharon's demands for years, stinting herself in her old age. They told Doris this, but Doris said she didn't have the money. She wanted to make sure there'd be a substantial inheritance for Darren and Sharon.


By September Darren's plans to kill Sharon and Doris were perfected. Although he had had little personal contact with Amanda since his return to school, he continued to phone her from time to time. Around the middle of September he called and asked if she'd like to go out with him on September 21st. Darren said they could have dinner out, and it would be a good chance for her to meet Derik and David, who would be returning from Tsawwassen after checking out a mailbox they had there.

Amanda accepted the date. Why she did this in view of Darren's threats is not known. Nor is it known why she failed to inform anyone of Darren's intentions to kill. She might well have feared the ridicule, the failure of the authorities to believe her, as Darren had predicted. His stories, which had once seemed the stuff of fiction, were now making demands on her imagination and resources beyond anything she was equipped to handle. Most likely, as she later claimed, she was simply too frightened to do anything, that she truly felt her own life and the life of anyone with whom she might share her secret would be put in danger. Whatever the case, she said nothing.

On the night of September 21st Darren picked Amanda up at her home and drove her back to the Huenemanns', where they waited for a call from Derik and David. To Amanda, Darren seemed nervous and jumpy, leaping up to snatch the phone when it rang. But it was David's concerned grandmother, checking to see if David was there. Darren said no, he didn't know where David was. At about 8:30 a call came through from the boys and Darren and Amanda drove to the Swartz Bay terminal to pick them up.

Amanda watched them walking toward the car. David was carrying a knapsack, which Darren told him to put in the trunk. Everyone seemed tense. The boys got in the back and at once Darren asked whether they'd found the mailbox. No, they hadn't, one of the boys said. They'd taken a cab from the ferry terminal in Tsawwassen, gotten off in downtown Tsawwassen, but hadn't been able to find the mailbox. Sharon was on the same ferry coming back, but she had not seen them. Darren was furious. When they reached the Lords' house the boys all went inside, while Amanda remained in the car. After a while they re-emerged and Derik walked around to the side where Amanda sat with her window partly rolled down. As Darren was getting into the car, Derik smiled at Amanda, leaned in, and moved the blunt edge of a knife across her throat. Darren started up the car and they drove off, leaving Derik and David at the Lords'. Amanda said nothing to Darren of Derik's gesture, an omission that could support her later claims of feeling powerless, intimidated, and fearful.

After a while Amanda asked Darren what was going on. He expressed surprise. "You mean you don't know? You haven't guessed?" Amanda said she hadn't. "Well, guess, then!" he said. She was silent. After a pause he explained. "They went over to do it tonight, but they couldn't find the place. They are absolute idiots! Such a simple task! Morons, the both of them."

Amanda shot back: "Well, maybe they didn't want to find the house—maybe they didn't want to do it."

"They were very excited about it," he said angrily. He seemed unable to cool down. He was particularly mad at David, who'd suggested that it was Darren's fault they couldn't find the so-called mailbox—Doris's house; that Darren's directions had been faulty. For an hour and a half Darren drove Amanda around the Oak Bay area and he was furious, name-calling the whole time. The job had to be done, he said. His grandmother was going to Europe for a holiday and before she went she was going to sign over $1.5 million to a retirement condominium and he didn't want to lose that money from his inheritance. (This is the approximate amount Doris's fortune would have been reduced by had she paid out on Sharon's new home and a retirement home for herself.)

There would be one more chance before Gran went to Europe, Darren said. In two weeks' time Mum would go over again to help Gran and they'd do it then, on Friday, October 5th. He'd draw a map so Derik and David wouldn't mess up again.

Amanda and Darren then drove back to the Huenemann house. They made tea and took it upstairs to the TV room. Ralph and Sharon were downstairs in the kitchen, but after a while Sharon came up and chatted about what she'd been doing that day. After Sharon left, Darren asked Amanda if she felt uncomfortable talking to her, knowing what was going to happen. Amanda said she did. Darren simply replied: "Don't worry. It has to be done."

Amanda said nothing. A little while later, a friend of Darren's called and suggested they all go to a movie at the University of Victoria. Amanda and Darren bade Ralph and Sharon good-night and went off to see *A Clockwork Orange*.

On Monday, October 1st, Victoria real-estate agent Joyce Russell received a call from Sharon saying she wanted one final look at the Oak Bay heritage home. Joyce had met the Huenemanns eight months earlier, when Sharon had phoned her regarding a house in the Victoria suburb of Uplands, and she'd been taking Sharon through various homes ever since. Darren often accompanied her. Mother and son would preview the house together, discuss its various points, then, if they liked it, would ask Ralph to look it over. Joyce Russell, a striking-looking woman with upswept jet black hair and dramatic makeup, apparently saw nothing odd in a boy Darren's age being his mother's constant house-hunting companion, adviser, and confidant.

Joyce became friends with Sharon, who expressed her friendship in her customary way by passing on her favorite recipes. She also started phoning daily to see if there was anything new on the market. ''She was,'' said Joyce, ''very thorough in everything that she did.'' The agent didn't mind the constant calls because she thought the Huenemanns were a fantastic family.

''I really admired them,'' she said. ''There was so much love and respect among everyone. All opinions were shared. Not just one person's opinion counted, but all of them. Darren didn't boast about money. He did say that if the house on Gibson Court didn't sell his grandmother would lend them the money. There was nothing out of the ordinary. They got along fine. They were really a model family.''

Early on Wednesday, October 3rd, Sharon kissed her son goodbye. She drove to the ferry; he drove to school for an enthusiastic rehearsal of his role as Caligula. He knew that if his careful plans went well he would not see his mother again. He had been specific in his instructions to David and Derik: they were to ensure that his mother and grandmother were dead, that they could not possibly recover from their injuries, and the only way to do that was to cut their throats. What Darren experienced as he sentenced both women to death, what he thought as he said goodbye, how he felt, or whether he felt anything, is not known.

On the morning of Friday, October 5th, Darren, Derik, and David went off to school as usual. Amanda Cousins slept in. She had seen Darren at school, but they hadn't been out together since they'd been to *A Clockwork Orange*. He'd phoned, and during the previous week he'd phoned a lot. Everything was set to kill his mother and grandmother as planned on this very evening. The one thing that had changed was that he'd decided not to give Dave, as he sometimes called him, any reward. Because Dave had suggested that it was Darren's fault they couldn't find Gran's house on their first attempt, he'd have to be punished; he'd have to pay for this "treasonous remark" with his life.

"What do you mean?" Amanda had asked.

"About three months after the murders, I'm going to ask Derik to go pick up Dave and bring him here," Darren replied. "Derik will somehow get Dave to hide in the trunk of the car so no one will see him come here. Then we'll get Dave to allow himself to be wrapped in chains as a game, a challenge to see if he can get himself free. Then I'm going to inject an air bubble into his bloodstream. Then I'm going to drop the chains, needle, and Dave's body into the ocean from my canoe."

A couple of days later Darren had phoned to say he had a much better plan for disposing of Dave's body. "I've found a dumpster," he said, "and I could put Dave's body into it and put it where it'll never be found." As far as Derik was concerned, Darren said he'd stick to their agreement—property in Sooke and an allowance.

"What'll happen if I tell anyone?" Amanda asked.

"If you tell anyone before telling me, I'm going to stuff you into a crawl space," Darren replied.

Late on the morning of October 5th, Amanda got out of bed, showered, dressed, and went downtown, driving her mother's car. She was supposed to be at school, but she had decided to skip it and shop for some tapes that she wanted. At about 3:30 p.m. she returned home. At 4 p.m. the phone rang. It was Darren.

"They're on the ferry, on their way," he said.

At 5:30 p.m. Darren phoned again.

"I'll pick you up at 6:30," he said. "It's either happening now—or it's not."

An hour later Darren picked up Amanda at her home and drove her to the Huenemann house. They were alone. He fetched a pack of tarot cards and pulled a black velvet cloth from a drawer. "I'd like to do your reading," said Darren. Sitting on the edge of his seat, excited and edgy, he spread the cards out on the cloth and studied them for a moment before looking at Amanda. "Your present is full of confusion," he said. "You have a secret that could get you into trouble. In the future you could become very greedy."

He then spread the cards for himself and scrutinized them. "It's all about my future," he said slowly. "I'm going to have a lot of trouble in the present, but in the future I will have power and wealth."

After the tarot reading, Darren and Amanda made a light dinner in the kitchen. Ralph came in a little after seven, chatted briefly with them, then went to another part of the house. Darren stayed in the kitchen by the phone, while Amanda sat upstairs in the TV room watching one of her favorite programs, *Night Court*. It had barely ended, when the phone rang. The time was eight o'clock. A few seconds later Darren came into the room.

"That was them," he said.

Downstairs they stopped to tell Ralph they were going out. And then they drove to Swartz Bay.

# THE KILLINGS

The day Doris Leatherbarrow and Sharon Huenemann died was wildly busy, just the sort of day that made Doris feel most fully alive. On the following Tuesday she was meeting her sister, Anne Ward, in Toronto, and the two of them were heading for Paris and a two-week vacation in France. Anne, slim, tall, and chic, bore little physical resemblance to Doris, but psychologically they were extremely comfortable together, which made them ideal traveling companions. Although Doris vacationed abroad once, sometimes twice, a year, she tended to be a reluctant traveler, apprehensive about disasters that could befall the business while she was away. Once she'd reached her destination, however, she knew how to have a good time.

Doris had asked her former bookkeeper, Betty Whyte, to come into the warehouse and give the manager, Mary Keighley, a hand during her absence in France. Doris had bought the warehouse some years earlier for storing and shipping her stock. Betty, a soft-spoken Scot, had kept Doris's books for nearly twenty years and retired after an aneurism had caused a small stroke two years earlier. Betty no longer wanted the stress of working full-time but enjoyed going into the warehouse on a casual basis when Doris needed her. On Friday, Doris had called Betty to make sure she'd be in on Tuesday, Monday being Thanksgiving. Betty assured her she'd be there.

All day long Doris and Sharon matched labels, phoned merchants, took orders from the stores, checked goods, gave orders, and wrote checks. At about two in the afternoon a longtime friend of the family, Irene Campbell, stopped by the warehouse to bid Doris bon voyage. Irene had originally been Anne Ward's friend. They had met at Woodward's department store, where they'd both worked some forty-five years earlier. Through Anne, who later moved to Toronto, Irene had become friends with most of the Kryciaks.

"I knew she'd be at the warehouse with Sharon and that if I wanted to say goodbye I'd better get over there," Irene said. "Sharon and I sat down and chatted. I had some coffee and Sharon popped some borscht Doris had made into the microwave oven. When Sharon asked what the heck she'd put into it, Doris laughed and said, 'Everything.' I could believe it, because Doris didn't waste a thing. Doris was too busy to talk. She was going in all directions, working over her books and racing around talking into the phone. Just full of life she was, full of life.''

As Doris bustled about, and Irene sat casually chatting to Sharon, David Muir and Derik Lord sailed toward Tsawwassen. For the young hit men everything was going smoothly so far. Darren had picked them up at school at 2:30 p.m. and driven them to Swartz Bay, where they'd walked onto the ferry. There was nothing to distinguish them from all the other teenagers who swarmed through the crowded ferry. They wore jeans, jean jackets, and running shoes. David's jacket was light blue and his T-shirt dark blue; Derik's jacket was acid washed and his T-shirt was white. A knapsack sat on the floor between them. At Tsawwassen they walked off the ferry with a couple of hundred other passengers. Most moved toward the parking lot. Derik, carrying the knapsack, crossed with David to the cab stand.

Parmjet Bhinder had been driving for Delta Sunshine Cabs for a year, and would later remember the two young white males, about eighteen to twenty, who got into his cab, the chubby one in the front seat, the skinnier one in the back. Parmjet noticed that the chubby one had a map of the Delta area. There was some small talk about the weather as he swung off Highway 17 onto Fifty-sixth Street. At the corner of Twelfth Avenue, he stopped by the strip of shops and let the boys out.

At the same time as the boys arrived at Tsawwassen's main shopping strip, Doris and Sharon left the warehouse in Surrey, driving off in Doris's white Cadillac. Office manager Mary Keighley had taken off a couple of minutes earlier after helping them pack their car, for Sharon was anxious to catch the 7 p.m. ferry. It was 5:15 p.m.

The afternoon was clear, crisp, the ground traced with long shadows over fading gold. The distance between the boys' drop-off spot and Doris's home was about one and a half miles, much of it uphill along streets thick with yellow and blood-red foliage. The air was chilly enough for a few fires to have been lit in the well-maintained homes that characterize this particular area. Some of the chimneys were smoking, and the smell of burning wood mixed with the salt smell of the sea, which lapped the wooded headland just a few blocks away.

The walk took about forty minutes. The boys knew the area vaguely, for this was the second time within a month that they had searched for Doris Leatherbarrow's home. Derik carried the knapsack containing two crowbars on his back; each boy was intent on killing a woman. When they had failed two weeks earlier to find Doris's home among the sometimes oddly ar-ranged streets that run along the coastline close to the U.S. border, they had simply returned to Victoria and resumed their pleasant daily lives as beloved sons and high-school students. This time they were determined to succeed. What their feelings other than determination were is not known. It's likely they felt that killing Darren's gran and mum would be a cinch. Evidence later indicated that they hardly considered the possibility of being caught, and there was no suggestion that they felt any hesitation or regret. When David had raised the possibility that they might get caught, Darren had dismissed it out of hand. Both boys were strong and Derik was trained in judo. They'd picked this time not only because Sharon would be there with her mother, but because it was virtually certain the women would be alone. But more to the point, both women were short and one of them was old. So they'd be easy targets. They were kind, too. Darren had said "hospitable," and this innocence would make it even easier to catch them off guard and kill them. The main thing was to first bash their skulls with the crowbar. After that, there'd be no chance of them fighting back.

Doris's home was easily recognizable. Darren had described it a score of times, and although the light was beginning to fade, the number on the wall was still clearly visible. The house was of a plain, subtly Oriental design, with a trellised screen wall to the side, some Oriental stonework, and low-maintenance grounds scattered with giant cedars. It stood next to the Weaver Continuing Education Centre, a modern building that filled the corner of the curving street and that, until recent years, had been the neighborhood primary school.

A few doors down the street, Gregory May, sixteen, was playing football with his thirteen-year-old brother, Daniel. They noticed the two boys walking through the school parking lot, then stopping and waiting. The parking-lot area is a popular spot with teenagers for meeting and partying on Friday nights, and Gregory figured they were waiting for a friend. However, he and Daniel noticed them again a couple of minutes later as David and Derik retraced their steps, looked around, then came back down the path by the side of the school. Both brothers stopped tossing the ball for a moment as the boys passed between them, then Daniel and Gregory went into their home for dinner. It was 6 p.m.

David and Derik walked in the fading light up the short driveway of Doris's home. A white El Dorado stood under a carport, its nose nestled close to the shoulder-high wall of patterned bricks that hid the backyard and swimming pool. There was a door at the carport side of the house, and to the right of this door were the kitchen windows.

Doris and Sharon were in the kitchen, preparing a quick dinner, when the doorbell rang. The plates were already on the counter, with the salad sitting on them, and the lasagna was almost ready. Sharon went to the door and a moment later Doris heard the sounds of some people being let into the house. Soon Sharon came back into the kitchen. They were friends of Darren's, she explained to her mother. One of them was over to see his dad and they'd just popped by to say hello. She'd offered them a ride to the ferry and something to eat, so they'd have to heat up two extra squares of lasagna. Doris popped the squares into the microwave, and Sharon crossed the tiled dining area off the kitchen and returned to the nearby living room.

The boys were ready. David had taken his crowbar from the knapsack and hidden it on his lap. Derik had his resting against the back of his leg. They had each slipped on a pair of black rubber work gloves. As Sharon approached the room across the tiled floor, Derik Lord emerged and, raising his arm, moved toward her. The blow fractured Sharon's left skull. She crumpled slowly, staggering back toward the U-shaped kitchen area. Again and again Derik struck her, splitting the skin across her forehead and pushing a portion of her skull into the base of her brain. Doris, apparently on hearing the strange, unidentifiable sounds, turned from the microwave and hurried to investigate. She had taken only a couple of steps, when she found herself face to face with a fresh-faced young man whom she had never seen before. The blow that struck her right skull was immediate and massive, shattering the bone and almost tearing off her ear. She fell to the floor, unconscious.

Sharon, despite her injuries, was conscious and lucid. Unable to get up, she lay on the floor a few yards from her mother, watching as her son's two young friends went behind the banquette area and started rummaging through the kitchen drawers. "Why are you doing this?" she asked. There was no reply. Again they went by her, this time into the bathroom looking for towels. Then they were back in the kitchen. Under the sink they found dishcloths. "Why are you doing this?" she asked, again and again.

The last thing she saw was the two boys standing over her and a red-and-white checkered dishcloth coming down over her face. Then Derik Lord bent down to her and, using a long, nonserrated knife, stabbed her in the throat. He knew he had to cut the jugular vein, but damned if he could find it. Then, with a swift right to left movement, he severed the major arteries of Sharon's neck. Blood spurted up over his jacket.

David stood over Doris, who lay face down, reaching awkwardly with the knife under her neck, trying to cut her throat. But the plastic handled knife with a straight, thin blade, which he'd taken from the kitchen drawer, seemed blunt. Giving up in disgust, Muir left to ransack the bedroom. When he returned a couple of minutes later, Derik had rolled Doris onto her back. A knife stuck out of her throat.

Hurriedly, they went through the house. They found two women's purses, one in the master bedroom, one in the second bedroom. They removed and kept the money, then scattered the billfolds and the rest of the contents of the purses on the floor. They opened wardrobe doors, pulled clothes out, and tipped the items in the built-in wall drawers onto the floor. They then unlocked the patio sliding door, went to the woodpile, and found the key that Darren had said would be there. They went back in through the patio door, closing it but leaving it unlocked. David threw the key up the hall, so that it fell on the floor near one of the bedrooms. They picked up their crowbars, stuffed them into the knapsack, then slid outside to the carport.

It was nearly dark. There was no sound; the streets were deserted. They removed their gloves, stuffed them into the knapsack too, and went down the driveway. The whole job had taken about fifteen minutes. Getting back to the main shopping strip was all downhill and easy. But even half running it was a touch-and-go situation, for they *had* to be on the seven o'clock ferry. Finally they reached the shopping strip.

Kathy Toyne, a tall, willowy blonde, was taking the calls at Delta Sunshine Cabs that evening. Sixteen years of age, she was employed to record the calls and pass them on to the dispatcher. At 6:45 p.m. a call came in to pick up someone at the corner of Twelfth Avenue and Fifty-sixth Street. The caller said he was trying to catch the seven o'clock ferry. Carefully, she wrote down all the information and asked for his name. "Dave," he said. Kathy passed the slip to the dispatcher, and a few minutes later cabdriver Paul Martin picked the two boys up and sped toward the terminal. But traffic was plugged bumper to bumper, and after crawling halfway down the single line toward the ferry, the cab came to a halt. It was almost seven. The boys leaped out, threw a $20 bill on the seat, grabbed their knapsack, and ran down the side of the road.

The ferry was also late. It would be another twenty minutes before David Muir and Derik Lord joined the mass of foot passengers walking onto the ferry for the one hour and fifty minute return trip to Swartz Bay. Once on board, there was nowhere to sit. Derik finally sat on a chest where life jackets are stored. Julie Anne McClung happened to be sitting across the lounge. She was a student at the University of British Columbia but recognized Lord from her days at Arbutus School and later at Mount Doug. Idly she watched him for a moment, then resumed reading. At about the same time, at Delta Sunshine Cabs, Kathy Toyne took the completed call slip from ''Dave'' and filed it with the rest of the day's records.

As the ferry headed toward Swartz Bay, another ferry was pulling out of Nanaimo on the east coast of Vancouver Island, heading for Tsawwassen. On board was Jim Kriss, Doris's nephew, with his wife, Barbara, and two children. Jim and Barbara had driven down from Campbell River with the intention of catching the ferry to Horseshoe Bay, which is slightly northwest of Vancouver. It was a convenient spot from which to reach the Kerrisdale home of Jim's parents, John and Sheila Kriss.

When Jim and Barbara reached the Nanaimo terminal it was clogged. A long wait for the Horseshoe Bay ferry was inevitable. As they sat there, a ferry employee moved down the lines of waiting cars, informing passengers that the ferry was leaving for Vancouver via Tsawwassen shortly, and that if they didn't mind taking that route, there was ample room and immediate boarding. For the Krisses it meant a slightly longer trip at the other end— maybe fifty-five minutes instead of forty—but that was nothing compared with a two-hour wait.

Doris was Jim's godmother and there was a particular fondness between them. Jim was a late bloomer. He'd been a restless, rebellious teenager, and it wasn't until his late twenties that he'd finally matured. In his struggle he'd gained a lot of self-knowledge. Now, at thirty-six he was plain spoken, responsible, and affectionate. Doris had watched Jim's growth with interest, and wished to help him in her own limited fashion. Because he wanted to buy his own home, Doris said she'd lend him $10,000.

Sitting in the Nanaimo terminal, with the children growing restless, Jim and Barbara decided to take the alternative route, and just before seven o'clock boarded the ferry for Tsawwassen. It was a decision that placed them close to the murder scene near the time of the deaths.

One hour and forty-five minutes later they were on the mainland and driving down Highway 17. Approaching the turnoff to Doris's home, they debated whether to pop in and say hello. Normally they would have, but the children were tired and the traffic was horrendous. They kept heading for Kerrisdale.

At the same time that Jim and Barbara were debating a visit to Doris, Derik and David were disembarking at Swartz Bay. Darren and Amanda were waiting. Darren had been quiet and intense on the drive in, wondering aloud whether the boys had pulled it off. Now, as the two boys got into the back seat, it was Derik who seemed nervous. He kept looking around and was almost totally silent. David was smiling and appeared happy.

"So?" asked Darren. "Is it done? How did it go?"

"Fine," David said, "fine."

"Well, what happened?" Darren demanded.

"What do you mean, what happened?" Derik shot back. "We just killed two people."

"Well, did you have any trouble finding the house?" Darren was on edge waiting to be filled in.

"A bit of trouble," said David. "Those streets are weird." Then he added that once they'd found the house, they went up to it, knocked, and Sharon had answered the door.

"I said we were over to visit my dad, and Sharon asked us in and offered us some lasagna," said Derik.

"She even offered to give us a ride back to the ferry," said David, and both the boys laughed. They then described how they had hidden the crowbars and how they'd used them to strike Sharon, then Doris.

"Was there any trouble?"

"I put a one-inch hole in Gran's head and she went out," David said. He seemed pleased and excited.

"I had problems with Sharon," Derik said. He was morose and tense. "She was lying on the floor, asking why we were doing it. There she was, saying 'Why, why, why are you doing this?' "

"Well, you didn't tell her, did you?" Darren demanded.

"No, I didn't tell her," Derik replied. But he said they couldn't stand her lying there, watching them, so they'd gone looking for towels, but couldn't find any.

"My gran never keeps towels around," Darren interjected. "Only for visitors."

"Well, we couldn't find any, so we got some dishcloths from the kitchen and put them on their faces so they wouldn't be watching us. Then we got knives out of the kitchen drawers and we cut their throats. I got blood on my jacket and David has blood on his shoes."

Darren advised them to burn the clothing.

"I can't burn my jacket," Derik replied. "If I do Mum will notice that it's missing. Anyway, the blood will come out with dry cleaning."

David didn't seem to care about the blood on his shoes. "We'll be getting new shoes soon," he said. He appeared happy, almost giddy.

"Did you get the money?" Darren demanded.

"We couldn't find any money under the stove," said Derik. He sounded upset.

Darren then asked if they'd taken the money from his mum's and gran's purses. David said they had, and produced $1,580 in bills from his pocket. Sitting in the back of the car, he counted them out, split the wad in two, and gave half to Derik. The two boys then described how they'd messed up the house, then left the key on the floor. They boasted that they'd made it look just as if thieves had been there.

"Did you get rid of everything?" Darren asked.

David laughed excitedly. "Yeah, we threw it all overboard from the ferry. It even hit the side on the way down."

Darren persisted. "Did the crowbars sink?"

"Oh, for God's sake," snapped Derik. "The bag had crow-bars in it, two crowbars. Of course it sank."

For a moment Darren was silent. Then he asked, "Are you sure they were really dead?"

"We're sure," they said. "Absolutely sure."

Darren wanted no details. After a few minutes he turned to Amanda and said, "You must be pretty nervous. You must be looking for us to drive down a dirt road." He then ran through their alibi again. Amanda was to say she'd seen the two boys downtown on the Friday afternoon, had later picked them up outside Cotton Ginny's in the main shopping area, then they'd all had dinner together in Chinatown.

"Now, you've got to swear an oath you'll stick by the alibi," Darren ordered. "You've got to raise your right hand and swear Aye." Obediently the three of them raised their right hands and said, "Aye." Derik said "Aye, Commander."

When they reached Derik Lord's house, David Muir picked up his bike and rode home. Then Darren, Derik, and Amanda drove to Oak Bay to look at the house Darren planned to buy with his inheritance. En route Darren asked Derik how David had been. Derik said he'd been okay and was proud of what he'd done. Darren then drove Derik home, and a little while later dropped Amanda off at her place. As soon as he reached his own home, he went upstairs to the rec room, where Ralph Huenemann sat waiting anxiously for Sharon to arrive. He stood at the doorway, bade his stepfather good-night, and went to bed.

# Part III

**Caligula:** Do you think, Cherea, that it's possible for two men of much the same temperament and equal pride to talk to each other with complete frankness—if only once in their lives? Can they strip themselves naked, so to speak, and shed their prejudices, their private interests, the lies by which they live?

**Cherea:** Yes, Caius, I think it is possible. But I don't think you'd be capable of it.

**Caligula:** You're right. I only wished to know if you agreed with me. So let us wear our masks, and muster up our lies. And we'll talk as fencers fight, padded on all the vital parts.

*Caligula,* Act 3

# THE INVESTIGATION

After Constable Darwin Drader checked out the house on Forty-ninth Street and saw the bloodied bodies of two women through the window, he'd radioed Delta police headquarters to send in the homicide team. Within the hour Staff Sergeant Raymond Oliver and identification expert Special Constable David Roberts were at the scene.

All the doors and windows of the house were locked and unbroken, except for the patio door on the south side. It was closed but slid open. The lag bolt was lying inside on the floor and there were tree needles on the carpet.

At 3:34 a.m. Roberts went into the house through the full-length sliding door. As he looked for trace evidence and recorded the scene photographically, he worked from a base of 35 years of police experience in the United Kingdom, New Zealand, and Canada, 27 of them in forensic identification. In his late fifties, he was as used to the scene in front of him as any human can be. A short, plump, elderly woman lay in the open hallway just outside the U-shaped area of the kitchen. Flat on her back, her right arm flung out and her left ankle crossed over her right, she could simply have been asleep if not for the matted hair that stuck to the dried blood on her face and the long, tapered knife that protruded from her neck. A few feet away, lying parallel to the kitchen cupboards, was the body of a younger woman, the neck and front of her cream, flowered pullover soaked in blood and a brown-handled, nonserrated breadknife sitting on her chest. The curly brown hair of the younger woman was visible, as was the

117

short gray-brown hair of the older woman, but their faces were hidden. The killer or killers had put a red-and-white checkered dishcloth over the face of each woman.

Moving carefully, methodically, through the paneled house, with its heavy beams and high-ceilinged living room, Roberts noted the signs of an interrupted burglary. In the master bedroom one wall of teak paneling faced another consisting entirely of drawers. All these drawers had been pulled open and the contents half spilled or tossed onto the thick carpet. A fully packed suitcase lay on the bed. In the cherrywood-paneled second bedroom a woman's purse had been flung to the floor and the contents strewn around. Lying on the floor outside the bedroom was a key. It later proved to be for the front door.

The house was stifling, although the thermostat was set at only 70 degrees. Returning to the kitchen, Roberts saw that the heat was coming from the top of the stove, where gas jets burned under two blackened pots. In one pot were the charred remains of beans; in the other, beets. Celery and tomatoes had been cut up on the counter and set out on two plates. The microwave door was open, and four servings of lasagna sat inside. There were two full place settings for dinner, but two more plates had been placed on the counter—as if guests had just arrived? Two knives lay in an open drawer, blood and hair stuck to one. Roberts nosed through the custom-made Polynesian-walnut cabinets in the kitchen. He checked the built-in oven more carefully, then groped about in the lazy Susan built beneath it. Stuck at the back was an egg carton and a quilted satin box. Both contained jewelry—some gold brooches, gold necklaces, and jade. There were several bills, and an envelope containing $259 in cash.

Neither body showed any signs of a sexual attack. The younger woman's cream pullover had not been torn or tampered with, and her black twill slacks were neatly zippered and in place. The older woman also wore black slacks, and her sweater, too—black with a large flower—was in a normal position, pulled down comfortably over her hips.

Just as it was obvious the attack had not been sexual, it was obvious that whoever had attacked the women had wanted them dead, and that the women seemed to have been caught totally off guard while they prepared their dinner. There were no visible bruises or cuts on the arms and hands of the type received when victims struggle to ward off anticipated blows to the head or upper body. And the two extra plates had been added later. Had the two women known the killer? Killers?

Roberts cruised the house again, now joined by his partner, Identification Officer Dave Black. There was no sign of forced entry. Constable Darwin Drader had reported that the sliding door off the patio was unlocked when he'd found the bodies. The bedrooms, Roberts noted, were in a mess, as they often are when thieves go on a rampage. But the scene simply didn't jell. There were too many valuables such as TVs and electronic equipment lying around, or cash and jewelry hidden in places familiar to any thief, for this to have been a genuine break-and-enter gone awry. It was, in fact, just the sort of mess some fool might create in an attempt to deceive the police.

As night faded, the number of police at the house grew. Inspector David Rankin, after reviewing the scene, had phoned Detective Bill Jackson in Delta and named him primary investigator; he was to work with Sergeant Hugh Davies. The Royal Canadian Mounted Police had been called in, and one of their specialists, Sergeant Herb Leroy, was already inside, scanning the house with a Lumalight, a portable laser that detects tiny fibers, hair, and other minutiae not visible to the naked eye. Coroner Michael Olifkey came and went. Soon after dawn—after calling Gordie Tregear in Victoria and asking him to notify the next-of-kin, then phoning Ralph Huenemann and telling him to stay by the phone—Jackson arrived at the scene.

Both victims had been struck on the head with massive force, but nothing in the house appeared capable of producing that type of wound. The knives used to cut the women's throats seemed to have come from the kitchen drawer. Officer Leroy of the RCMP, a blood-splatter analyst, told the investigating team that his findings were consistent with the women's throats being cut as they lay on the floor, where they were found. For hours, identification specialists crawled over the house in what turned out to be a futile search for suspect fingerprints. At 1 p.m., New Westminster pathologist Ruth Sellers arrived to examine the bodies and determine the time of death.

Twenty hours after Sharon and Doris had been murdered, their bodies were still lying on the kitchen floor. At almost precisely the same time that they were finally removed to the New Westminster morgue, Darren and Ralph Huenemann arrived at the police department in Delta. They had left Saanich at 1 p.m. and, on arriving in Tsawwassen, had immediately driven to the police station, where Bill Jackson was expecting them. Jackson, a burly, comfortable man with soft gray hair and an understated manner, had heard of Darren's gut-wrenching, hysterical reaction to the deaths of his mother and grandmother. He was sensitive to the loss both men had suffered and was pleased with their willingness to cooperate when, as he later told other officers, ''they must both be going through sheer hell.''

Darren had by this time ostensibly pulled himself together. He assured the police he would do absolutely anything to help find the killer. Both he and Ralph gave full, clear statements as to their activities and whereabouts the previous evening. It was straightforward stuff. Ralph Huenemann said he had arrived home from the tennis club at 7 p.m. and had stayed at home all evening. He had chatted with Darren and Darren's friend, Amanda Cousins, then waited for his wife. When Sharon had not arrived home by midnight, he had driven to the ferry, both to check the route and to see if by any chance her car was still at the terminal.

Darren said that he had picked up his friend, Amanda, at her house at about half past six, and brought her back to his place, where they'd both gone into the kitchen and prepared dinner. At about eight o'clock he and Amanda had gone down to Chinatown, where they'd picked up a couple of schoolfriends and driven around town until he'd taken Amanda home. He had returned to his house about 10 p.m. and had gone to bed. Darren then gave Jackson a description of the valuables in his grandmother's house—about $100,000 in jewelry and some cash. ''I'll inherit everything,'' he told Jackson, estimating that ''everything'' would be about $4 million and included four women's dress shops. Darren said that his aunt, Mary Matheson of Victoria, was the executor of the estate. Chattering on, his manner one of a person desperately anxious to assist, Darren volunteered, "And by the way, if you're looking for ways to break into the house, my grandmother sometimes left a key outside. Through the carport, down the steps, there's a woodpile on the left. At the bottom of the woodpile is a plastic key stone. It's like a stone, but underneath is a place for a key."

Jackson found it an interesting comment, because a key *had* been found inside the house. But what made it more than interesting was that police had already learned from a neighbor close to Doris that some months earlier Doris had decided to stop hiding the key outside. Only if a family member specifically called her to leave it out, would she do so. Jackson tucked this information into the back of his mind and, after the two men had left, phoned Gordie Tregear in Saanich and asked him to interview Amanda Cousins.

A couple of hours later Tregear phoned back to say that Amanda's statement looked okay. Amanda said that Darren had left school after classes at about 2 p.m. on Friday and that he had driven Derik Lord and David Muir to Chinatown. She'd had the use of her mother's car that day, and had followed Darren's car downtown. She'd then visited a couple of stores and driven back home. At about 3:30 p.m. Darren phoned her, and three hours later he picked her up and they'd driven to the Huenemann house. Once there, they'd gone into the kitchen and prepared dinner for everyone. At 7 p.m. Ralph had come in from playing tennis, and at 8 p.m. Derik and David had phoned from Chinatown and asked to be picked up. Amanda had gone downtown with Darren, they'd picked up the boys, then they'd driven around for a while. David had to get home, so they dropped him off. Darren then drove Derik home at 10 p.m. and dropped Amanda off at her house a half hour later.

Jackson agreed with Tregear: it looked as if Darren was in the clear. The following morning, Jackson met again with Darren and Ralph at the Delta police station. By then Jackson had located Doris's will and a copy of Sharon's will and confirmed the fact that

Darren was to inherit everything upon the deaths of both his grandmother and mother. Ralph had been left out entirely from the main fortune and stood to gain nothing—or at least nothing of great significance—from the death of his wife. This fact, apart from any other consideration, removed Ralph Huenemann as a suspect in the deaths. In the course of the Sunday-morning interview, Jackson was intrigued to learn from both Ralph and Darren of the long and bitter battle that the Huenemanns had had with the Victoria contractor who had built their Saanich home. Jackson noted the name—Norman Porter—and decided to investigate that lead further.

Meanwhile, he wanted to pursue another possibility. It was almost inconceivable that money wasn't somehow involved. What other motivation could there be? The crime wasn't sexual, the "mess" in the house looked phony, it wasn't a crime of passion, there was no suggestion of drugs or any criminal involvement. With sex, hatred, and revenge wiped out, the only motive left was money—in this case plenty of it. Who had had financial dealings with Doris?

Early Monday, Jackson interviewed Mary Keighley, Doris's 57-year-old manager. Mary had been with Doris only two years, but she told them all she knew. From this and another source he learned that Doris had intended to lend her nephew, Jim Kriss, $10,000 as a down payment for a house after his father had given his request for help short shrift. True to form, the $10,000 was to be a loan rather than a gift!

Five days after the murders, Jim's wife, Barbara, was alone in her Campbell River home when two police officers—Jackson and Tregear—came to her door. Her two children were at school, her husband was away on business. They stayed two hours, during which Barbara claimed she became "scared out of her mind." She says they asked over and over why anyone who wanted to go to Kerrisdale would take the ferry to Tsawwassen and not to Horseshoe Bay, a more obvious route? What were she and her husband doing in Tsawwassen? She tried to explain they'd taken that route because they would have had a long wait for the Horseshoe Bay ferry, but it seemed to make no difference to the officers. They demanded the ferry receipt. By some miracle she'd kept it. The officers then said they were just making inquiries, but they left Barbara bewildered and frightened. Sobbing, she called her mother-in-law, Sheila Kriss. Sheila in turn called her cousins, Pat and Ed Crowe, in Campbell River. When they arrived at Barbara's home they found her in hysterics and took her home with them, and later picked up the children from school. It was Barbara's first contact ever with the police.

The next day Jim Kriss returned home. He immediately phoned the Delta police and asked if they wanted him to make a statement. Neither Jackson nor Tregear felt it was necessary. All of Doris's bank accounts and books had been checked by then and there had been no withdrawal of $10,000, or any check written for that amount. Jim and Barbara Kriss were simply not viable suspects. Nonetheless, a few days later the RCMP visited the Kriss household and asked Jim to come down to the police station to be fingerprinted and to take a lie-detector test. Confused, still stunned by the death of an aunt to whom he felt exceptionally close, and wanting to help but feeling outraged, he asked if he was under suspicion. He was assured that he was not. "We're simply clearing up some loose ends," an officer said. The test cleared Kriss completely.

Delta police felt it was time to take a closer look at Victoria contractor Norman Porter, whose bitter relationship with the Huenemanns had not only been so vividly described by Darren and Ralph, but whose reputation—preliminary police inquiries indicated—was that of a gifted, quick-tempered man who enjoyed a day in court challenging any client who'd had the temerity to question his professional judgment.

On Friday, October 12th, one week after the murders, Porter was visiting a friend in a Saanich body shop he frequented, when, in his own words, "Detectives Bill Jackson and Hugh Davies came roaring down the driveway and stopped in front of the shop, while at the same time a Saanich police car (with Gordie Tregear) pulled up at the back. It was wild, like television. I couldn't believe it." Porter, with the help of his lawyer, Richard Margetts, made a lengthy statement. It included the fact that he had been with his friend, Gary Cunningham, in the same body shop until 8:30 p.m. on the evening of October 5th. Cunningham confirmed Porter's statement.

Three days later, on Monday, October 15th, a double funeral service was held for Doris and Sharon at the Ocean View Cemetery in Burnaby. It was a chilly, gray day, but the parking lot was filled with the big, solid automobiles of the sort that Doris favored. About 450 people had come to pay their last respects— some 70 family members, plus fellow merchants, staff members, members of the minichain group (merchants who had acquired several stores in the lower mainland but had not gone national), salesmen and suppliers, a few neighbors, and a lot of police officers.

The presence of two coffins, mother and daughter side by side, the lids covered in red and white roses, affirmed not only the deaths of Doris and Sharon but the senseless brutality that had marked their end. The mourners were edgy as they struggled to cope with an experience unlike anything any of them had known. As the service proceeded, a series of incongruous events intensified the ambiance of tension and confusion.

Ralph Huenemann had a lifelong interest in chamber and choral music. He was on the Board of the Vancouver Chamber Choir, and in choosing pieces for the service, which the Vancouver Chamber Choir was to sing, he selected those that meant something to him and Sharon. The hymns included Bach's motet *Lobet den Herrn* (Praise to the Lord) and the Crimon arrangement of the Twenty-third Psalm (The Lord Is My Shepherd), both highly traditional. But some of the other selections were more esoteric and unfamiliar to many of the mourners. Sung a capella, Ralph's choices floored Doris's family and infuriated some of her friends, who thought the music "absolutely weird, fit for a concert hall, maybe, but not for these circumstances."

When the choral works were over, the Reverend Ross Manthorpe proceeded with the service. But the audio system in the chapel was wrongly connected to the system in another room, which nobody was able to locate. As the Reverend Manthorpe spoke, rock 'n' roll music blasted out of the wall and filled the packed chapel. This was followed by loud youthful giggles and chatter.

Sheila Kriss stood to give the eulogy for Doris. After describing her prairie childhood and early years, Sheila spoke of Doris's business sense—"a unique style that was a crazy mix of procrastination and brilliance"—then turned to her relationships. "Family was important. She helped us all in one way or another. When Anne would visit from Toronto, Doris would plan a big dinner party, invite all the brothers and sisters with their families, and cook up a storm with garlic as the main ingredient. We were all great at spending her money for her—why not buy a condo at Whistler or Palm Springs, perhaps a new boat or whatever? She would laugh about our schemes, yet we knew Sharon and her grandson Darren were her two most precious possessions.

"Darren was the light of her life. Through the years even his swimming lessons and birthday parties were held at her house. Their closeness and companionship brought warmth and love to both their lives. He was the answer to all her hopes and dreams for the future."

Then Dr. Huenemann read the eulogy for Sharon. It was at first simple and touching, emphasizing the strong bonds that had made the blended family of his two children and Darren into one happy, loving unit. "Sharon had the capacity to put others completely at ease. She had a transparent decency that appealed to everyone she met, except for those few pathetic individuals who have no capacity for decency. She made absolutely no distinction between people, not by skin color, nor by religion, nor by age, nor by gender, nor by any other label—and especially not by social status."

Ralph then referred to Sharon's interest in aerobics, and the fact that some years earlier she had become so keen she'd trained to be an instructor. Aerobic instructors, he said, are "young, slender, supple, and enthusiastic." Sharon, as "a short, middle-aged, slightly out-of-shape Ukrainian, made an odd member of the team, to say the least. But her students loved her classes because of her less-than-perfect human form, and she became an inspiration to them all."

The mourners filed out to gather for coffee in a small hall. Sharon's body, which was to be cremated, was left in the chapel; Doris's coffin was wheeled off for burial. At this point Chuck Gowan broke away and ran across the lawn, with Darren chasing after him. Gowan was sobbing. Embarrassed mourners paused to see the loving, solicitous son with his arm across his father's shoulders comforting him, "It's all right, Dad. It will be all right."

Dr. Huenemann departed immediately, leaving some mourners free to express their astonishment at his remarks. "To have called neat, stylish, clever Sharon 'a short, middle-aged, slightly out-of-shape Ukrainian' is bizarre," one woman exploded angrily, wiping away tears. "Especially after him saying Sharon never labeled anyone!"

"Forget it," her husband said testily. "It's just Huenemann's way of dealing with it. Christ, can you imagine what he's going through?"

Ralph Huenemann might have been going through hell, but there was no sign Darren was. Police who'd dealt with him during the previous week had remarked on his emotional flatness, the absence of any of the normal signs of grief. Now he seemed to be almost on a high. He greeted mourners with a lively, "Hi, good to see you." As he held one woman at arm's length, his eyes swept her outfit: "Hey, that suit looks terrific!" She felt his attitude was so incongruous that she later remarked to a friend, "It was as if we were at a party, with Darren playing the happy and solicitous host. When I got home, I started to wonder if we actually were."

Nearby, Nancy Poirier watched Darren's charm-school performance with a growing sense of nameless apprehension. On the Sunday following the murders Darren had phoned her to inform her of the deaths. "I suppose you know Mum and Gran have been murdered," he'd said bluntly. After that he didn't mention their deaths, but kept repeating how he'd tried to get hold of Nancy earlier and how important it was to him to do "the right thing." The call left Nancy perplexed and uncomfortable: it was as if the deaths of his mother and grandmother were secondary to his obsessive desire to be seen as polite.

Among the mourners was George Garrett, a respected veteran news and crime reporter for radio station CKNW. Garrett had known and admired Doris Leatherbarrow for years. Wryly he summed up the obsequies: "It was the strangest funeral I've ever attended and Ralph Huenemann's eulogy was the weirdest I've ever heard."

Darren's self-control and cheerfulness in the face of his tragic double loss had surprised many people that week. One of them was Mary Matheson, the sister Doris had chosen to be executor of her estate. Mary had known nothing about this decision until after Doris's death. On the previous Tuesday Darren had phoned to say how pleased he was that she was executor. He told her he thought the estate was worth about $4 million and listed the things he believed were now his. He told Mary that he fancied selling his gran's El Dorado Cadillac, and that he just might sell his own car and get another that wasn't so "racy." He was undecided what to do with his gran's jewelry, but there was one thing he was sure of, and that was sponsorship of the play *Caligula*. He pointed out to Mary that he was playing the lead role, and that a $2,000 sponsorship jointly by him and Mary would be the perfect tribute to the memory of Gran.

Darren's exuberance surprised the police, as well: his anguished reaction on hearing about the deaths of his mother and Gran was widely known. His grief had not only aroused deep sympathy but had given a particular edge to the police's determination to find the killer. So they were interested to learn that Darren had returned to school on the Tuesday, four days after the murders, and that he'd made a considerable effort to assure everyone he was all right. It was unusual for a victim to bounce back like that. He'd gone out of his way to visit the school counselor at his former public school simply to say, "I suppose you've heard what's happened. Well, don't worry. I've got everything under control." But while it was strange, the boy was unusual in other ways, too—really courteous, respectful in a way kids seldom were anymore. And very, very cooperative. A couple of kids in Doris's neighborhood, Greg and Daniel May, had contacted Darren and said they'd seen two teenagers loitering the evening of the murders and he'd told them to report it to the police at once. He'd also offered a reward of $12,500—a reward that Ralph Huenemann had matched—for any information leading to the arrest and conviction of the killer.

On the Wednesday, Darren had phoned Roche-Bobois, the fine furniture store that specializes in high-quality leather, and explained that his mother had ordered a new couch. Well, she'd died, he said, but the order was not to be canceled. He wanted the couch and he'd be responsible for payment. The following day Darren visited two of "his" four stores and received the loving hugs and teary condolences of Doris's devastated staff.

One store manager, who requested anonymity, said that she had never been so sorry for a young man in all her life. "Over the years he had often come in with his mother or beloved gran. To have lost them both seemed so terrible. After I'd hugged him I held him at arm's length to commiserate. I had a small, almost-electric sense of shock that left me unable to say anything. His eyes were so bright. He seemed to be almost smiling."

Darren's drooling anticipation of the fortune that was now at his fingertips might have been tempered had he known that on the same day as the funeral, Bill Jackson was in Victoria consulting with Gordie Tregear and Tregear's superiors, Inspector Al Hickman and Sergeant Barry Peeke-Vout. Hickman and Peeke-Vout had a wide network of contacts, both in police agencies and on a personal level, throughout the lower mainland, but particularly in the Victoria and Saanich areas. They promised to deliver any support needed by Jackson and Tregear to wrap up the highly publicized case.

Police by now suspected they were dealing with two carefully planned executions. David Roberts's intuition that the robbery scene had been faked was now a working hypothesis. The forensic lab had concluded that the blunt-force injuries had likely been caused by a medium-sized, heavy bar, probably a crowbar. There were flecks of black grease in the women's skulls and nothing was found in the house that could have inflicted such wounds. Whoever killed the women took the weapon away, just as they'd brought it there with the intent to kill. The knife left in Doris Leatherbarrow's throat had the bloody imprint of a household glove with a marigold pattern. The rubber gloves under Doris's sink had a daisy pattern. There were no marigold-patterned gloves in the house, so they'd been taken away, too. These details indicated a premeditated attack.

As Hickman, Peeke-Vout, Tregear, and Jackson reviewed the case, the big question remained one of motivation. Money looked to be it, but Jim Kriss had been the only one with a personal money connection to Doris, and he was clean. Darren stood to gain everything, so he'd been suspect from the start. But he seemed a pretty nice kid, hadn't ever been in any trouble, and there was nothing whatsoever to tie him to the crime. Now, Norman Porter—there was a possibility. He had made a statement, as had his buddy Gary Cunningham, that they'd been together at an automobile body shop in Saanich on the evening of October 5th. But had they been? Porter was convinced the Huenemanns had bilked him of $55,000, and he claimed they'd given him a very bad time to boot. Could he have been revengeful enough to have had a contract put out on Sharon? And had Doris bought it simply because she happened to be in the wrong place at the wrong time?

The more the investigating team chewed the facts over, the stronger that possibility seemed. Norman Porter now became their prime suspect.

Casually asking around, police found that Porter's personality triggered strong reactions. Everyone had an opinion about him and the opinions were all extreme. Some people thought him "brilliant," others "too controlling." Some thought him "unpredictable;" other saw him as "solid." But although Porter's personality didn't match any pat psychological profile, just about everyone agreed he was a guy who loved a good legal fight. So it came as a slight surprise when after police asked him if he'd be willing to go to RCMP headquarters and take a polygraph test, he agreed—in spite of his lawyer's advice not to. Police told Porter they'd set it up and be in touch.

On the same day (October 16th), Detectives Hugh Davies and Monty Macri of the Delta force met with Ralph Huenemann in Victoria. They told him that because they couldn't rule out the possibility of a contract killing, they wanted Darren and him to take a polygraph test simply to eliminate them as suspects. Ralph indicated he'd probably take the test, but he wanted to discuss the matter with Darren first. Davies and Macri then went out to Mount Douglas Secondary. They wanted more background on Darren. What sort of a student was he? Who were his friends? They spoke to principal Don Neumann and some of the teachers, and left with one name—Derik Lord.

It was a little before four o'clock when Davies and Macri, in plainclothes, drove to Lord's home in an unmarked police car. Although they felt there was an outside possibility they might turn up something interesting about Darren from his friend Derik, there was little doubt that Porter remained the leading suspect. When they reached the address, there were a couple of youths in back—one riding around on a bike and another standing in the driveway.

"I asked the youth in the driveway if he was Lord," Davies said, "and we identified ourselves. I then asked Lord if we could talk to him in the car and he asked, 'Are we going somewhere?' I said, 'No, we'll just park here, but I don't want any of your friends overhearing our conversation.' "

Davies opened the back door of the car and Lord got in. Then Davies got in the front with Macri.

Davies asked Lord if he was a good friend of Huenemann's. Lord said yes.

"Did you know Mrs. Huenemann?" Davies asked.

Lord smiled. "Yes, she was a nice lady."

Davies was concerned that Lord would report the conversation to his friends, so he assured Lord that he thought Darren was a nice guy, that he wasn't a suspect, and all they wanted was a little background information.

"Have you heard anything about the murders?" Davies asked. "You yourself, do you have any suspicions?"

Lord shook his head. "No."

"Do you play Dungeons and Dragons?" Davies asked.

Lord said he did, and that only recently he'd purchased the pieces for the game from Darren.

Davies then spoke about a case in Surrey, British Columbia, where the body of a boy was discovered in a park. When the RCMP investigated, they found that many of the students in the local school had known the body was there but hadn't said a word about it to anyone.

"Have you by any chance heard any rumors at school about these [the Huenemann/Leatherbarrow] murders?" Davies asked. Lord said he had not. Later Davies noted, "Lord smiled and joked periodically. It was a usual conversation with a youth. He didn't seem to be too nervous."

"Have you ever been to the Leatherbarrow house in Tsawwassen?" Davies asked.

Again Lord shook his head. Then he volunteered, "But I was over in Tsawwassen about a week before the murders."

"Why did you go to Tsawwassen?" asked Davies.

"I just went to see the Tsawwassen Mall," said Lord. "I went with David Muir."

"What's there? There's nothing much to see there."

"Yeah, it's dead. So we just went back to Vancouver Island on the ferry."

"Did you go to the Leatherbarrow house while you were in Tsawwassen?" Davies asked again. Again Lord shook his head. "And who's David Muir?" Davies asked.

At that moment Muir pulled out of the yard and rode off on his bike. "That's him," said Lord.

"What were you doing on the day of the murders?" Davies asked casually. He smiled at Lord as he asked the question, and Lord chuckled. He said he'd been downtown with Muir and then Darren and his girlfriend, Amanda, had picked them up, driven them around, and taken them home. He'd been dropped off at about 10:15 p.m.

"Does Darren have any other friends?" Davies asked. Lord said he did—Jack Lee and Tim Hunt—and at Davies's request, Lord ran back into the house and got their phone numbers. The two officers then left, drove to the home of Jack Lee, spoke to him briefly, then went to Tim Hunt's. They didn't stay long; they were too curious about Lord's statement that he'd been in

Tsawwassen with David Muir a week prior to the murders. It wasn't much, but it would certainly bear a closer look.

While Davies and Macri were talking to Lord, Tregear and Jackson were having a friendly, if astonishing, chat with Toby Hicks.

The evening before, Saanich police had received a very surprising phone call from a female student at Mount Douglas. She said there was a rumor floating around the school that Darren hadn't liked his grandmother and wanted to kill her. Had Darren said this to anyone? police asked. Yes, she said, he'd told a classmate named Toby Hicks. What had he said? " 'I wish I could kill my grandmother for her money,' " she replied.

Tregear and Jackson found Hicks to be a slim, quiet youth with a neat and shiny ponytail and a heavy interest in rock 'n' roll. They told him they'd heard a story about Darren's saying something about killing his grandmother. Did Toby know anything about it?

Sure, Toby replied. In fact, he'd thought it was such a weird thing for Darren to say he'd told several of his friends about it.

What had Darren actually said? the officers asked.

Toby replied, " 'If I kill Granny I'll get half the money, but if I kill my mother I'll get it all. It's worth about $4 to $5 million.' "

Jackson and Tregear received the statement with a mix of elation and caution. Was it fact or fantasy? Toby seemed solid, then again murder brought out some pretty nutty reactions. But what if Darren *had* said that? Darren—the same kid one officer had described as "the sort of young man you'd like to see your daughter date."

It was to be a week of surprises. The following day, Phil Harden, a staff sergeant with the Delta force, who was later to become administrative manager of the investigation, called to say that Ralph Huenemann had phoned him, disturbed and angry that Officer Hugh Davies had spoken to Darren's friends. Darren, complained Huenemann, was deeply upset. If police wanted any further communication with either him or Darren they'd have to do it through a lawyer. He had, in fact, hired Christopher Considine to represent them.

Police were incredulous. What did Ralph and Darren Huenemann need a lawyer for? They were the victims' family. And
Chris Considine? At 37, a high-profile member of Victoria's legal
elite? A $350 an hour man? What the hell for? Although police
were naturally suspicious of Darren because he stood to gain a
fortune by the deaths, not one substantial fact connected him in
any way with the murders. There was only Toby Hicks's statement. Fascinating in itself, it was worthless unless backed up by
hard evidence. And the facts were simply that when the murders
had occurred Darren Huenemann had been more than 40 miles
away, happily whipping up dinner at home with his girlfriend. This
lack of evidence was the bottom line. Yet there was another
element operating in Darren's favor. Despite their experience,
the investigating team still found it hard to associate the premeditated depravity of the crime with the charming student who'd
never been in a day's trouble in his life. Unwittingly, both Ralph
and Darren Huenemann were about to make that tie-in much
easier for them to accept.

On Wednesday, October 24th, Jackson went out to the Gibson
Court area to do two things: talk to some of the Huenemann
neighbors to see if they had anything to offer and give Ralph
Huenemann the jewelry that had been removed from Sharon's
body at the morgue. The substantial houses on Gibson Court are
occupied by professionals who, by and large, enjoy substantial
incomes. As Jackson left one of the homes—where the residents
had incidentally assured him that Norm Porter had given the
Huenemanns good value for their money and that Sharon's complaints were unfounded—he ran into Ralph Huenemann. Huenemann complained again that Darren was upset with the way the
police were acting. Specifically, Hugh Davies had been speaking
to Darren's friends and had asked them whether Darren kept
dirty pictures in his school locker. Darren, said his stepfather,
had found this most embarrassing.

Within a couple of hours of this curbside meeting, Chris Considine was once more on the phone to Jackson and Tregear. There
was to be absolutely no more contact by police with either Ralph
or Darren Huenemann, Considine warned. If the police wanted
to talk to them, they would have to do it through him.

Later that day, Jackson and Tregear went out to Mount Douglas Secondary and spoke again with Tim Hunt and Jack Lee in the presence of the vice principal. Hunt and Lee denied that Davies had asked them or anyone else embarrassing questions on the first visit. They mentioned, however, that when Darren had learned that police officers had visited their homes, he had become extremely angry. The two officers then talked to Toby Hicks again. Hicks reaffirmed his earlier statement that Darren had spoken of "knocking off" both his mother and grandmother for their money.

Both investigators felt it was time for Darren to take a lie-detector test. They phoned Considine to set up an appointment convenient to everyone. Considine replied that Darren refused to take the test: he was simply too outraged with police for having spoken to his schoolfriends. Furthermore, Considine said, Ralph wished to show his full support for Darren and had instructed Considine that he, too, would refuse it.

The situation was bizarre. The immediate family of the victims of a double murder were refusing to talk to, or cooperate with, the investigators seeking the killer! None of the team could remember anything like it. The more usual thing was for relatives to drive police crazy, needling them night and day with calls and visits, offering endless, often useless, information in the hope of finding the killer. So what was going on in the Huenemann household? Jackson and Tregear believed that Darren was manipulating Ralph. Using his flair for dramatics, he had made a scene over the routine investigation, and Ralph, predictable and decent, had moved to protect his teenaged stepson.

Darren's behavior became even more startling. Within hours of Considine's call he'd hired the lawyer to represent Derik Lord, David Muir, and Amanda Cousins. Darren told the three teenagers that none of them need talk to the police: Considine would look after everything. When police, curious now about the alibis of Lord and Muir and wanting to take a closer look, attempted to speak to them, they were told to "see their lawyer." Furthermore, on their next trip to Mount Douglas police were baffled to find that in this middle- and upper-class Canadian high school with a reputation for academic excellence, none of the students would talk to them. Why not? they persisted. Finally some students reluctantly admitted that Darren had warned them all to shut up, saying, "I wouldn't talk to the police if I were you." His influence was such that none of them would.

Darren's reaction to what had been a routine investigation among Mount Douglas students convinced police he was involved in the murders. There is, in law and in police work, a theory known as "the consciousness of guilt." First set out by American jurist John Henry Wigmore in 1905, it holds that the commission of a crime "usually leaves upon the consciousness a moral impression that is characteristic. The innocent man is without it, the guilty man usually has it" (*Wigmore on Evidence*, Vol. 1A, par. 173). In other words, a person who knows he's done something wrong will act in a way that reflects the fact he knows he's guilty. This "consciousness of guilt" is a powerful indicator of guilt, as there is no other reason to explain why a person would act in a guilty manner: the only exception would be a person who suffered from *delusions* of guilt, even though innocent. Although Wigmore states that the evidential value of the consciousness of guilt has never been doubted, he concedes that it is difficult to prove this consciousness of guilt by other evidence.

That was precisely the problem the investigating team now faced. A "moral impression" of guilt marked all of Darren's attitudes and actions—yet so far they had their hands on absolutely nothing that connected him to the crime.

Meanwhile, Darren was busy using his money and cunning to make life as difficult as possible for "the idiots"—as he began to refer to the police—involved in the investigation. He encouraged Derik's mother, Elouise Lord, to file a written complaint about Detective Hugh Davies talking to Derik without a lawyer present, which she did. He told all his friends not to talk to the police and offered them the services of his lawyer. He went to work on his natural father, Chuck Gowan, telling him that Jackson was harassing him; his complaints were sufficiently convincing for Gowan to naively attempt to have Jackson removed from the case.

None of Darren's ploys succeeded in slowing down the investigating team's plodding work. Gradually they were gathering enough bits and pieces of evidence to give credibility to the shadowy picture of a murderous conspiracy against Doris and Sharon. On October 26th, Delta Sunshine cabdriver Parmjet Bhinder told Delta police that he had driven two youths—about eighteen to twenty years of age, he thought—to the Tsawwassen Mall on Friday, October 5th. They had flagged him down at the Tsawwassen ferry terminal at 4:55 that afternoon. Jackson immediately ordered photos of Darren, David Muir, Derik Lord, and another close friend of Darren's, Niles Guthrie, to show to Bhinder. Guthrie had so far refused to talk to Jackson because Darren had ordered him not to.

Five days later, Tregear and Jackson drove out to David Muir's home on Casa Marcia in Saanich. David's parents, John and Vivien, were present. Police were still unaware that the well-spoken boy with the superior vocabulary and shy manner was running a weapons importing business on the side, and that only the day before he'd placed a $600 order with a American guns-and-weapons shop in Ohio. Muir raised the subject of knives, however, saying that he and Derik Lord shared an interest in them. In fact, he and Lord had gone to Tsawwassen on the 3 p.m. ferry on September 21st to rent a post-office box at the summer resort town of Point Roberts, a bluff adjacent to Tsawwassen but in the United States. Knives had a 15 percent duty on them, Muir told the investigators, but with a post-office box in the States they could smuggle the weapons in and avoid paying any duty. He then gave a slightly different version of his October 5th alibi, and for the first time police learned that on Fridays, everyone got out of school an hour earlier—that is, at 2 p.m.

The following day, Jackson and Tregear revisited Amanda Cousins, who revealed that Darren had driven Derik and David to the ferry on Friday, September 21st, and had picked them up on their return some hours later. As they once again ran through Amanda's version of events on October 5th, obvious inconsistencies in the account given by her and the account given by Muir emerged. Attempts to clarify these inconsistencies got nowhere, although when Amanda had given Tregear her alibi on October 6th, she'd claimed that she and Muir had been together. A few days later, Jackson learned that Amanda had been lying on at least one point: she had not—as she had told police—gone to school on October 5th.

During that week, the first week of November, the case began to crack. Ian Stabler called from Delta to say that cabdriver Parmjet Bhinder had been shown a photo lineup that included Muir and Lord. Bhinder had earlier told police that of his two passengers, one was thin and one chubby. The chubby one, about 5 feet 8 inches, had sat next to him and chatted about the weather, all the while holding a map of South Delta, including Tsawwassen, on his lap. Shown the photo lineup, Bhinder fingered David Muir, saying, "That looks like one of them. Rings a bell."

Further, a search of the Delta Sunshine cab slips for October 5th had turned up the record of a call received from a "Dave" at 6:45 p.m. to pick him up immediately at the Tsawwassen Mall at Twelfth and Fifty-sixth Street. Paul Martin, a 38-year-old cabbie, had responded, picked up two youths outside a store named Robinson's, and rushed them to the Tsawwassen terminal. Martin described both boys as white. One, in his late teens, wore a jean jacket and appeared to have blond hair. The other seemed to be smaller and had dark hair. They appeared frantic to make the 7 p.m. ferry, and when the cab became caught in the holiday lineup, they'd dropped a $20 bill on the seat and run to the passenger boarding area.

Shown the photo lineup, Martin fingered Lord. "That kind of looks like one of them but I thought his hair was longer," he said. Although the identification was tentative, Martin's overall comments fitted perfectly into the puzzle.

On the same day (November 7th), the photo lineup was shown to thirteen-year-old Daniel May. Daniel browsed through the pictures, searching for the two who had interrupted the football practice. "Yes, that sort of looks like one," he said, his finger hitting the picture of David Muir, whom he had earlier described as having "dark wavy hair and a husky build." Holding the picture of Derik Lord, he said, "And that looks like the skinny one, the one with the crew cut."

So Derik and David had been in Tsawwassen not only on September 21st, but on October 5th from about 5 to 7 p.m. And they had been in Doris's neighborhood. Sharon Huenemann had been at her mother's both evenings. Had the September 21st visit to Tsawwassen—allegedly to arrange for a post-office box—been a trial run for murder? Maybe an actual attempt that had for some reason been aborted?

Jackson and Tregear were now certain that Darren had had the motive and the means to set up the executions of his mother and grandmother. However, their efforts hadn't turned up one shred of evidence that tied him to the crime. Getting that evidence was the next step. They decided to go for a wiretap on the three suspects' phones and on Darren's car, which the suspects all used. The strategy was simple. If they could get an authorization for interception, Jackson would separately confront Amanda, Muir, and Lord with the evidence already in the hands of the police. It was likely that these confrontations would trigger phone calls among the teenagers in an effort to stick together and control the damage.

On November 8th, Peeke-Vout and Sergeant Jim Bland, who was experienced in obtaining wiretap authorizations, traveled with Tregear and Jackson to Delta for an overall strategy meeting. Interception is costly: it involves specialized equipment, experts, stakeouts, excessive manhours, and intensive planning and cooperation with other agencies. Permission from their Delta superiors, who would ultimately foot the bill, was required before the two chief investigators could proceed. After a lengthy discussion, the team got the green light.

Returning to Victoria, Jackson and Bland prepared the Judicial Authorization to Intercept Communication application, while Tregear tackled the organizational aspects.

Despite growing suspicions against Darren, Norm Porter still looked like a good bet. The possibility that he and Darren were somehow in it together could not be ruled out.

On November 8th, over a period of four hours, Porter under-went four polygraph tests at RCMP headquarters.

"Do you have any idea what happened to Sharon Huenemann and Doris Leatherbarrow?" he was asked time and again. By the end of the sessions, Norman Porter had been cleared completely.


Five days later, Mr. Justice Owen Flood granted the interception order. In less than 24 hours, RCMP and Saanich police had bugged the Lord, Muir, Cousins, and Huenemann phones, as well as Darren's car.

The trap was now set. The following day, Jackson and Tregear visited Amanda Cousins.

# THE ARRESTS

The two officers making their way out to the town house where Amanda Cousins lived with her mother had a lot in common: both were a comfortable ten pounds overweight; both had been married twice; both had raised families; both were shrewd and quietly spoken; and both couldn't imagine being anything but a cop. Like Tregear, Jackson had been raised in Victoria, and working there was like coming home. Since getting together as a team—they'd not known each other before—they'd found they shared one other powerful interest besides the Huenemann case: they were both crazy about fishing. In fact, for weeks they'd been talking about getting away from the case for a few hours and taking off in one of Tregear's boats; the salmon run was at its height and the weather was still, cloudless, and perfect. But so far they'd had no luck.

Today they sensed they were about to get lucky—professionally, at least. They were confident that Amanda Cousins held the case for the Crown locked inside her capable mind, scared though she probably was. What they didn't know was that Darren had dropped her at the end of October, saying that she knew so much it could cause complications. He told Amanda he'd phone sometimes, but he didn't want to date her again. Amanda's immediate reaction had been one of humiliation and anger. She later testified in court that she "felt used," had called Darren "ridiculous and egotistical," and had marched out, slamming the door on him. She had not confided in anybody about the events that had swirled around her, but as Jackson and Tregear drove up on the afternoon of November 16th, she was convinced that she was an accessory to murder. She knew she had to choose a course, but in what direction? When the two officers sat down and quietly tossed out the nonspecific fact that they knew she had lied to them, she made up her mind.

"Yes, I was lying when I told you"—she indicated Tregear—"that I'd followed Darren to Chinatown after school on October 5th and had seen him drop off Dave and Derik. I said that because the day before, Darren had told me to say it if anyone asked me. On the Saturday morning, Darren phoned me and said that his mother and grandmother had been murdered, and he reminded me to tell the police about seeing him drop off Dave and Derik—if they asked. So I did."

The two officers—knowing that Amanda had not been to school on October 5th—made no comment when she continued, "What happened was, I saw Darren leave school at 2 p.m. with Muir and Lord in the car, but I didn't follow. I spent the evening with Darren and then went downtown with him to pick up Dave and Derik. We dropped Dave off at about 9:15 or 9:30 p.m. and then dropped off Derik."

Jackson and Tregear thanked Amanda and left. They had let the lie about being at school slide by; she was obviously frightened, confused, uncertain whom to trust. They sensed, too, that she was ready to jump, but that the big leap into truth telling was terrifying to her. They were sure she was getting ready to take it. All she needed was a little more time.

On the same day, Tregear put in a call to Chris Considine. When Darren had first met with the police he had, in an attempt to reinforce the notion of a burglary, mentioned that his grandmother kept a key hidden outside. Police had discovered that she had not done so for months unless someone close asked her to. Yet when the bodies were found, a key had been lying on the floor near a bedroom, as if tossed there by the intruders. Police also knew that Sharon had her own key to her mother's house. That key was missing, and they suspected that the key—which Darren had intimated had been taken from the outside hiding place—was in fact Sharon's. Now, as Tregear phoned Considine, it was to ask

Ralph Huenemann to search his Gibson Court home for the missing key one more time. After a while Considine called back to say that Ralph had not found it.

On November 22nd Tregear and Jackson re-interviewed David Muir. He was at home with his parents, John and Vivien, who were still essentially unaware of the events that were overtaking their lives. They had retained their own lawyer, Malcolm Macaulay, a criminal and civil trial lawyer, to help them sort out the inexplicable information they now had to deal with. As they sat in the pleasant living room they'd put together with such care and effort, the nightmare of every parent unfolded. David was advised of his right to consult with counsel, parents, or other adults. He read the Young Offenders form and signed it. The detectives then told him that he had been positively identified in Tsawwassen on the evening of October 5th. They suggested that he think about telling them what had really happened, and a short while later they left.

The next day David anxiously waited for his mother to get out of the house. As soon as she left in mid-afternoon, he dialed Derik, who answered by his preferred, self-chosen name. The police recorders started to roll:

"House of Lords, Lucifer speaking," said Derik.

David was cool and to the point. The police had been at his house. They had a positive identification.

"They've got to be lying," said Derik. "They haven't said anything to Darren, so they've got to be lying to you."

"We've got to change the story," David insisted. "Tell them we were there to pick up a package, but we went the wrong way. We went back or we'd miss the ferry. Let's get together this weekend."

"Could you call Darren and—"

"No! I'm not even supposed to be talking to you," David said. "My mum's left and I've got to do this real quick."

"Okay, I'll do it. So they said we were over there! We'll have to say we were picking up a package. Are you allowed to see people?"

"Only Chuck [his friend]. Like we're paying $350 an hour to lawyers—they say they've got positive identification."

"They have to be lying—otherwise they'd have done something," said Derik.

A few minutes later Derik called Darren and told him to get right over.

"Why?"

"Just come on over!"

"It's David!" Darren knew it. "Is he saying something? What did they say to him?"

"They say they've positive identification he was over on the day of the murders. They have positive identification on the ferry and taxi."

"I've got to call Dave!"

"He's not allowed to accept calls."

"Oh, God!" For the first time Darren sounded concerned. "I'm calling Considine right now. Just calm down and don't panic. I'll be right there. Do—?"

"I *can't* tell you on the phone."

"Tell me basically..."

"I *can't* tell you on the phone," Derik snapped back. "Okay? They are insinuating they've positive identification. Okay?"

"You mean over there?"

"It must have something to do with there, because I'm Dave's alibi."

"Ssh, calm down. Is that all you have to tell me?"

"Dave's got a lawyer. He's changed his story—he's saying that, yes, he was over there."

"But he wasn't, though," Darren shot back.

"But he's changed his story! Went over to pick up a package..."

"On that other thing, as well..."

"It was two weeks before...I don't know what Dave is doing but he's got this new lawyer...he was over there to pick up a package."

Darren remarked that Dave could have taken a bus. "Did he say I took him to the ferry? Are you sure you didn't go over there on the night...on the bus...?"

"He just changed his story and said he was over there! Not the night of the murder, not the night of the murder."

Darren told Derik to calm down, adding, "I'm going to call Amanda."

He then called David, but Mrs. Muir refused to let her son speak to him. A derisive Darren called Derik back.

"He's let the police bully him into this thing. I'd start to sue! I'd laugh in their faces. They are a bunch of idiots! They don't know! If Dave was somewhere else in his own little mind, that's something else. Have you talked to Dave at all?"

"No. Iron Lady wouldn't let me past."

Darren said that Considine was going to give him a list of things. "He's just meeting with my father, my mystery father. Tell your dear mother. She'll go through the roof. Now, what about that identification on cabs and ferry—God, my lawyer didn't even know [they had it]!"

Derik once again said that the identification was positive. "And Dave was over there...and if I was with Dave that night...it means..."

"No!" Darren cut in, loud and angry.

"But I'm Dave's alibi," Derik wailed.

"No, you weren't over there. Right?"

"No, I know I wasn't over there. But I'm Dave's alibi!" Derik persisted. "If he was over there, I was over there."

"Dave is out of line, out of line. And *you* are into a puddle up to your knees!" Darren scolded him, his tone superior and his voice beginning to rise. "Dave is the most malleable boy I've ever met. Don't panic! Don't allow them to push you around." His voice now high pitched, he advised, "And tell his mother to fuck off." Then he added in a high effeminate voice, "Oh, I can't believe this bunch of weirdos. I love you all!"

Darren then phoned Amanda, told her about David's changing his story, asked her to call Chris Considine, and ordered her to say nothing whatsoever to the police.

Three days later Jackson and Tregear went to the Kmart Shelbourne Street in Victoria, where Derik Lord was working. They warned him of his rights: "Do you want to give a voluntary statement? Do you realize anything you say can be used against you? Do you wish to consult with anyone? Do you wish to consult with an adult relative? Do you wish to consult with any other adult?''

"Yes," said Derik, "I want to talk with Darren Huenemann." He then said he'd make a statement only in front of his lawyer.

The officers said that would be fine with them, and prepared to leave. On their way out they paused. Bill Jackson said quietly, ''It was you who killed Darren's mother and grandmother, and not David, I believe. I wonder what Darren will say when we tell him that it was you who killed his mother. We're not arresting you now. But we will be seeing you again. Now, go back to work.''

A short while later a frantic Derik phoned Darren at home and ordered him to be at Mount Douglas in 10 minutes. When Darren asked why, Derik snapped ''Just *do* it!'' and hung up.

Seated a short distance away in an unmarked car, Constable Scott Brandon watched as a few minutes later Darren wheeled out of his red brick driveway and headed for the school. Brandon, his thick wavy hair falling over the back of his collar in routine undercover style, followed him at a distance.

At the school a male whom Brandon could not identify got into Huenemann's car. Darren drove down to the Kmart parking lot, stayed awhile, then took the road in the direction of Derik's house. Cunning enough to realize that his car was probably bugged, Darren kept the radio on full blast for the entire trip, swamping the conversation the police were so keen to tape. But apparently the idea of being under visual surveillance hadn't entered his mind, judging by the antics that followed.

A marked police car had been parked in front of the Lords' residence. Darren spotted the car some distance away, stopped his Honda, and opened the trunk. His passenger, now identified as Derik Lord, leaped out of his seat, jumped into the trunk, and Darren slammed the lid and drove on. Sometime later, convinced there were no police around, Darren stopped again, sprang open the trunk, and Derik crawled out and into the passenger seat once more.

Back home, showing the first signs of tension, even panic, Darren again phoned Derik. Curtly he ordered Derik to stay away from Dave. The police, he said with contempt, were lying. They really knew nothing, he claimed as once more the police recorders rolled:

"Considine told me that they are trying to get you against each other. If they get David alone, they'll say you said these things. Don't run anywhere. I'm saying nothing to nobody. When the police take out handcuffs, that's arrest. So far it's just harassment."

Derik wasn't so sure. "Tregear said, 'I wonder what Darren will say when I tell him you killed his mother and grandmother.'"

"Well, I was talking to a guy who is taking law and what they did is against the Young Offenders Act," Darren replied. "And I think I can sue them."

"My father is really pissed off," Derik fretted. "As soon as he's found out, he's going to be really pissed off."

"Had they had the evidence to arrest you, they'd have arrested everyone so far," Darren calmly retorted. "They are trying to put you and Dave against each other, and me in the middle."

"Well, they can come to your place and arrest you," Derik whined. He then suggested that it was "defamation of character! It's libel!"

Darren concurred with an inspired suggestion: "They can't get away with it—if we charge them *now*."


Darren, already sour because his father, Chuck Gowan, had found his old contacts at the Delta police department impervious to his attempts to get Jackson and Tregear pulled off the case, now pinned his hopes on Considine. Claiming harassment, Darren had Considine write to both Delta police chief Patrick Wilson and the police commission asking that the case be transferred to other investigators.

But it was too late. Police felt it was time to move. Just before 10 a.m. on Tuesday, November 27th, seven and a half weeks after the murders, Jackson and Tregear went to David Muir's home in an unmarked car and arrested him on two counts of first-degree murder.

A short while later, with Muir in the back seat and a marked police car following at a short distance, the two men drove to nearby Mount Douglas Secondary. En route they cell-telled principal Don Neumann and asked that he call Derik Lord to his office without explaining why. When they arrived, they were told Lord wasn't in his class. A few anxious moments ensued before he was located in a different classroom and brought to the principal's office. There he was charged on two counts of first-degree murder, frisked, handcuffed, and escorted back to the waiting police car.

While this was going on, another officer checked out the boys' lockers. In Muir's locker they found a starter pistol converted to take .22 bullets and a spring-back knife with a fitted handle.

Both boys, silent and displaying no emotion, were now seated together in the back of the unmarked police car. The wiretap evidence showed all the ingredients of a conspiracy—a real closeness among the three boys, a cover-up, their changing stories to obstruct the police. But this wasn't the solid evidence police now desperately needed before they could charge Darren. In the hope that Muir and Lord would panic and unwittingly provide it when put together, the car had been bugged. But Lord and Muir said nothing.

When the group arrived at Saanich police headquarters, Malcolm Macaulay, Muir's lawyer, was already there. Lord phoned his own counsel, J. M. Peter Firestone, whose involvement in a couple of bizarre, high-profile cases had brought his name into prominence.

Several days before Muir's arrest, Macaulay had intimated to police that he'd be interested in making a deal. Now, after talking privately with Muir, Macaulay asked Jackson if he was considering using his client as a Crown witness, and he volunteered the fact that David was a follower. Jackson said he wouldn't discuss the matter then but would keep it open. Macaulay told Muir to say nothing to the police, and gave Jackson both his office and home phone numbers.

Jackson and Tregear then escorted the morose pair from Saanich to Tsawwassen, where they were placed in the Delta lockup cells at 3 p.m. after having their shoes and jackets removed. Police felt that there was a strong possibility the Crown would use Muir to testify against the other two boys. About an hour after their arrival at Delta, Jackson and Tregear took the husky sixteen-year-old to an interview room and told him so. Muir, acting on Macaulay's advice, told the two detectives that he didn't want to make a statement. Well, if he was going to testify, they said, they had to find out what he knew about the murders and the events surrounding them. How else would they know if his testimony was worth anything?

Jackson and Tregear then told Muir that any statement he made would be inadmissable, which meant it would be excluded as evidence in court. They also told Muir that it wouldn't be their decision whether he was a Crown witness or not; that was something Macaulay and the Crown counsel would have to work out.

At that point Muir volunteered that he had already told his lawyer "some things."

"Well, we've got to know what you're going to say to know what you'd testify as a Crown witness," Jackson said again.

For a few moments David continued to look down, silent. Then he looked up and, in a normal voice and indifferent tone, told his bloody tale.

Sometime during the last summer holidays I was over at Darren Huenemann's house. There was just the two of us and he started telling me about the valuable things his family owned and he told me that his grandmother owned some clothing stores in Vancouver and that she was worth about $4.5 million in assets and that he was going to inherit it someday but that he didn't want to wait. He said he'd like his grandmother killed so he'd inherit the money but that his mother would also have to be killed because she would inherit half the money. He asked me about ways to kill them so that he wouldn't get caught. I suggested a couple of ways that wouldn't work—at least, I was sure they wouldn't. We talked about it a couple of times but at this point I thought it was just a joke. After this Darren brought Derik Lord in and asked if he would be willing to help. Derik thought it was a good idea, the basic plan of killing Darren's mother and grandmother so Darren could get the money.

Sometime in August Darren, Derik and I went on a canoe trip to Chatham Island so we could talk in private. We talked about Derik and I killing Darren's mother and grandmother, and Darren came up with the idea of us going to Tsawwassen when his mother and grandmother were together there, rather than wait until his grandmother was at his house in Victoria. We all thought that was a good idea and we talked about that. Darren suggested that we go to his grandmother's house on a Friday when his mother was there and that we should kill them and try and make it look like it was a burglary. He told us what the house was like, where it was, what vehicles we might expect to find there, what time they'd probably be home, and the explanation we should tell them for being over there. That explanation was that we were here to visit Derik's father who was working in Vancouver at the time. We all discussed how to kill them and the plan we came up with was to wait until they were in the same room and then when they weren't looking, to hit them on the head with crowbars knocking them unconscious. After they were unconscious we were to put on some rubber gloves, go to the drawer in the kitchen and take out a knife each and to get a rag from under the sink to make sure we didn't get any blood on ourselves, and then to stab them until they were dead. We were supposed to stab them in the throat. It was Darren's idea to use the kitchen knives so we wouldn't have to take any knives and it wouldn't be traceable from us.

It was also Darren's idea to wear rubber gloves and to use a cloth to keep blood from getting on our clothing. Darren also told us about a key that was hidden outside in a small box that was hidden in some logs in a woodpile. We were supposed to take that key and leave it somewhere in the house to throw the police off track because a lot of people knew where that key was hidden. Darren said there was usually $1,000 to $2,000 underneath the stove and we were supposed to take that but leave everything else alone. We were supposed to check in their purses and Darren said his grandmother sometimes had a couple hundred dollars in cash in her purse. If Derik and I killed Darren's mother and grandmother so he could inherit all the money, he said he was going to buy a 50-acre plot of land up-island quite a bit and he told Derik he would build a cabin on the land and Derik could live there. Derik wanted to be away from his family. Darren said he was going to buy both Derik and I motorbikes and he would provide money for me to buy weapons for myself and Derik. The weapons Derik and I wanted were knives, some of which were Japanese. We were also going to try and import throwing knives and throwing stars. We planned to spend all together about $20,000 and use Martin Lankau's post-office box in Point Roberts to have them sent there and he would bring them across the border for us. Martin is a friend of Darren's and he was to be paid about fifteen percent of the value of the knives. Martin knew nothing about the murders but was involved in smuggling the knives across the border. He brought one package across the border and he was paid $15. Darren picked the package up when he was over here and I believe it was on October 13, 1990. That system came to an end when six packages arrived and Martin's mother sent them back. Darren was going to buy me a car for killing his mother and grandmother, a souped-up Honda CRX, and he was going to be giving me a couple of thousand dollars a month until he got his inheritance and then he would give me a large amount which I expected to be $100,000 in cash. Darren was going to pay for Derik to take martial-arts classes, support him living in the cabin and give him spending money. Derik was going to be getting all these weapons and taking martial arts because Darren wanted him to be his bodyguard.

We talked more about doing this plan in September and Darren started talking to his girlfriend Amanda Cousins and I think he may have mentioned to her what [we] were about to do. On September 21st, a Friday, we all planned that Derik and I would go over to Tsawwassen to kill Darren's mother and grandmother. It was still just Derik and I and Darren involved. We had bought the crowbars and rubber gloves at Capital Iron in the summer. Darren, Derik, and I went to buy the gloves and crowbars. The gloves were black rubber gloves, thicker than dishwashing gloves, and came up halfway to the elbow and probably were for gardening. The two crowbars were about eighteen inches long and were not round but six-sided, curved at the top with a nail puller and flattened at the other end. They were black in color. The bars were about $7 each and the gloves about $3 a pair. Around September 7th, Darren told Derik and I that his mother would be at his grandmother's house in Tsawwassen on September 21st and asked if we were ready to kill them. We told Darren yes. On September 21, 1990, Darren drove Derik and I to the ferry and we went over on the 1 p.m. ferry as there was no school. I took an old black carrying bag of mine and we put the crowbars, the gloves and a black plastic bag in the old bag. I had a map of Tsawwassen that I got when I was over with my dad at Vancouver in the summer. It was a map of the whole lower mainland and I bought it at the newsstand on the ferry. I had the map in my jacket pocket. We took a cab from the ferry terminal and he dropped us at the mall at Twelfth Avenue and Fifty-sixth Street. We walked around looking for the house and went to a Forty-ninth Street close to the border and couldn't find the house. Darren had given us the address of 811 Forty-ninth Street. We went to a Chinese store near there and got directions to a pay phone at Diefenbaker Park where we called a taxi to take us back to the ferry. We went home on the 7 p.m. ferry and Darren and Amanda Cousins picked us up and drove us home. After Derik and I were dropped off Amanda apparently asked Darren if we had been over there to kill his mother and grandmother. I think Darren told her that was right. I know Darren told her that that was what we went over there for but it might have been later. Then Darren told Derik and I that his mother would be at his grandmother's house in Tsawwassen on October 5, 1990, so the three of us decided that Derik and I would go over again and try again. Darren asked Amanda to say that she had followed the three of us in Darren's car to Chinatown after school to alibi us as we then couldn't have caught the 3 p.m. ferry. I didn't find out until after we came back. After school got out at 2 p.m. on Friday, October 5, 1990, Darren drove Derik and I to the 3 p.m. ferry in his car. We had the same old black bag with the two crowbars and the two pairs of gloves with us, and also my map. When we arrived at the Tsawwassen ferry terminal we went outside and approached a cab and got a ride to Twelfth Avenue and Fifty-sixth Street by Robinson's store. The cabdriver was East Indian and I think skinny. Then we walked through Winskill Park and we went up Eight A Avenue. We took a couple of side streets until we came out on Eight A Avenue from the Winskill Center, then we went up Eight A Avenue to Forth-ninth Street and walked past 811 Forty-ninth Street and no one was home. We went to Weaver schoolyard next door and waited there. We walked back to the house and no one was there yet because there were no vehicles in the driveway at all. Darren had told us that there may be a gray company van in the driveway but if the white [car] wasn't there that they probably weren't there either. We waited again [in] the schoolyard until after

6 p.m. and then we walked out onto Forty-ninth Street to check again if they were home. We walked to the corner of the front yard and we saw the Cadillac in the carport and the brake light was still on so they had just arrived. We then walked up the path by the school and waited a couple of minutes at the end of the path. There were two boys on the street throwing a football on the street where Forty-ninth Street curves around in front of the school. They saw us, but we didn't think they'd be able to identify us. Darren told us afterward that they just described two boys wearing dark clothing. I was wearing a blue jean jacket, light colored, blue jean pants, white Nike running shoes, and a blue T-shirt and I was carrying the bag in my hand. Derik was wearing a tan-colored jacket, white shirt and runners and I can't remember his pants.

After we waited a couple minutes at the end of the path we walked back to the house, 811 Forty-ninth Street, and we went to the carport door. Before I knocked and could think of what to say, Mrs. Huenemann opened the door and invited us in. She asked us what we were doing over there and we said we were over to visit Derik's father. She asked us if we'd like to have anything to eat and we said no. She told us she was just making a quick supper for herself and her mother, before they went to the ferry. She asked us if we'd like a ride to the ferry and we said yes. I don't remember the conversation after that but Derik and I were trying to decide when to hit them. We had taken the crowbars out of the bag in the schoolyard and we had them under our jackets when we went to the house. [I hit] Mrs. Leatherbarrow on her head and she fell to the floor. I don't remember if I hit her any times after that. Derik hit Mrs. Huenemann repeatedly on the head, maybe even ten times, and she was unconscious. He hit her the first time and she fell to the floor but was making noises and her eyes were moving around so he kept on hitting her, until she was unconscious. We put the crowbars on the counter with my bag and we took out the gloves and put them on. We went and opened the knife drawer. We knew where it was because Darren had told us. We each took out a knife and we got a rag each from under the sink. Derik started stabbing Mrs. Huenemann in the throat while she lay on her back. I went over to Mrs. Leatherbarrow who was lying facedown. I tried to reach under her neck and cut her throat but the knife wouldn't cut. I had a plastic-handled knife with a straight thin blade. It wasn't a bread knife but it was long and quite thin. I said, "It's not working," and I left the kitchen and went up to the room on the right up the hall. I emptied the drawers out on the floor, because this is what we had planned to do with Darren, to make it look as if they were killed during a burglary. I scattered some of the contents around a bit too and then I went back down to the kitchen. Derik had finished stabbing Mrs. Leatherbarrow as well as Mrs. Huenemann. Mrs. Leatherbarrow had been rolled onto her back and was laying on her back. Derik went up to the master bedroom while I went through Mrs. Leatherbarrow's purse and checked under the stove. There was a lower portion of the stove that swung out and there was a bunch of documents there. There was $1,580 in Mrs. Leatherbarrow's purse which I took and there was no money under the stove. I put the money in a brown bag that we had and I put that inside my coat. I went up to the master bedroom to see how Derik was doing and dumped out a couple drawers there too. Derik had searched Mrs. Huenemann's purse and he found $20 there, which he put into the bag. We unlocked the patio sliding door and walked around to the woodpile and Derik searched and found the keys. We went back in through the patio door and I threw the keys up the hall. We went back out the patio sliding door and I locked it. Darren had told us we could flit [*sic*] the lock from the inside and then push it closed and it would lock. When we left the rags were over the women's faces and the knives I believe were in their throats. Derik had left them that way. Derik told me to put the rag over Mrs. Huenemann's face because her eyes were still moving around when he was stabbing her.

When I came back down to search Mrs. Leatherbarrow's purse and she was on her back after Derik had finished stabbing her, I put the rag over her face because I didn't want to remember her face. After we were out the patio door and locked it, we went over to the corner of the yard closest to the school, in the backyard and we were going to jump the fence into the schoolyard but there was a man sitting in a truck and a lady drove in in a station wagon so we went back out through the carport onto Forty-ninth Street and then onto Eight A Avenue. I looked at my watch at that time and it was 6:36 p.m. When we came out I noticed the boys weren't playing with the football there— they had left. When I stopped trying to cut Mrs. Leatherbarrow's throat I put the knife back in the knife drawer and left it there. After we left we quickly walked back the way we'd come to the shopping center, where I called for the cab to pick us up at about quarter or ten to 7 p.m. When I called I gave my name—Dave. The taxi was Sunshine Cabs and the driver was a white guy about 30 or 40 years. He drove us to the ferry and we found that there was traffic backed up in the passenger dropoff area, so we paid him a twenty-dollar bill and we got out and ran to the passenger ticket booth. We ran all the way up the ramp to the ferry and the ferry was late, so we made it. It was about 15 minutes late leaving, so it didn't leave for a little bit after we got on it. We waited until the ferry was a few kilometers away from the first islands we came to, and went to the back of the top outside deck and threw the bag over the side that had the crowbars, gloves and map in it. Then we went down and phoned Darren from the phones and we told him our ferry was a little late, and we also told him that we had gone through with the plan. Darren and Amanda picked us up at Swartz Bay at before 9 p.m. Darren asked how much money we had and if there had been any problems. We told him what had happened and I counted out the money and divided it between Derik and myself. Amanda was present during this. She didn't say much and I asked her if she was okay, and she said yes.

Darren drove back to Derik's house and Amanda stayed in
the car while Darren, Derik and I went into the basement
to get my bike. We talked for a few minutes and then I rode
home and Derik went back out with Amanda and Darren
for a drive. I arrived home at approximately 9:35 p.m. and
my parents were home and I was supposed to be home at 9
p.m. so was grounded. Since then Darren has given me
$100 cash. He told me he wouldn't be able to do anything
about money with us until after all his legal affairs had been
settled. When we were driving home from the ferry, we
talked about the murders with Darren part of the way.
Amanda just listened and said nothing. Darren has told us
that he has heard that there were no fingerprints at the
scene, no witnesses, and the police had no leads. He told
us some people wouldn't give interviews and that the
police hadn't had a case like this where people were just
clamming up and telling them to go away.

David sank back, his confession over.

It was now 9 p.m. Jackson, who had written down the statement as Muir made it, and Tregear, who had asked clarifying
questions, leaned back, wrung out and exhausted. More than
exhausted, the two detectives were stunned. They felt as if
they'd been shoved over an abyss. They couldn't connect this
beloved son and well-raised lad, this pride of his parents' heart,
with such callous premeditation and such cruel, barbaric acts.
Their sense of incredulity was so powerful they felt no elation, no
triumph, not even relief, that they now knew everything. They
fully believed the confession. It filled out details that only the
killer could have known, and it was made in a voice so devoid of
emotion that the killings and the voice in which they'd been
recounted somehow belonged together.

"The hair stood up at the back of my neck, Muir's voice was
so flat and so cold," Tregear said.

"His tone was absolutely chilling," said Jackson. "He recorded all those details without a flicker of emotion. It was like he
was talking about a sailing trip."

There was another revelation that had taken them aback: Amanda Cousins knew everything and had been lying to them from the beginning. They'd been surprised when the wiretaps had shown that Darren still phoned her regularly, but they'd never suspected that from the start she'd deceived them according to a well-prepared plan. Now Muir's confession made it clear why she'd been hanging in there: she thought Darren would kill her if she didn't.

At ten that night Jackson called Macaulay at home and outlined Muir's statement. Macaulay mulled over the alternatives and then asked Jackson not to show the statement to Amanda Cousins until he and Crown counsel had had a chance to work out some deal together. Jackson agreed not to re-interview Amanda until Macaulay had had a chance to negotiate, but he warned Macaulay that there wasn't much time and he could not wait long. He also said he would not disclose these negotiations to Darren Huenemann or his counsel, Chris Considine. At 11 p.m. Jackson phoned Macaulay again and the two arranged to meet the following morning at 9 a.m. in Macaulay's Victoria office.

When Jackson arrived the following morning, Macaulay's associate, Harold Rusk, was also present. As they discussed a possible deal, Jackson felt very strongly that neither Macaulay nor Rusk wanted the police involved any further in the negotiations, that it would be Rusk and Malcolm Macaulay who would work out any negotiations with the Crown counsel.

While this meeting was going on, Tregear was meeting with Sara Cousins at Saanich police headquarters. From her past performance, Amanda would probably not cooperate easily. Tregear, knowing that a meeting with Amanda was inevitable, if not imminent, hoped that Sara might be able to help them gain Amanda's cooperation.

Like many a mother with a daughter who is neither a woman nor a child, 47-year-old Sara had had a somewhat strained relationship with Amanda for some time. Sara had always trusted Amanda, but knew that for the past year her quiet and willful daughter had been skipping a lot of school. Amanda had not told her that but

Sara didn't need to be told. She knew her daughter well. A warm, calm woman, Sara felt that Amanda was simply going through a stage. Besides, when Amanda turned sixteen the law said that if she didn't want to go to school, she didn't have to. Like all children, Amanda knew her rights.

Sara was now within weeks of completing several courses required for her degree in education. Tina, Sara's 26-year-old daughter who lived on the mainland and attended Simon Fraser University, already had a degree in communications and was going for one in fine arts. Sara was confident that Amanda, too, would find her way. But over the past few weeks, it had become clear that something was really bothering Amanda. Sara noticed that she was eating little and was sometimes very depressed. Going into her room one morning, Sara was alarmed to find that Amanda was sleeping with a long knife by the side of her bed. Amanda said simply that she felt very nervous.

Now as she sat in an interview room at Saanich police headquarters, Sara listened with mounting distress as Tregear informed her that David Muir and Derik Lord had been arrested for murder the previous day, and that Amanda was far more involved in the situation than she had imagined. Tregear explained that Amanda had been privy to the conversations of Muir and Lord after they had been in Tsawwassen both on the night of the murder and following an earlier attempt.

Tregear told Sara Cousins that police had just obtained Crown-witness status for Amanda if she cooperated fully. But, if Amanda did turn Crown witness, Mrs. Cousins would have to terminate her studies immediately, relocate the entire household, and live indefinitely under 24-hour police protection. As a large part of Sara Cousins's world fell apart, she replied that she did not believe that Amanda would cooperate.

At 3:30 that afternoon, Jackson received a call from the Crown counsel in Delta, ordering him to get a statement from Amanda. The order profoundly upset Jackson. He'd promised Macaulay he wouldn't see Amanda until Macaulay had negotiated some deal for Muir, and although he'd warned Macaulay he couldn't wait long, the meeting with him to discuss a possible deal hadn't broken up till noon, only three and half hours earlier. At 4:15 Jackson got hold of his boss in Delta, Phil Harden, administrative supervisor of the case. He told Harden he couldn't get anything from Amanda without disclosing information taken from Muir's statement, and this was contrary to the agreement he'd made. A few minutes later Jackson received a call from Crown counsel Lothair Kiner, saying they needed to know that night whether Amanda Cousins was going to be a Crown witness or an accused. Jackson again spoke to Harden. Harden was clear; there had been an attempt at negotiations between the Crown and Macaulay, but it had gotten nowhere, as Macaulay had said he believed there was simply not enough evidence to convict David Muir.

Jackson felt satisfied that negotiations had broken down, that Macaulay was not interested in pursuing a deal further, and that the time had arrived to re-interview Amanda. He then told Harden that he and Tregear were excluding themselves from taking any statement Amanda might make. A freak coincidence had made Jackson's withdrawal desirable. During the course of the investigation he had learned that he was distantly related to Amanda through marriage—that Amanda was, in fact, his wife's cousin's child. Detectives Ian Stabler and Lyle Beaudoin, who'd been in the thick of the case since the beginning and were at that time involved in the surveillance of Darren's bugged vehicle, were asked to take Amanda's statement, instead.

Sometime after Sara returned home and told Amanda that police wished to speak with her, Stabler and Beaudoin arrived. Stabler is a big ox of a man in his mid-forties, with a London accent and a comfortable manner, while Beaudoin, wafer thin and tall, with a dark mustache and sleek black hair, is some years younger. They told Amanda what being a Crown witness meant, advised her to think about it, promised to return, and left. There was no need to tell them what they knew; Sara would have filled her in.

Amanda had seen Darren only at school since the murders, with the exception of one night when, at the suggestion of Dr. Huenemann that Darren ''relax,'' she and Darren had gone out for dinner. But Darren, although keeping his distance from Amanda, still phoned frequently, prattling on endlessly about the investigation. Guessing that his phone was bugged, he scrupulously avoided any discussions of the murders. Only fear can explain how Amanda could have endured his hypocrisy or borne, even for one evening, the company of a young man cruel and dangerous enough to order the executions of his mother and grandmother.

When Stabler and Beaudoin returned to the small town house at around 9 p.m., Amanda told them she did not want to talk to them.

"You don't have to talk," said Beaudoin. "But you could listen."

At that, Amanda nodded okay and sat down on a small couch with her mother, opposite the detectives.

"Derik and David have been arrested for murder," Beaudoin said. "Make no mistake! They will be charged! We know they were in Tsawwassen on September 21st and October 5th. They've been identifed in a photo lineup. We know, in fact, Darren was involved, and that you were deceptive in your statements to detectives Tregear and Jackson. You did not tell the truth. We want you to tell the truth now."

Amanda, very fair and pale skinned, turned pink. "I think I should call my lawyer."

"It's my understanding you're a witness in this situation and not an accused," Beaudoin replied. "What would you need a lawyer for?"

Sitting with her legs tucked under her, her arms crossed, Amanda said nothing. Stabler then told her that Crown counsel was offering her immunity to charges provided she had not been involved in the actual murders or in planning them.

At that moment Amanda's face once again became suffused with color.

"Are you scared?" Beaudoin asked.

She nodded.

"Well, I am, too," Beaudoin said.

Later, when testifying, Beaudoin described the scene as very emotional. "I held my hand out. I said she could trust me, to tell me the truth. I asked her if she trusted me and she said she did. At that point I told her that she reminded me of my own daughter when she is afraid to tell me the truth.''

Hearing this, Amanda began to cry uncontrollably. Sara put her arm around her daughter and held her. ''Tell me the truth, Amanda,'' she quietly pleaded, ''tell me what happened.'' Turning on the detectives, she said sharply, ''How can she tell you anything? You're too close!'' Defensively, she held her daughter closer.

Both men, sensing they were on the edge of getting the evidence that would convict Darren Huenemann, had been leaning forward and were almost in Amanda's lap. They sat back immediately.

''And then it was like a floodgate opening,'' Beaudoin said.

With Sara holding her arm protectively around her sobbing daughter, Amanda started to speak. As she calmed down, Stabler and Sara Cousins moved a little distance away into the sitting room and Amanda and Beaudoin sat at the dining-room table. At no time was David Muir's statement ever mentioned. Every hour Amanda and Beaudoin took a few minutes' break. Sara remained close to her daughter throughout the night, but did not intervene in the discussion. At 3:30 a.m. an exhausted Amanda sank into her mother's arms, her statement finished, her life— and that of her mother—never again to be the same. The statement was filled with detail that could only have been known by someone who had either been at the murder scene—which was out of the question—or who had heard the killers themselves describe it.


On the following morning, while a still-confident, even ebullient, Darren drove his gleaming car to the Mount Douglas school grounds for what was to be the last time, Lord and Muir were taken from the Youth Detention Centre on Willingdon Road, Burnaby, to Delta Youth Court for a bail hearing. There they were met by their lawyers, Firestone and Macaulay, whose task was to persuade the court of two things: that neither Lord nor Muir would pose any risk to the public should they be released, and that they would appear for trial when ordered. The Crown's task was to persuade the court that the seriousness of the offenses alone warranted holding both boys on remand until trial.

During the three-hour hearing before Judge Philip Govan, Elouise Lord swore that her son, Derik, was at home at 8:30 p.m. on the evening of October 5th. In her early forties, her thick, curly black hair framing her unlined face, Mrs. Lord also testified that David Muir was there as well. The credibility of this claim was to become a crucial and extremely contentious issue in the subsequent trial of Lord and Muir.

The Crown's case was seriously weakened by Elouise Lord's testimony. Bail hearings presume the innocence of those charged but not yet convicted—unless there is ''compelling'' evidence to the contrary—so the Crown decided to make full disclosure of its case, although unable, of course, to make any use of, or reference to, the inadmissable confession already in its hands.

The doubts raised by Elouise Lord's testimony could not be ignored. Judge Govan ordered the boys released into the custody of their parents and set their bail at $10,000. He instructed the youths that they had to visit a bail supervisor once a week, had to be home Monday through Thursday by 9 p.m. and could not stay out later than 11 p.m. on weekends. Because of the protection afforded by the Young Offenders Act, publication of the boys' names, or anything that could identify them, was automatically banned.

Tregear and Jackson were having a leisurely late breakfast in a downtown restaurant that morning when they were told that the Crown in Delta had made full disclosure. They knew that someone would soon break all contents of the disclosure to Darren, and it was time to act.

A couple of hours later, they drove their unmarked police car into a parking lot a short distance from Mount Douglas Secondary and walked over to the school. They went immediately to the door of Darren's classroom, while principal Don Neumann cleared the corridor of a couple of chatting students. Darren was then called out of class and, as he stood in the corridor, was charged with two counts of first-degree murder—charges he would automatically face in adult court. He was frisked, hand-cuffed, and escorted off the school grounds and down the street to the unmarked car.

On his way, Darren passed a couple of students, whom he breezily greeted with words and a gesture with his cuffed hands. Passing his black Honda, he asked what would happen to it. Police told him they would make arrangements to have it towed away. When the group arrived at the Saanich police station, Darren phoned Chris Considine and his stepfather, Ralph. A little while later, Darren and his escorts boarded the ferry at Swartz Bay for Tsawwassen.

The group arrived at the Delta lockup just as Lord and Muir were being released on bail. An hour or so later Chris Considine and Ralph Huenemann arrived and, after spending some time with Darren, sat down for a briefing with Staff Sergeant Phil Harden. Ralph then learned for the first time that Darren had planned to kill him. His life, Harden explained, had been spared only because he had been excluded from any role in administering Sharon's will. What Ralph's reactions were to Harden's words are unknown. Later, however, Ralph would say in court, "The Darren I knew could not have done those things."

Judge Lee Skipp, when he presided over Darren's bail hearing in the British Columbia Supreme Court two weeks later, found the evidence sufficiently compelling to think otherwise. He refused Considine's motion for bail, and Darren was returned to Oakalla, an antiquated provincial prison that has since been permanently shut down. He was held there until he was transferred to Wilkinson Road Jail, outside of Victoria, in mid-December. Darren had requested the transfer in order to be closer to his stepfather and friends.

Both Oakalla and Wilkinson Road jails were overcrowded, smelly, and brutal places. Those who had thought Darren's coolness was mere posturing and phoniness were amazed at his indifference to his surroundings. "A cocky and manipulative kid," an Oakalla guard said. "But really young. He seemed to be more concerned about the zits on his face than his upcoming trial."

# EASY TIME

While Derik and David were living in their Saanich homes, keeping their 9 p.m. curfew and battling against a Crown application to move their cases to adult court, Darren was a mere couple of miles away, adapting to the routine of life in jail with the agility of a seal sliding into the sea.

Wilkinson Road Jail is a classic red brick monstrosity. It was built in 1913 as the Saanich Prison Farm, was later used as a mental institution, then reconverted to a prison in 1964. Despite its fortlike appearance and oppressive high-security atmosphere, Darren seemed to suffer neither apprehension nor angst; seemed, in fact, to be almost content in the new all-male world in which he now found himself. Regardless of his confinement within the walls; the regimentation of mealtime, shower time, cell time; regardless of the 24-hour elbow-rubbing with strangers, Darren appeared to be almost enjoying himself, as if he were savoring a degree of independence and freedom he had never before experienced. But while incarceration was providing Darren with his first chance ever to relate to other adults free of all the standards and expectations that his mother had scripted for him, it soon became obvious that he remained cocooned in his own fantasy world, a world not only impervious to reality, but one that seemed to be nourished by the particular tensions and dramas that every prison setting spawns.

Darren's truncated ability to recognize reality and his need to feed on the solaces of fantasy were to yield strange results. Once inside prison, he started talking about killing again. This time the victim was to be Amanda. It is impossible to say what Darren's actual intentions were. Lying, exaggerating, posing, and wallowing in dramatic effect were what he did best. Perhaps his fantasies of killing Amanda were nothing more than jailhouse bravado: however, when he'd spoken about killing before, nobody had taken any notice until after his mother and grandmother were dead. Whatever his actual intentions, two fellow inmates were to later testify that while in Wilkinson Road Jail Darren considered not only escaping, but making arrangements to have Amanda Cousins murdered by a professional hit man.

"I started a seven-and-a-half-month sentence on March 14th," said Stanley Dick, a rangy, bearded 39-year-old with a record for theft and alcohol-related offenses. "Huenemann and I were on the same C Unit and we spoke every day from the time we were let out of our cells in the a.m. until lockup at night. He said he was in for the murder of his mother and grandmother, but that his co-accused were the two who had actually done the killings. He said they had stabbed them."

Dick said Darren wasn't worried about the co-accused, nor did he express any concern about the deaths of his mother and his gran. One day while they were lounging around talking, Darren mentioned his grandmother. He made a snapping noise with his hands between his legs, and said, "Dirty Jewish pig."

"Darren talked about Amanda Cousins. She was his ex-girlfriend and he said she knew a lot. He was afraid of her and the damage she could do to his case. He offered me $10,000 if I would kill her, and there was another witness he wanted killed, a minor witness—I can't remember the name—and he asked me if $5,000 would be enough. He said he had the money, a bond worth about $30,000 and $2,000 in a bank account."

Dick claimed that Darren often spoke about his father's house and about $100,000 worth of jewelry that was in the drawers, on a night table, and scattered around. There were a lot of paintings in the house, but they were fakes. The real ones were in storage in a warehouse in Vancouver.

"I asked him if there was a security system and he said there was, but it wouldn't be a problem. He'd tell me how to get into it."

Because Amanda was in a safe house with 24-hour protection, Darren figured it would be difficult to kill her.

"He favored shooting her on the courthouse steps, but said I could do it anywhere I want, but she always had a cop with her. He then asked if shooting a cop would cost extra. I said that if the contract was for $10,000 that was the deal—the cop wouldn't be extra. He talked about it every day. I told him I wasn't into killing."

When Darren wasn't talking—or fantasizing, whatever the truth is—about killing Amanda, or down on his hands and knees, compulsively checking the chairs and table to make sure there were no bugs, he was chatting Dick up about escaping to the United States.

"He talked about escaping right from the beginning," said Dick. "I was to be transferred to a camp on April 24th. Once I was there I was supposed to write to [another inmate] Gus Paquette and tell him where I was. Gus would tell Darren, who'd send someone to the camp with $2,500 in cash, city clothes, and a ride. I was to get out of camp, go to Vancouver, and find a hooker who'd visit Darren. She'd inform Darren as to the date I'd be ready, waiting for him outside the jail. I was to bring a hydraulic jack, drills, a wire cutter, and a hand gun. Darren said he'd have $30,000 ready in cash and a car waiting."

Dick said his job was to get Darren into the United States, hide him out there, and arrange for plastic surgery on his face and hands. Darren said he'd sell some of his paintings, and with the money left over would buy drugs (for trafficking).

"If Darren escaped," said Dick, "one way or another Amanda was going to get it. As I was leaving Wilkinson Road to go to camp, he said to me, 'If you fuck me, you'll have to pay.' "

It's reasonable to wonder how much of this spacy testimony was lifted out of context, concocted, or merely a fine example of the absurdity jailhouse talk abounds with. But a second inmate, Randy Brown, a 31-year-old coke user being held on remand on a robbery charge, also found Darren interested in the subject of wiping out witnesses.

"I was also on the C Unit," he said, "and I was explaining to Darren about my robbery charge and how I was getting screwed by this guy I'd made a deal with. He went to the police and he was going to be a witness against me. Darren said that he had a girlfriend and *she* was going to be the problem for him. He didn't know where she was and she had two police officers with her all the time. I talked about having this witness taken care of, and Darren then asked me if I could check into his case. You know, have her taken care of...done...killed.''

Brown said that Darren didn't tell him his girlfriend's name, nor did he have any idea where she was. They never got down to swapping details. Still, Brown mentioned it to a girlfriend of his who knew a hit man. The girlfriend called the hit man on his pager, but the hit man had his standards, and no way would he touch the job because of the cops.


Whether Darren was ruthless enough to murder Amanda is not the question, as he obviously was. There were already two down, and Amanda would be just one more to go. Still, the testimony of Dick and Brown might have lacked all credibility if not for the single occasion when Darren dropped his mask long enough to allow for one look into his mind. The day before New Year's Eve 1990, Darren phoned his former Dungeons and Dragons master, Colin Newall. Newall hadn't forgotten Darren's murderous fantasies and believed he was involved in the killings. He recorded the conversation.

> Colin: Hello.
> Darren: Hello, Colin. How are things? Good?
> Colin: Don't you have anything else to do over there?
> Darren: No, I don't think so. Don't you? Of course you do.You know, I was looking at Thomas...Does he live in Oak Bay?
> Colin: I guess so.
> Darren: Okay, that's good, that narrows it down. There are only about, oh fuck, there are only about four people...
> Colin: What was that you said?
> Darren: Fuck.

Colin: I never heard you say that before...prison's reformed you.

Darren: (laughing) Oh dear...

Colin: [About the play *Caligula*] I didn't know you ran the whole thing. I didn't know you had total control over it.

Darren: Yeah, didn't you know?

Colin: No, I just heard about that recently actually.

Darren: In the paper?

Colin: No, from Andy [Thomas]. I didn't know that you were funding it.

Darren: God, yes! Oh yes, Grandma put up the money long ago. How did Andy get to know that?

Colin: He went with Peter.

Darren: Yeah?

Colin: And Peter made the statement.

Darren: He went with Peter where?

Colin: To the police department.

Darren: Ohhh...Okay.

Colin: But Peter made the statement. Andy had nothing to do with the statement.

Darren: Oh, well. God! You know Peter's tendency to ...well, let's say his girlfriend and him...the carving session...Do you understand? [Months earlier Dungeons and Dragons player Peter Tyrrell had allegedly cut his hand with a knife in a manipulative gesture to arouse a rejecting girlfriend's sympathy.] Do you understand what that means? With his hands...? That'll all come out on the stand.

Colin: That's...that's irrelevant to the testimony.

Darren: No. It pertains to his image...that will stop his ...statement...his credibility as a witness...

Colin: Well, realistically, an objection would be ruled.

Darren: But the jury would still hear it completely...yes. And the jury frowns upon that [sort of] thing as my lawyer says...Oh, they hate that. No, it's not irrelevant. It's quite relevant. We're going to be doing it to all our witnesses. Because they'll dig up my past, I can dig up any witnesses' past that come against me. And it's relevant completely, it's the credibility of the witness.

Colin: Uh-huh.

Darren: You should enjoy them on the stand. I hope Peter's strong. If he isn't, he's in big trouble. So Andy went with him. So who told him at the police station that I was in charge of everything?

Colin: One of the officers.

Darren: Well, I wonder who told them that. Probably Cloak [the drama teacher].

Colin: Maybe the principal.

Darren: No. He didn't know. They hadn't done those audits yet. Well...so they told him that? Ummmm...I don't even know where they find these things out.

Colin: Well, that's just as well because you're probably finding things out they don't know...

Darren: Oh, I've got piles of things they don't know! But they're for me to know!

Colin: The thing is, though, who are the two guys...like, who are these two guys you knew? They were friends of yours. It looks pretty bad.

Darren: Who? The news is saying this? Who's saying they were friends of mine?

Colin: The news is. That's where I heard it from.

Darren: Well, they certainly weren't...they were acquaintances. I knew them.

Colin: So what do you feel about them?

Darren: Well, I've no idea. The prosecution won't show me anything.

Colin: Well, what do you feel about them? They were the evil doers and you were the mastermind.

Darren: Not yet. No. I haven't had that proved. I know what they have against me, which is...ummm...but I don't know what they have against them. The prosecution will never tell me anything.

Colin: Well, in the news...those guys were your hand.

Darren: My hand?

Colin: Basically, from what I can tell, they did it because you paid them. That's what the papers say.

Darren: Oh, yes. But you see the thing is you can check every bank account I ever had. It has not been depleted at all.

Colin: But you paid for the play. You said you did.

Darren: I never made any money payments on that play. I was going to, we were in the midst of doing it. But I'm afraid my check stopped when everything else was frozen that I own. So, God, no! I'm not still paying for that thing since I'm not in it (laughing). Helloooooo...Oh, no! I was going to pay for the play, that was no problem, my grandmother had already arranged that. That's nothing new, that she'd arranged it already for publicity's sake. So that was no problem. I cleared it with my aunt and everything. No...none of my accounts had moved.

Colin: Oh, I can't...I really can't believe that you don't know that the other guys are involved. They're your servants.

Darren: I know they're involved, but...the thing is, if they [the police] have the same kind of evidence they do against me, then I know they're not guilty, because I know I'm not guilty and I look at the evidence.

Colin: Yeah, but the problem is, though...there was no break-and-entry like you said.

Darren: Yes, there was. The police are lying.

Colin: You said yourself there wasn't one earlier.

Darren: The police never told us there was. There was a breach in one of the things [patio door]. There'd been one before, see, so you couldn't tell how many there were. She used to break in herself (laughs) so there was many a time...but we haven't proof on that. Oh, yes. I'm covered there. Don't worry about that, pleeeease. I'm going to go into court with enough cards at my feet to sink everyone who takes the stand and lies. Peter, too. Sorry, Peter!

Colin: So what's so bloody dumb about his testimony? It's totally true—[it's] what you said...I haven't read it myself of course, but what you...I've been told it's in the testimony...everything that was said.

Darren: Yeah, well, there's some weird pieces missing...I certainly don't remember...There's a person [called] Thomas in his statement...I never heard anything being said about Thomas. I don't even know a Thomas! There's no Thomas in my school.

Colin: They may have made a mistake on the name.

Darren: Yeah.

Colin: But everything else...you know...about cracking your granny's neck, and then Andy would crack your neck ...that's all down there, isn't it?

Darren: I think so. I haven't read the statement. My lawyer burst out laughing. He said, ''This is the most creative statement.'' He said, ''Who cares what you said? You're eighteen. You're with a bunch of guys.'' And then he said, ''I daresay that Peter person seems to have problems of his own.'' So I explained them to him.

Colin: (laughs) Yeah?

Darren: Then he said, ''The statement's fried.'' And so is Andy. I told him I had stuff on everybody. Andy, too. And my lawyer said that it was a good thing I was funding the play, [because] if you were in a play and you're an actor, what you say doesn't matter. So I'm not too concerned. Oh, pleeeease. So when did he make this wonder statement, by the way?

Colin: I don't know. It was shortly after you were arrested I think.

Darren: Oh, was it? Or was it before?

Colin: It wasn't before.

Darren: Oh, I see...So Andy went with you?

Colin: Yes.

Darren: Andy's a nut case.

Colin: I'd rather not be subpoenaed myself.

Darren: Oh, yes. I have dirt on you, too. Don't worry.

Colin: What? You have dirt on me now, too? What is it?

Darren: Yes. Oh, shush! Quiet! Let's just say Andy spoke of you, and you spoke of Peter, and Andy spoke of...(laughter) Let's just say I remember everything. I certainly do. As my lawyer said, "That's a good boy, just write it all down and we'll fry them on the stand." Yes, sir! Oh, I'm not at all concerned.

Colin: Yeah, but you also remember that the other guy, the prosecutor, is going to be as bad [as the defense lawyer].

Darren: Against who? Me?

Colin: The prosecutor could be as bad as Considine.

Darren: Mr. Considine? Mr. Considine is the best. They're finding the best prosecutor to combat him. But they're frightened of him. And they're frightened of me! 'Cause I was like this when I was arrested…(laughs) They kept asking me, "Aren't you a little nervous, kid?" [I replied] "No, no, not at all, I like silver. What the hell!"

Colin: Silver?

Darren: My wardrobe…my shackles and things.

Colin: Yeah, right.

Darren: They were all nice and they jingled. I made little noises, little tunes with them and stuff. Drove 'em crazy on the ferryboat over. Oh, God! They take themselves very seriously. I laughed. I shook both their hands and I told them and this really unnerved them. Shook both their hands and I said, "There will be no hard feelings, gentlemen. When I'm acquitted I'll sue you both for everything you own." They didn't like that.

Colin: The two of them? The two cops?

Darren: Sue the department, too. I'd sue anyone who lied. So that's no problem. And false arrest and all the rest of it and what's-his-name's stuff…Peter's?…that's no relevant testimony. It's not relevant. As my lawyer said, "A, it's a game, and B, whatever you say is fine—let's have Peter's past record." And I said, "Very well." (laughs)

Colin: Yeah, but the game…well, is very good character witnesses of people…

Darren: Actually, no. My lawyer said it's the worst character witness of people, and he said, "The best character witness of people is what you were like when you were arrested and they knew it and that's why they're frightened, because you stood like you were going to sue them.'' And you bet I am. Oh, please, Colin! I have my cards up my sleeve all the time. Granny always taught me to keep a full deck up there.

Colin: Well, we'll see, we'll see what happens. They are using press right now, though.

Darren: Well, of course! Oh, I want that! Then I can sue for more later. The more they degrade my reputation...

[Darren then spoke about his forthcoming preliminary hearing and the bail application that would follow.] Oh, it would be all very interesting to see. I hope Peter comes to court! Oh, dear! Oh, dear! I pity the boy in front of my lawyer. My family—my God, they're 110 percent, my whole family's 150 percent behind me. Everyone's behind me. No, that's no problem—except for these few odd ones—like my girlfriend, who I call a variety of names. And she didn't tend to like those. No, no. I wouldn't be too concerned.

Darren has given us a self-portrait in this secretly recorded conversation. His guard is partially down, lowered just enough to allow a short but sharp glimpse of the real Darren: the poisonously thwarted child hiding beneath the veneer of charm. There is a possibility that the testimony of Stanley Dick and Randy Brown, although taken under oath, might have been unwittingly exaggerated, distorted by time and dramatized by the process of the trial itself. But there is no room for speculation in this self-portrait, no drawing on the analysis or interpretations of others. Darren himself fills in all the lines with clean, bold strokes—his cunning, callousness, pretentiousness, dangerousness, his childishness, and his naïveté. ''I have dirt on you, too,'' he says smoothly when he learns that Newall has made a statement. His voice is that of a stranger. His normal honeyed tone has disappeared, and sneers, giggles, sarcasm, threats replace it. ''Let's just say I remember everything.'' Anyone who witnessed against him would pay for it by being ''fried'' on the stand. ''Oh, dear! I pity the boy!'' he sneers. The words are thick with loathing.

If the mind could be X-rayed like the bones of a body, we would find in this tape the skeletal frame of the dwarfed child whose individuality and potential had been crushed by the powerful needs of others. "They're frightened of me," he boasts, this little boy with all his fantastical, magical powers pitched against the dragons of the police. In the theatrical scene he depicts—all of which was fabrication—he drives the police "crazy on the ferryboat," jingling his "silver" handcuffs. Strutting centerstage in his own mind, he shakes the detectives' hands and grandly says, "There will be no hard feelings, gentlemen...I'll sue you both for everything you own." He depicts the police as frightened by the character and control that he exhibits. "Aren't you a little nervous, kid?" the police gasp in awe. Not him, for he knows "piles of things they don't know. But they're for me to know." He finds it amusing that the marks left by the phony break-in of the patio door staged by Muir and Lord are mingled with the marks made by his own grandmother. No pity for dead Gran from the "light of her life." Just laughter at his own cunning in using her: "She used to break in herself, hee, hee, hee...Oh, yes. I'm covered there. Don't worry about that, pleeeease."

Later, when this tape was played in court, a look almost of relief settled on the faces of the riveted jury, for now there was no uncertainty about the well-dressed, mild-looking young man seated in the stand. Darren's witness against himself shouted aloud. It said: Here is the real Darren, not the polite Darren with the air-conditioned car and lots of money and oodles of charm. Here is the Darren who plotted to have his mother and grandmother killed with a hit by two high-school friends for a trifle of money and a promise of belonging.

# TRANSFER BATTLE

Soon after Sean Madigan, Q.C., was named Crown prosecutor in what had become known as "the Huenemann murders," he moved to have Derik Lord and David Muir raised from juvenile to adult court. In his opinion the youths were contract killers, and only a jury trial would satisfy the public.

The objective of a transfer hearing is to arrive at some understanding of the accused's intellectual and social maturity so that, if convicted, he receives a penalty that is appropriate to the crime. The factors used in making this assessment are highly individual, so separate hearings were held for Lord and Muir, even though they were charged with the same offense.

Lord's hearing was scheduled first. It opened in a Surrey courtroom before Judge Jack Varcoe on February 25, 1991, in an atmosphere tight with tension. The preliminary hearing for Darren Huenemann, resulting in his committal to trial, had been held two weeks earlier. During Huenemann's preliminary, Crown evidence had revealed some of the brutal details surrounding the women's deaths, including the careful planning that had preceded the attack.

Doris's family felt that the evidence against Derik was compelling, and were shaken by the sight of him free on bail, chatting in the corridor with friends, or sitting with the rest of the spectators in the body of the courtroom, surrounded by his parents, two grandmothers, sisters, aunts, uncles, and cousins. The very size of his support group seemed, in some irrational way, to exacerbate their own sense of victimization. But the presence of Derik as a spectator, and the elbow-rubbing proximity of the two families crowded together in the small courtroom were comparatively minor sources of stress compared with the stakes involved.

What is an appropriate penalty for killing another human being? The maximum penalty for first-degree murder under the Young Offenders Act is three years. Trials are held before a judge, are open to the public, but are protected by a ban on publication. In adult court the same conviction, after a public trial with its attendant media publicity, carries a mandatory sentence of 25 years without parole.

The stakes, therefore, were enormous. If Lord's lawyer, Peter Firestone, could defeat Madigan's application and retain Young Offender status for his client, Derik Lord would be home free at age 21, even if subsequently found guilty. Furthermore, his crime would remain forever under wraps, and he could lead the rest of his life free of any stigma. But if Firestone lost and his client was later convicted in adult court, Lord would re-enter society as a middle-aged man, under parole for the rest of his life and marked wherever he went and in whatever he did as an ex-con.

While the main issue in a transfer hearing is the appropriateness of the penalty, deciding just what is appropriate depends largely on the considerations raised in subparagraph (b) of Section 16 of the Young Offenders Act. Would the accused benefit from treatment? How suitable are the resources available? Is the best program for this individual in a federal or juvenile institution? Is the accused mature enough to adapt to the federal system? Is the accused likely to kill again, and should the public be protected as long as possible? Only when the court knows the answers to these questions can the matter of appropriate penalty be decided. Ultimately, while the facts of a crime are easy to come by, it's the judge's assessment of the mind-state of the offender that can result in either a treatment-oriented three-year slap on the wrist, or 25 years mopping floors as a lifer.

Both the Crown and defense in the Lord case had enlisted forensic specialists—in this case psychiatrists and psychologists—

to assist the judge in reaching the "right" decision. (A forensic expert is a person from a specific profession who gives expert testimony in legal proceedings.) Assuming for the sake of argument that Lord had killed the women, what was his motive? Was he psychotic, on drugs and unaware of what he was doing? Did he drink heavily? Had he been abused as a child? How did he behave at school, at work, among his peers?

Unfortunately, expert witnesses do not always agree. The law deals in black and white; psychiatrists and psychologists inhabit a world of grays, a murkier and more speculative one. However experienced and of recognized competence, it's not unusual for expert witnesses on either side to be hesitant and indecisive, and sometimes in total disagreement. In these instances, "experts" may be of little help to the court's decision making. Such was the case in the transfer hearing of Derik Lord, and even more so in the hearing two weeks later of David Muir.

Lord's hearing got under way with a series of witnesses who testified to the facts of the case, specifically those that dealt with the seriousness and premeditated nature of the crime. On the question of treatment, Dr. Wesley Carson Smiley, a psychiatrist with Correctional Service Canada, took the stand and outlined the programs available for 140 adult "patients" at the Regional Psychiatric Centre at Matsqui, British Columbia, an adult institution with no specific program for adolescents. Inmates were paid to do grades 10 to 12, he said, and post-secondary education was available through Simon Fraser University and the University of Victoria. When asked about violence inside prisons, he reported that there had been 62 incidents of stabbings, murders, riots, and sitdowns in the federal system's 62 prisons the previous year.

Wiry, pale-faced, and dressed totally in white—jeans, shirt, running shoes—Derik Lord followed the proceedings with varying degrees of interest and indifference. From time to time bitter whispered comments about the law in general and the police in particular were tossed out by Derik's father, David, and were clearly audible.

Fran Maclean, Madigan's 33-year-old assistant Crown counsel, opened the second day of the hearing by calling David William

Huggins, a probation officer and youth worker under the Young Offenders Act, to the stand. Maclean's voice is distinctive, calm, and tinged with a languor that makes it almost a drawl. Her voice and her poise seemed to mesmerize the edgy courtroom as she asked Huggins about Lord's level of emotional maturity. She wanted to establish the fact that Lord was intelligent—and therefore responsible for his acts—and that when Lord faced a problem he felt it was all right to use violence to solve it.

Huggins had interviewed Lord twice in addition to meeting with him a half-dozen times while supervising his bail. He thought Lord's general demeanor was a "little bit different" from what most people would have been like under the same circumstances. "He'd often smile or smirk at times I didn't think anything was funny," said Huggins. "It was out of place, like when he'd be sitting in the waiting room laughing and joking with his mum. Otherwise, he was ordinary."

As for his intelligence, Huggins said Lord probably rated a bit above average. But Lord didn't like school, and didn't apply himself, although his teachers said that if he'd make an effort he'd do well.

"Have you any other observations regarding his emotional response?" Maclean asked Huggins.

After a long hesitation, he replied, "He was on a pretty even keel most of the time. There were a couple of occasions discussing behavior at school where he'd been involved in inappropriate behavior. He became angry, felt the school was making too much of it. You [could] see the anger build in him. When he was kicked out of his classroom, for instance, he placed himself up over a beam at the second-floor level. When we discussed that, he became agitated and annoyed. He'd been sent to the counselor and saw the counselor as a bit of a joke. He also threatened to blow up the staff room. When we discussed that, he became agitated and said the school was making too much of it."

When Maclean asked what Lord's emotional response to the charge of murder had been, Huggins said that Lord certainly had not reacted the way he, Huggins, would have. "I'd be a nervous wreck. There was nothing of that nature with Derik. Apart from giggling and anger."

Maclean then inquired about a collection of weapons belonging to Derik.

Huggins replied, "I phoned Mrs. Lord and asked to see his collection of knives. She said okay and I indicated I'd be over in half an hour. Derik wasn't home when I phoned, but he was there with a friend of his when I arrived. Derik opened a shoebox on the table. There were a couple of boot knives in leather sheaths, combat knives of poor quality, and a lock-blade knife. This was an awesome weapon. It had an eight-inch blade, jagged, a buck-knife-type blade. The handle was molded to fit into the hand and fingers. It had a button on the back that sprang the blade. It was shaped so you could have the knife in your hand and punch with it. Awesome. There was also a BB gun and another gun, a .37 caliber, I believe. His mum had taken the collection away and kept it in a secret hiding place."

"Derik had an interest in knives at age eleven, is that right?" Maclean read. "And he began carrying them at—"

Judge Varcoe interrupted, referring to Huggins's official report. "Where did you find that?"

Maclean named the page and read: " 'Derik often played with a knife, flicking it around. He enjoyed pretending to strike, then flicking it around so that the handle, not the blade, struck the person.' "

The courtroom was silent. Elouise Lord whispered to Derik, who shrugged and stared ahead without replying. Maclean took her time, letting the words sink in, as she then perused the report. Finally she found what she was looking for. "What is this reference you made to dynamite?" she asked Huggins.

He replied that he'd gone up to Mount Doug regarding Derik's threats to blow up the staff room. Lord had told some classmates that he could get dynamite, a rumor got going, and it got out of hand.

"Derik thought it was a joke that the school was considering kicking him out [as a result]. I asked him if he could get dynamite, and he said yes. I asked him if he had said he would blow up the staff room, and he said yes. He said he knew a guy who supplied firecrackers and he'd asked him if he could get dynamite. The fellow said yes, but he never got back to Derik. I asked Derik why he threatened the staff room and Derik replied, 'Teachers are in the staff room and nobody likes teachers.'

"Some students felt intimated by Derik showing knives," Huggins continued, "but others felt Derik was just playing around. A girl at the Kmart where Derik worked said she had complained about her supervisor to Derik. Derik had responded, 'Why don't you stab him, stick him? I'll sell you the knife for $25, or do it for $50.' The personnel manager at the store said that two women had complained to him about Derik playing with knives."

There was little that Peter Firestone, Lord's lawyer, could do to soften the emerging portrait of Derik Lord as a nasty and potentially dangerous thug, other than to faintly hint that Lord's home life might have been less than ideal. To Firestone's query as to whether Derik came from a stable home, Huggins simply replied that it was an older house in the Gordon Head subdivision, and yes, there'd been some conflict.

At that point Judge Varcoe recessed the court for the day, reconvening it for Thursday, April 4th, after discovering that one of the experts was in the Caribbean and unable to appear. A member of Lord's family then asked Crown counsel Sean Madigan for a copy of Huggins's report. There were several spares available and soon they were circulating in and out of the courtroom among Derik's relatives and friends.

Doris's family also asked Madigan for a copy. He explained that most of the material was confidential, and confidentiality precluded his giving it to anyone outside of the subject's family. Madigan suggested they ask Firestone. Firestone politely refused. Out in the corridors Derik's friends pored over the report, making wisecracks and comments, while a frustrated John Kriss vainly tried to obtain a copy and swore he'd hire his own lawyer "to get some real representation for my family."

That evening, John Kriss received a phone call that did little to improve his feelings of victimization. A Delta police officer informed Kriss that Elouise Lord had complained to Peter Firestone that Kriss had poked her in the back as they were returning to the courtroom after a recess. Furthermore, Derik's sister, Dawn, said that Kriss had insinuated they were "the scum of the earth." "This is just by way of a friendly warning," the officer told Kriss. "You must not make loud remarks or act in any way that could be thought aggressive toward the Lord family." The call floored Kriss, who later informed Firestone that the credence given the charge "insulted my integrity."


Psychiatrist Thomas Ripley, of the Youth Forensic Services of Victoria, was the first on the stand when the hearing resumed in Surrey on April 4th. Madigan's plan—based on an assumption that Lord had killed the women—was to show the court that Ripley had no knowledge or insight as to why Lord had killed, nor did he know whether Lord would ever kill again. If he could make it clear that there were no definitive answers to these critical questions, the chance of Lord going to adult court would be greatly increased.

Holding Ripley's report, Madigan had the psychiatrist confirm the fact that all the anecdotal material in it was received from Lord or from his parents.

"Now, there's no suggestion in it that Derik ever loses the ability to distinguish between fantasy and reality," said Madigan smoothly. "You found nothing medically wrong with him. You found nothing of a psychiatric nature that prevents him knowing [what's going on] just like any other normal eighteen-year-old. He does not suffer from any mental illness. Now, do you have *any* experience, or *any* knowledge from your training, as to why a young man would have the capacity to commit the offense?"

Unhesitatingly, Riply said no, he didn't. He'd read the complete reports on the crime and had no explanation to offer.

Madigan pressed on with his questioning about motive. He knew that Ripley had found no motive, but he wanted to rub it in. It strengthened his own theory—that the killings were cold-blooded contract murders for profit.

"You know the fact pattern—they were hired to kill two women. Is there *anything, any* explanation, that would explain why a young man would commit that crime?"

"No." Ripley shook his head. "There was no abuse. There was nothing in the past history or the psychological testing that would explain it."

Madigan then tackled the issue of whether Lord was a danger to society. "Is there *anything* that would assist the court in [predicting] whether he would do it again?"

"Repeat offenses are quite low, particularly with someone with no history of repeated violations of the rights of others. Derik does not have such a history," said Ripley.

"What about distinguishing right from wrong?" Madigan countered. "You realize that whoever did it had the capacity to stop their actions. A person of conscience could have stopped after knocking the two women out."

Ripley agreed. Yes, at any stage the actions could have been stopped.

"If he did it," Madigan persisted, "is there anything you can see in this young man's behavior that would indicate it would not be repeated?"

"There are two factors to consider," replied Ripley. "The rarity of this type of event, and Lord's own history. There are no previous episodes of not appreciating the rights of others, which would therefore lead—"

But Madigan cut him off. "On October 4th Lord was a Grade 12 high-school student. He came from a good family, had a decent background, was an ordinary kid. Yet on the next day he crossed on the ferry to kill two women to collect money. And there was nothing different about him."

Ripley agreed. "You are right. Violence is extremely difficult to predict. As far as giving an absolute prediction as a psychiatrist, I am unable to do that."

"On the 4th of October you could not have predicted what was going to happen the next day?"

"I would have said it was extremely unlikely."

Madigan pressed the point further. "So you cannot assist the court in predicting the dangerousness in the future."

"It's impossible to give any assurances of that nature." After a pause Ripley added, "We can deal only in probability and likelihood."

"If we had *that* opinion the day before the murders, time would have proven us to be wrong." Madigan let his words hang in the air for a moment before adding, "In fact, these deeds were planned. In fact, these deeds were done."

With the psychiatrist's clear admission that there was no way to predict Lord's future behavior, Madigan moved to his next objective—to establish the fact that Lord did not need psychiatric treatment.

"This young man has picked up all the proper goals of parents and his moral development has been correct, internalized, and incorporated in his own values, and he could accept and act on them. His rejection of those values was not the result of a deficit in his mental state. He was not a drug taker, not an alcoholic."

"Yes, it's not the result of a deficit," said Ripley. "He is not a drug or alcohol user." He continued, "The depression he experienced in the fall of last year [when he lost his girlfriend] is the result of a certain inability to shape and modify his reaction to events. He would have benefited from treatment then."

"A depression?" Madigan's voice rose in slight derision. "That's not unusual in adolescents. You said he'd be better off in a juvenile system."

"If there was appropriate treatment. The treatment in the juvenile system is the best available."

Madigan pointed out that Lord was now eighteen, and that the age for admittance to the adult system was eighteen and over. "If this young man doesn't need any treatment, why would treatment be necessary?" he asked. "So that he would benefit from psychiatric intervention for his depression?"

"Yes."

Firestone, Lord's lawyer, then asked Ripley for an overall assessment of Derik. "Because of his immaturity, would this young man be better served by the youth system?"

Ripley's neutral reply concluded his testimony. "Youth Forensic in Victoria has a psychiatrist and psychologist and a program could be set up."

Dr. Melvin Stangeland, a Victoria psychologist brought into the case by the defense, then took the stand. Stangeland said that he had interviewed Derik Lord and taken social and family histories, and questioned Lord about his relationships at school and with his family. He found no indication of mental disorder.

"I found he suffered from excessive anxiety, and difficulty in communicating interpersonal relationships—an avoidance personality disorder. He also suffered from post-traumatic stress disorder—the sort of thing suffered by those who had been through the Vietnam War, crashes, abusive situations. I had read the police reports of the crimes, but I did not discuss the events with Derik."

"Did testing reveal anything?"

"People who commit murder aren't easily classified. It's sometimes done by people who are antisocial, who have difficulty communicating their feelings, until they build."

"You know that these killings were not explosive acts but long-term planned killings," Madigan said flatly. "Was there anything to indicate why such a thing could have occurred? If you took the test results and tried to say if they would commit murder, you couldn't say it?"

"That's right."

"Your testing didn't reveal why a high-school kid would have been involved with it?"

"No, it didn't."

"...[didn't explain how it could have been done] by someone who'd been brought up properly?"

"I wouldn't say he'd been brought up properly," retorted Stangeland. "Cursorily he'd been brought up properly, but if you look deeper—no."

"I think Derik has a reasonable understanding of right and wrong," said Madigan. "He should know killing was wrong. If he stuck a knife in someone, he'd know that was wrong?"

"Yes." Stangeland then added, "There was some preoccupation with fantasy. Derik didn't discuss a lot about this, but information from other sources indicated that there were some elaborate and fantastic schemes, for example, importation of weapons. Derik was caught up in a rather fantastic way of looking at things, so that they [the three boys] were able to justify their actions as reasonable. Their involvement together was more like those in early adolescence before any heterosexual relationships.''

In a mildly incredulous voice Madigan asked, ''Talking about killing your friend's mother and grandmother to inherit money is a fantasy?''

''There was a fantasy to share a lot of money, that Derik was to be put in some cabin in the wilderness. It wasn't based on any real understanding of how the world works. The whole scheme, plan and idea, goes beyond simple killing for money. A contract killing is a business-type transaction. This was more complex than that.''

''You're aware of the great lengths the group went to to cover up?''

Stangeland hesitated. ''All I can do is look at the psychological testing. I'd need a lot more information...''

''But you did call it 'an immature conspiratorial fantasy'?'' Madigan insisted.

''I'd call it a plot to kill,'' Stangeland countered.

''The way the money was to be used, the power—that was *not* fantasy.''

But Stangeland was as insistent as Madigan. ''The *scheme* was fantasy, something not well based in reality.''

''The scheme! Throwing the weapons off the ferry, making it look like a robbery, the alibi in Victoria...''

''I'm not talking about *everything* that went along with it! He would not have been fantasizing when the act was committed.''

Madigan was finished. He'd accomplished his objective. He'd shown that while Lord *did* have fantasies of wealth and freedom, he could still distinguish right from wrong, and had used that ability to cover up his tracks. He looked toward Firestone, perhaps anticipating a full barrage.

But the serious, stocky 34-year-old Firestone was apparently saving both his arguments and his energies for his summation. When he stood up, it was to deliver a single, brief statement. ''Your bottom line analysis is 'A personality profile that would not be best served in an adult institution.' ''

Stangeland nodded assent.

Back on his feet, Madigan started his summation with an overview of the factors to be considered under Section 16 of the Young Offenders Act. "Sometimes very confusing factors seem to arise," he said, "but one factor continues through all of them. What is the evidence of the offense and, arising from that offense, does the public have to be protected from the offender?

"We are dealing with one of the worst crimes imaginable. The killings took place for the basest of motives—greed. The killers were hired to kill and were promised payment. The killers, other than greed, had no motive to kill. The crime was planned over a long period of time, at least from July to October, 1990. The details of how to do it were hashed and rehashed by Huenemann, Muir, and Lord over this period of time, but the ultimate objective remained consistent. The objective was that Doris Leatherbarrow and her daughter, Sharon Huenemann, were to be killed so that Darren Huenemann could inherit all the money, become a rich man, and share his wealth with the persons whom he, in essence, hired to kill."

Madigan then explored details of the crime itself. Repeatedly he stressed the variety of murder schemes considered by the boys, the degree of premeditation involved in the plot that was finally chosen, and the lack of any clear evidence of mental illness.

"There is no doubt that the fertile imagination behind all these schemes was Darren Huenemann, but he was using Lord and Muir to do his dirty work for him. Drugs and liquor don't feature in this case at all. These plotters were sober and sane. They weren't drunks or drug addicts. They were people who knew what they were doing and why. The first time when they failed to find the Leatherbarrow house, they returned and were met by Amanda Cousins and Huenemann. There wasn't a sign of remorse or troubled conscience. The killings were reset for when Sharon would be back in Tsawwassen in two weeks' time. We can see the planning that went into it—the buying of crowbars, the decision to use knives taken at the setting, the setting up of an alibi.

"If this case had been committed by an adult, it would appall. It's a case that should go to trial by jury. The trial court would then be a judge and twelve ordinary citizens, and everyone would be able to see how the law is enforced. This trial would have all the benefits associated with our criminal law, a trial in which our fellow citizens can judge."

Madigan then made an offer that left the courtroom in silence. There was more than a trace of awkwardness in his voice as he declared, "The Crown will make one concession. If Your Honor reaches that stage where you cannot transfer because of the 25-year mandatory sentence, we would be prepared to indict Lord for second degree under Section 16."

Despite Madigan's powerful submission, this maneuver revealed the uncertainty that lay behind it. Madigan's certainty that a transfer to adult court was appropriate was offset by his fear that Judge Jack Varcoe would not transfer Lord simply because he, Varcoe, found the potential imposition of a 25-year sentence on a teenaged youth to be excessive and repugnant. Madigan's offer was a compromise that only the insane disparity in sentencing—three years or life—could explain.

"That would be a serious error," said Firestone in a slightly derisive tone. Taking his time, he poured himself a glass of water and rocked his plump body back and forth as he emptied the glass. He continued, "The Crown has spent almost the entire submission saying that because of the seriousness of the offense, this case *must* be raised. Now we have this concession, and if you adopt it, it could be a trialable issue." Presumably Firestone meant that the defense could claim that the prosecution had doubts about the appropriateness of the first-degree charge.

"We have to look at the interests of society having regard to the needs of the young person. There is *nothing* that would require the public to be protected from Derik Lord for 25 years. There's a very supportive family. There are no psychological problems. Section 16 says you must consider the psychiatric report. There is no need to reject it. Also the Huggins report, on balance, is a positive statement.

"My client is not perfect. He has some problems which relate to his level of adolescence, the way he deals with his family, with his father in particular. He's immature for his age, and has trouble dealing with the real world. Bail was granted by Judge Goven—it is quite clear that special conditions are made for young offenders.

"There's an absence of physical corroborative evidence at the scene of the crime—no fibers, no fingerprints, no hair. There's just a theory—and what Amanda Cousins says. And perhaps she got that information from other sources.

"The Lords have had to put their home up for surety. We have the counselor's assessment from Mount Douglas, and the letter from his English teachers, which is a positive statement. He still takes judo classes, and in April will start at Camosun College. [In a decision made in a previous case] Judge McEachern [chief justice of the British Columbia Appeals Court] has sent a clear message that 25 years is clearly excessive for someone who comes under the Young Offenders Act. And the intent of that act is the least possible interference with freedom.

"The nub of the issue is the needs of the accused and the needs of society. The length of sentence should not exceed the needs of protection of society. It would be an error of law not to emphasize the interest of society—but also the rehabilitation and needs of the young person. The dangers to society must be considered, but this is not an overwhelming case. The penalty of 25 years must be taken into submission. This is too much for a young offender."

When Firestone mentioned the "rehabilitation and needs" of Lord, the faces of some of Doris's family and friends darkened with anger. From their grim expressions, they objected strongly to Firestone's describing the murder of Doris and her daughter as "not an overwhelming case." "Not overwhelming for whom?" one grieving woman commented to another.

On the other side of the courtroom, Firestone's words brought a sense of relief and hope. As Firestone concluded with the comment that adult prison programs are not specifically geared to adolescents, a couple of members of Lord's family nodded in eager agreement.

"The accused has wide family support"—at this point Firestone turned slightly and gestured to the family, who packed two benches—"he has part-time work at the Kmart, and he has not been proven incorrigible. The court must consider the dangerousness of placing this young man into the adult system. As for the raising of this young offender to adult court on a second-degree charge—that could be considered cruel and unusual punishment."

Madigan's response was blunt and brief. "If he needs it [a treatment program]—and he doesn't seem to need it—he can be treated at Matsqui. He is an adult now. This decision should not be up to a psychiatrist or a psychologist, or whether he does or doesn't have a mental disease, or whether he does or does not have a marvelous family.

"The doctors have made it quite clear they can't help the court. What they have said today could just as well have been said before the offense. They are of absolutely *no* assistance as to whether the public needs to be protected. All they can say is 'I don't know.' We have here a young man of impeccable background, for argument's sake, who, according to the evidence, went out and killed—not one—but two women in a brutal and uncivilized fashion. There is no bar to transfer."

With the arguments of both sides completed, Judge Varcoe set April 15th for his decision, the clerk ordered everyone to rise, and the Lord family and Doris's family filed out side by side, avoiding one another's eyes and aching with resentment and anguish.

One week before Judge Varcoe delivered his decision on Derik Lord, the transfer hearing for David Michael Muir opened before him. Once again the Crown sought to discredit any claims that the accused merited the protection of the Young Offenders Act, while the opposing counsel sought to uphold it. Psychiatrist Dr. Wesley Carson Smiley again appeared on the scene. This time, the slight, neat-looking Dr. Smiley had more to offer the court than a routine outline of federal programs.

"How do you avoid becoming a victim once you're in prison?" Muir's lawyer, Malcolm Macaulay, asked.

Smiley summed up the brutal reality. "If you're small and inadequate, you're a victim. If big, intelligent, socially skilled, you're okay."

Macaulay pointed to David Muir. He was dressed in gray slacks and blue sweater, and sat with his parents, John and Vivien, in the body of the courtroom. As attention shifted to him, Muir turned deep red.

"Do you see a young man there, hardened and tough?"

"Well, to be candid, I've never seen a hardened, street-smart-looking youth in the courtroom," Smiley replied. "The fact is, some look tough and their criminal background is comparatively mild, while other offenders look angelic and their backgrounds are horrendous."

"He has no priors," Macaulay pointed out. "He tends to be a follower rather than a leader. Is he typical of the young offender?"

"He's typical of the young offender who in the past has been raised to adult court."

Smiley was followed by psychiatrist Emily Murphy, who had worked at Youth Forensic for five years and Adult Forensic for three. Murphy, brought in by the Crown counsel, told the court that Muir showed no indication of any criminal, medical, or psychiatric problems, although in importing and selling weapons he was transgressing the "loyal norms and hopes" of his family, who knew nothing about it.

The crime itself raised the question of Muir's ability to feel guilt. "It involved cruelty, the use of knives to draw blood, and a slow death," said Murphy. "This indicated a lack of empathy, which is simply the ability to get into the shoes of another person. This could mean a diminished ability to feel guilt, or to learn from mistakes."

Murphy said she found David "intellectually well beyond his years and financially mature," with no "deep psychological conflicts." She felt that his interest in knives, which had a long history and was highly developed and intense, would continue.

"However, no psychiatric treatment, medication, or psycho-therapy is needed," Murphy concluded. "It was an atypical crime in that it was planned for a long period of time."

Faced with Murphy's clear opinion that Muir could gain nothing from psychotherapy, and was therefore not treatable—and hence not releasable in short order—Muir's lawyer homed in on the issue of public safety, hoping to show that Muir did not need long-term imprisonment.

"Could you say if he'll be a danger to the public in the future?" Macaulay asked.

"No, I can't," said Murphy.

"If you presumed innocence," Macaulay persisted, "is there anything in David's behavior outside of the norms of adolescent behavior?"

"He chose a group of peers interested in weapons, his social skills are poorly developed, he did not have any girlfriends. He doesn't appreciate the moral aspects of importing weapons. There's a restriction in the emotional range," Murphy replied.

When Macaulay remarked that lack of empathy was common with adolescent and adult murderers, so this shouldn't be taken as an indicator of later adult behavior, Murphy dryly retorted, "To find someone who feels triumph and jubilance [after murdering another] is definitely a lack of empathy."

But Macaulay persisted. "David said, 'I feel bad about it. I cringe when I hear their names mentioned.' Doesn't that indicate remorse?"

"Not necessarily," said Murphy. "I'd have to know the context, have to know if it was said with tears or flatly."

After commenting on the fact that Muir was impressed with Huenemann's flashy style and possessions, Macaulay went on to wonder aloud if it was possible "that David's immaturity, his desire for peer acceptance, and his desire for money *plus* meeting Darren Huenemann at this time, might explain his involvement in this matter." For instance, Macaulay said, "If David had had his own car, a relationship with the opposite sex, had finished his education—given his background, might he not have been able to resist the spell of Darren Huenemann?"

Not in Murphy's opinion. "He was as attracted to Derik Lord as to Darren Huenemann," she pointed out.

The following morning, when psychologist Steven Sigmond took the stand, Crown counsel Madigan started his examination by wondering aloud if Muir had ever expressed remorse or shown any indication of it.

For legal and ethical reasons, Dr. Sigmond said, he had been instructed (by Macaulay) not to talk about the crime or how David felt about his victims. However, David had said he "felt bad about it all."

"These tests"—Madigan waved some papers—"adolescent tests and adult tests—are they the same? Oh, they are? So it's a conduct disorder at eighteen and an antisocial disorder after eighteen! Why is eighteen chosen—what's so magical about it?"

Sigmond said that the personality "jelled" at that age. He described David Muir as "very superior in intellectual abilities but immature." There was no mental illness, no personality disorder. His verbal skills were in the upper limits of the superior range. He had much-better-than-average judgment, reasoning, creative, and cognitive resources on which to rely. "He was brought up very well by his family," Sigmond concluded, "but he certainly has a social-skills deficit."

When Dr. Roy O'Shaughnessy, the clinical director of Juvenile Service, took the stand he also spoke positively of Muir's family. "The father's a strong stand of support, the mother is having a hard time." He continued, "David's family is highly functional, with appropriate roles of intimacy and contact. David himself has long-standing affective [emotional] relationships with family and friends, and does not show any of the features of the prognostic indicators of future violent behavior...My own feeling is that it [the question of transfer] comes down to protection of society. Almost all kids are better off in juvenile than in adult courts. This is a boy from a nice, protected, middle-class family, not exposed to street life, not hardened, has never been in youth court."

At this Madigan exploded. "You have described *a choir boy*!" Leaning over the Crown counsel table, he snatched up the book containing photographs of the murder scene. The plastic-covered pages flopped open as he thrust the book at the psychiatrist. "A choir boy did that? Absolute nonsense!"

O'Shaughnessy glanced at the scene, but this didn't satisfy Madigan. "Look at those women! Look at it! Look at them!" Photos of the women's heads pooled in blood could be seen. The courtroom froze.

"The boy you've described wouldn't even have shoplifted," Madigan said derisively. "You're a medical doctor. You know the death that's been involved, the slow, painful death imposed on those women. And while they were getting the boys lasagna!" He threw the exhibit back on the table. When he resumed speaking, his voice, if not his intent, was kinder. "And what about weapons, eh? You've clearly untapped that part of his fantasy life."

"We didn't pursue anything about weapons," O'Shaughnessy admitted. "To be frank with you...I don't know."

"Now, we're not talking about Darren Huenemann. He didn't do it," he said, indicating the book. "Lord! You say this young man has empathy. But he imported weapons! And you didn't go into that?"

O'Shaughnessy, who had done his forensic psychiatry at Yale and whose reputation is impeccable, held his peace.

After one seemingly interminable minute of silence, Madigan slowly said, one emphatic word after another, "The facts are he plotted to kill in August. He couldn't do it on September 21st. *So he went back*. Where, tell me, is his empathy?"

"I can't answer that question." O'Shaughnessy was blunt. "I'm impressed as to how people can turn off empathy."

"He has a decent home, decent parents, decent siblings."

O'Shaughnessy attempted to explain the process by which David Muir drifted into murder. Through peer association, he said, Muir's inhibitions were diminished. Through fantasy, talk, there was a gradual acceptance over months.

Madigan didn't budge. "How could this be possible? You know he is a very bright young man. If he's the person you describe, how could he lose the inhibition to kill? He went to do it September 21st. It failed, so he came back on the ferry two weeks later to do it. *Where* is the conscience, *where* is the empathy?"

O'Shaughnessy said quietly and firmly, "Buried in a desire to be one of the group."

"You say he might not do it again?"

"That doesn't mean he won't do it again. We have no way of predicting. We'd have been absolutely wrong if we'd said on September 21st that David would never do anything like this."

"Yes, yes," said Madigan, "ever so wrong. Because this is first-degree murder. But he had the chance to get out of it after September 21st, and you would have said that, if he was normal, he would have taken it."

Again O'Shaughnessy reiterated his simple but basic belief. "He was under strong peer pressure to please."

"Derik is only a year older. Are you saying to please him he would kill? He had a chance to quit September 21st, and for two weeks after that he had his home background, his environment, and so on. And that could not change his desire to kill for money. What happened to him? Tell me!"

"I don't know," said O'Shaughnessy quietly. "He's no different today—now that he's done it."

Again in an effort to highlight the enormity of the cold-bloodedness involved, Madigan recounted the planning—the bars, gloves, and the intent to kill. Again he drew a picture of the murder scene and the meeting back in Swartz Bay with Darren Huenemann and Amanda Cousins. "And from Amanda Cousins we learn of David's mood. And what kind of a mood was it? 'A little excited and giddy.' Can you please explain to His Honor, did you know all these facts? Do you think counseling for three years is sufficient?"

"Yes." O'Shaughnessy's reply was firm. "You don't treat what is not there. Treatment is not needed. I have some explanation, but it is not sufficient. The pressures of peers overrides parents and society at large...whether it's sufficient..." He hesitated, seemed to consider, then simply said, "In any case, there is *no* evidence of psychiatric illness or personality disorder."

Madigan wouldn't let go. He wanted to make it crystal clear that psychiatry, unable to come up with any reason as to why Muir had killed, was scarcely in a credible position to rule on appropriate treatment for him. He pointed out that O'Shaughnessy knew Muir had committed the crime, yet he still didn't know why or whether he'd do it again. "And now you say that counseling is enough. Isn't that a complete non sequitur?"

"No, it isn't. [That's] trivializing what we do." There was an edge of distaste in O'Shaughnessy's calm response. "He does not need treatment now."

"As far as you know!" Madigan shot back as he concluded the interview.

Robert Ley, a clinical psychologist and an associate professor at Simon Fraser University, who'd been brought into the case by the defense, then took the witness stand. Like previous witnesses, Ley described Muir as a conventional teenager, responsible, compliant, who held down a part-time job and had a good relationship with his family. But he was also self-conscious, lacked self-confidence, and was not self-assured even with his peers. But there was nothing abnormal about him. Ley then traced the development of Muir's friendship with Lord and Huenemann, starting over the 1989 Christmas break, and his introduction to Dungeons and Dragons, a game he did not care for.

"During the summer of 1990 the relationship developed at the Huenemann house. David described Darren as narcissistic and grandiose. He bragged about money and possessions, which impressed David. Darren was prone to tease and embarrass his friends. David had had no heterosexual experience and once, on going to Darren's house, Darren told him he had a chemical that would make David black out, after which he, Darren, would take off his clothes and rape him."

"Why did David continue to see Darren?" Madigan asked.

"He was impressed by his material possessions and had difficulty objecting to his behavior. David admired another youth who stood up to Darren, but he couldn't do it himself. Because of his wealth, Darren exercised considerable psychological and social control over David. When David and Derik Lord ordered a Damascus steel dagger through a mail house, Darren announced he would wear it when he was an emperor on Brunei.''

Ley went on to discuss David's interest in knives and guns. Most youths did not have this interest in guns, Ley said, but David's was quite specific. He'd always been interested in how things worked, in trains, office machines, taking things apart. It was a normal development with parental support.

''When I asked David his reaction and that of others to bringing back some knives from Hawaii, he said that they'd been a real hit. Lots of kids wanted to buy them from him and he'd enjoyed the attention. That's why he'd made the order in summer.''

Muir was not, Ley said, an animated or spontaneous kind of fellow, but was reserved like his father. He embarrassed easily; his face, neck, and cheeks flushed. Through his collection of knives he received attention from his peers. It conferred uniqueness and status on him.

Ley reported that Vivien Muir was uncomfortable with her son's relationship with Huenemann, who never went into their home but always waited outside in his car. She disliked, too, David's craven manner when Huenemann phoned, and the fact that her son began to talk about money. At about this time David started to show antisocial attitudes, a development that Ley attributed directly to his association with Huenemann.

''He began to shoplift small items like gum. Once he dropped a stolen key chain into an open packet of potato chips and felt a minor accomplishment. When he was caught stealing gum, and his parents were informed, he experienced guilt. On another occasion he glued a penny to the school hallway floor and watched students trying to pick it up. Twice he released stink bombs at school, essentially to show off.''

Peering over the bench, a testy Judge Varcoe cut into the saga of schoolboy antics. ''Assuming that David Muir committed the offense, is it correct we are dealing here with an intelligent, normal, young man who killed for profit?''

Ley balked at the description of Muir as greedy and acquisitive, and responded with a succinct but perhaps critical assessment of David Muir as "essentially a compliant youth who was seeking social acceptance, recognition, and a sense of membership."

As for the rewards of the crime, Ley said, they were quite impractical. "How could David drive a flashy new car or own some land? What would his parents say? This doesn't support greed as the sole motive. What emerges is a picture of a youth who is extremely susceptible to other youths whom he admires and is dependent on."

All this time Madigan had been listening with the air of a tiger dozing half-hidden under the bushes. Now he stepped forward and asked mildly, "You're a psychologist?"

"Yes."

"Just what *is* the expertise of a psychologist?" He paused. "What can you actually *do*? For instance, are you trained, are you qualified, to predict the future?"

"No."

"Then...why...are...you...doing...it?"

"Because I have an opinion about it."

"Do you know what the crime of first degree is?" Madigan asked. "This is the crime that carries with it the most serious level of blameworthiness—subjective foresight of death. The penalty is severe, and deservedly so. If any of the facts that David gave you were inaccurate, then your conclusions would be inaccurate."

"They could be incorrect," Ley conceded.

"*Would* be incorrect," Madigan countered.

After further jousting over the validity of some of the psychologist's judgments, Madigan charged, "You have branded David an immature this and that—and yet all you have said is based on what David told you. What do you know about the murders? Tell the court what you know."

"They traveled to the home of the victims, struck them with steel bars, and purportedly slashed their throats."

"Not purportedly! They did it! You never asked Muir anything about this?"

Ley said he had not. Not a single, solitary word? inquired Madigan. Ley replied that discussing the crime would have been unethical, and improper from a legal viewpoint. "[In my role] you are not acting for the court."

Madigan brushed this consideration aside. For him the fact remained that the missing information was of such significance that Ley knew nothing about Muir's true emotional and intellectual state, his planning, or reaction to the crime. Again, he made sure the court was getting the message. "You've described him gluing a penny to the school floor, and stink bombs. But you are missing the gold nugget. Compared to murder, they pale to insignificance."

Ley agreed that if he had such information, it would probably change his mind. He nonetheless felt he had some valid answers.

"Guesses," snorted Madigan. And when Ley said very calmly, "No, opinions," Madigan snorted again, "Guesses!"

"When you are missing the most important information in his life, they are guesses. You know nothing about the most dangerous, the most cruel, act he ever committed. His disloyalty to his parents, to his young siblings, to society, to his friends—not to the loony ones—to his school. All that's missing. Is it fair to give His Honor a guess?"

Ley said yes, he believed it was, and for another half-hour the struggle between the black-and-white world of law and the multi-layered grays of the mind continued, Ley steadily maintaining that while "some things" were missing, other information about Muir that was knowable and true was available.

In summing up the significance of his struggle with Ley, Madigan said, "You say 'he's not aggressive or violent—excluding his current charges.' But these charges stand out like sore thumbs. How *can* you say he is not aggressive or violent? You can't say he isn't. Everything you say is subject to the missing information!"

"Ethically, and for potential legal reasons, I couldn't discuss it [with Muir]," Ley replied. "Your questions imply we could achieve a perfect understanding of a person's motives. And we can't."

"So it's a guess."

"A professional opinion."

"A defective opinion."

"I do not believe that," said Ley.

When Madigan was finished, Macaulay told the court that David Muir's parents wished to make a statement. Leaving her place, Vivien Muir moved forward and stood before the judge in the body of the court. Red-eyed, her voice shaking, she read from a prepared statement held in trembling hands:

" 'We have always found David to be reliable in looking after the house when we were away. He took responsibility and was no problem at all. He was very caring for his siblings, our cat and dog, and when the cat had kittens always made sure there was a bed for the kittens. He always knew if a pet was wounded, and would put medication on it.

"David always made us proud of his accomplishments at school, with his music, and in sports. He did not have many friends, but those he had were wonderful people from very nice families. David has always participated at all levels of family, including younger children. When there is a case-load sale, he always unloads the groceries, and participates in family chores, working in the garden and on the lawn for hours. He worked hard, diligently, and was reliable. We always played family golf together. He gave us, and we gave him, love and support."

David's father, John, conservative in grays and tweed jacket, then stepped forward. A qualified horticultural-agricultural expert, John Muir read his brief statement in a clear, strong voice: "We love David very much. We keenly regret these circumstances. But I feel David is a responsible young man and, regardless of the outcome, feel he will make a contribution to our society."

The strong, clear voice was a reflection of John Muir's dignity; as he turned and resumed his place beside his wife, his face was ashen.

Although Doris's family and friends were exhausted by the intensity of the Muir hearing, which they had attended daily, it had lacked the irritable, confrontational edge that had saturated the transfer hearing of Derik Lord. Usually the Muirs were alone, or with two or three friends or older relatives. They stayed away from the crowd around the courtroom door and seldom spoke, even to each other. They seemed numb with sorrow. David carried a paperback and read continuously.

Now, as the Muirs resumed their seats beside their son, a few tears were shed on both sides of the court for the couple. Among the spectators, the feeling of bewilderment was palpable. They had relied on the experts to explain everything—to say, "*This* is why he did it, *that* is how it all came about." But the experts had explained nothing. One woman voiced the confusion of many when she later commented in the courtroom hallway, "The things that mother said—it could have been my son she was talking about."

Both Crown and defense gave brief summations, the final skirmish in the struggle to draw, from the twilight zone of psychiatry and the harsh illuminations of law, something that would recognize the tensions involved between the needs of society and the needs of the individual, and create something akin to justice for both.

Madigan stated they were all seeking "a right and proper solution based on the probability of rehabilitation and the danger to the public" and that it was his task to persuade the court that a transfer was "necessary and imperative" and that it "must appear as the right and proper solution." It did not have to be exceptional, unusually clear, or even necessary. He lambasted the psychiatric opinion as "worthless" because none of the experts had discussed the crime with the accused, and pointed out that the public interest was not confined to the rehabilitation of the offender.

"We are dealing with an execution-style killing, senseless, premeditated, brutal. Three years is clearly inadequate...The real issue is what this offense is, and the punishment associated with it. The killings couldn't be worse. We can use all the words we want, but the women were murdered for money...They had to be disposed of so that Darren Huenemann could become rich. And for reasons we don't know, two young men from Saanich decided to carry out the murders as described by him.

"A jury trial would satisfy the public—it would have the benefit of participation of citizens in the outcome. David Muir was a contract killer hired out to kill for profit. It would," Madigan concluded, "make a mockery of the law if he is not tried in an adult court before judge and jury."

In launching his submission, Macaulay stated that it was legal precedent and opinion that should inform the court's final decision, and declared the comments of Chief Justice Al McEachern as being of "crucial importance."

"To quote the Honorable Chief Justice, 'The provisions of the Young Offenders Act, with its maximum of three years' detention, is clearly inadequate in cases of first-degree murder, and the Criminal Code, with its mandatory imprisonment for 25 years, is equally inadequate in cases where a sixteen-year-old youth may be convicted of that offense. Applying both the liberal philosophy of the Young Offenders Act and ordinary criminal-law principles, it is my view that when both statutes are inadequate...the view most favorable to the youth should be adopted. Similarly, a youth has a 'right,' under Section 3(1)(f), to the least possible interference with his liberty that is consistent with the protection of society. It seems to me that the proper operation of the Young Offenders Act can hardly ever accommodate a transfer to the regular courts if the youth risks a mandatory sentence that may be more than is consistent with the protection of society.' "

Macaulay wrapped up his summation by pointing out that the psychologists and psychiatrists who'd assessed Muir had had good reason not to discuss the crime with him. Although the Crown followed a convention of not calling them in later as witnesses at any subsequent trial, there was no law to prevent this.

"Huenemann," Macaulay said in his conclusion, "described himself as the duke of Borneo. As Caligula. As His Celestial Highness. As legal counsel. As an appropriate subject for a bronze statue at his school." And David Muir, he said, was just "a malleable little boy."

He paused. "As for the second-degree charges offered by Madigan—that's a tail-wagging suggestion, inappropriate and improper. If Crown felt there was evidence for a second degree they should have stayed the charges and started all over again. They are not entitled to ask the court to participate in this unholy bargain.''

The transfer hearing for David Muir was over.


On April 15th, Judge Varcoe handed down his decision on the transfer hearing of Derik Lord. After citing the premeditation involved in the crime, the disparity in sentencing between youth and adult court, the question of Lord being a danger to society, and the appropriateness of a jury trial, Judge Varcoe ordered that Lord be proceeded against in adult court.

On April 29th, he ordered David Muir to also stand trial in adult court. In addition to the same considerations cited in the Lord decision, His Honor noted that no psychiatric evaluation had reconciled ''the intelligent, respectful personality'' of Muir with the callous deliberate murder for the purpose of profit. The professionals who had interviewed him had made ''no attempt to understand the crime.''

Muir and Lord immediately appealed. When their appeal was rejected by British Columbia Supreme Court Justice William Esson, on August 23, 1991, the youths proceeded to the British Columbia Court of Appeal.

During the first few months of the sixteen that elapsed between the arrest of Muir and Lord and the end of their battle to block their transfer to adult court, the Crown made several unsuccessful attempts to have the bail of Lord and Muir rescinded and the accused taken into custody until trial.

After Lord and Muir were initially released on bail—two days after their arrest on November 27, 1990—Mount Douglas Secondary School principal Don Neumann asked the court that the youths be held on remand because of the high level of anxiety being experienced by some staff members. In a letter he stated that staff and students felt at risk, were suffering sleepless nights, and were generally distressed. He backed his claim with statements from school psychologist Dr. Nancy C. Reeves.

By early May, when the court heard another application to rescind bail, Neumann had changed his mind. On May 10th he wrote another letter, stating that there would be "no problem to students or staff if Lord and Muir remained on bail." In fact, if Muir wished, Neumann said, he could return to school to sit for his exams. Neumann gave no explanation for his turnabout.

The initial decision to release the youths in the high-profile case had surprised both Mount Doug students and their parents, who were sometimes distressed to run into the accused downtown shopping or at the movies. Some parents expressed deep concern at the message they felt the courts were delivering to their own teenagers, and could not understand the court's apparent willingness to put the image of the criminal-justice system at risk in this particular case.

The judges deciding on the disposition of Madigan's applications to rescind bail were caught between a "brother judge's" initial decision to grant it [based on the testimony of Elouise Lord that her son was home with David Muir at 8:30 p.m. on the night of October 5th], the gravity of the charges, and the core of the Bail Reform Act, which is the presumption of innocence. To lock up an accused who has not yet been convicted is considered justifiable only if there is reason to believe he or she will commit another offense, or will not show up for trial.

Members of Doris's family were among the spectators who attended the courtroom for these bail hearings. Ordinary, law-abiding Canadians, they had had no previous exposure to the criminal-justice system and, until the deaths of their sister and niece, had never dreamed of questioning the wisdom of the court or the legitimacy of its decisions. They had accepted, without thinking about it, the formality of all judicial procedures as a reflection of an ultimate rightness of an almost transcendent order. Because they believed that these judicial procedures were the bedrock of a civilized and safe society, they took it for granted that there would be a place in the system for their own viewpoint and sensitivities.

The continuation of the accused on bail, in face of compelling evidence of their involvement in the crime, quietly devastated them. The horrors of the immediate past, which they were still trying to deal with, appeared to be less real to those involved in the processes than the future and well-being of the accused and the maintenance of the concept of "the good of society."

"We don't count," John Kriss said after one Crown attempt to rescind bail had failed. Reminded by a veteran member of the media that victims do count—that their counting is the core of the criminal-justice system—Kriss responded, "Well, the system sure has one hell of a dumb way of showing it."

Muir graduated from Mount Douglas Secondary and enrolled full-time at the University of Victoria. Lord did not graduate but attended Camosun College for a couple of semesters as a part-time student and then dropped out. He continued, however, to work at the Kmart on Shelbourne Street—selling sporting equipment and knives.


On March 13, 1992, judges Brian Carrothers, David Hinds, and Harold Hollinrake unanimously dismissed the final appeal and confirmed the transfer of both Lord and Muir to adult court. Their trial date was set for May 11, 1992.

# THE RECKONING

The case of Her Majesty the Queen vs. Darren Charles Huenemann got under way on Monday, June 24, 1991, in the Supreme Court of British Columbia, Courtroom 10 of the New Westminster Court House. The sober mood surrounding the proceedings was set by Judge William Stephen Selbie when he addressed the potential jurors—a crowd of about forty people, who stood pressed together beyond the bar. Although his words were textbook routine, the careful tone of their delivery could well have been a reflection of the solemnity that His Lordship himself was feeling. Bill Selbie, a silver-haired, distinguished-looking 60-year-old, had been a county-court judge for ten years. A year earlier, the county courts and the Supreme Court of British Columbia had merged, and in July 1990, Bill Selbie had been appointed to the Supreme Court. Although he had sat on murder cases in juvenile court, this was his first time presiding on the bench at a murder trial with a jury.

Before him sat two lawyers for the Crown, two for the defense. Sandy-haired, 57-year-old Sean Madigan was the chief Crown prosecutor. He was assisted by prosecutor Fran Maclean. Hair falling to her waist, but neatly held back with a barrette, Maclean was as serene and unflappable as she had been at the Lord hearing in February, leaving it to Madigan to supply the acerbic wit. The team for Darren's defense was composed of his lawyer, boyish-looking, delicately featured Chris Considine, and his assistant, Dan McDonagh. Thirty-two-year-old McDonagh, whose hip hair style—brush cut on top, hair down to his collar at the back—was the antithesis of Considine's pudding-bowl trim, had been called to the bar only five weeks earlier.

The center of all eyes—never stared at but covertly watched—was Darren Huenemann. Sporting a neat gray suit and looking as composed as if he were at a concert, Darren sat in the glassed-in, bullet-proof defendant's box a small distance behind the lawyers, directly facing the judge and with full view of the jury.

"We are about to take part in a very important function of our society," Judge Selbie said in his opening remarks. "We will administer—together—justice. This affects all our society. It will be your aim in the days ahead to see that justice—as perfect as we can make it—is done. It will be your aim to see that no one is made to suffer more than necessary for the administration of law. This just means a fair trial.

"This will mean financial sacrifices and personal inconvenience. You must serve willingly. If you all ask to be excused, trial by jury will cease to be. It is a cherished right. It deals with the basic freedom of individuals. The inability to speak the language, physical disability, personal acquaintance with the accused—these are reasons to be excused.

"Your function as judge of the facts is to be impartial, indifferent. If you can't be indifferent between the Crown and the accused, tell the sheriff. As you will hear when the accused is asked to plead, he has been charged with the murder of his mother and grandmother. There was publicity. If you were exposed to it, and if you feel you are unable to be impartial and indifferent, you can be excused.

"Even if your name is called, you may not be chosen. You should not feel hurt or embarrassed. It is no reflection on your integrity. There are many reasons for challenging and rejecting. You will be sworn before you enter the jury box, as I was sworn. It is one of the responsibilities you accept as citizens."

Within 90 minutes the procedure for jury selection was completed. The defense was entitled to challenge twenty times, the prosecution four. As the black-gowned clerk of the court, Linda Russell, pulled the names from a box and the sheriff called the prospective juror forward, prosecutor Madigan and defense lawyer Considine scanned them as they stood to the side, one by one. Like youngsters called up in front of the class, they were exposed, waiting, the center of everyone's attention. Considine challenged seven times, Madigan three. Six who passed asked to be excused, two citing overexposure to the publicity that had surrounded the case.

Once sworn in and seated, the jury could have been a cross-section at a lunch counter in any middle-class neighborhood shopping mall in North America, but for the fact that everyone was white-skinned and Caucasian. Two male citizens of Asian descent—one Japanese, one Chinese—had been on the roster and were challenged. The end result was six males, six females, aged from early twenties to mid-fifties, but the majority in their thirties. As a group they reflected the variety of dress, hair, and personal style that is the legacy of the 1960s to the 1990s. In tailored suits, ankle-length denims, miniskirts, and slacks; shirts and ties, T-shirts; sandals, high heels; hair bobbed or kinked or cascading over the shoulders; flashy jewelry or no jewelry at all; married and unmarried—they were a perfect mix of individuals, with nothing in common except society's pressing need to uncover the truth.

Addressing the newly sworn jury, Judge Selbie reminded the members that they, and he, constituted the court. "You have become with myself the judge in this trial. Your responsibility will be the determination of the facts. Mine will be what is applicable to the law. You will weigh this evidence as calmly and dispassionately as you can. There are two counts—that on or about the fifth of October, in Delta, Darren Charles Huenemann did commit the first-degree murder of Sharon Huenemann and Doris Leatherbarrow. Each of these elements must be proved by the Crown beyond the shadow of a reasonable doubt. It is not necessary for a person to commit murder to be guilty of it. A person who aids is equally guilty."

He then delivered the required warnings: that jurors were not to discuss the case with anyone, not even among themselves until all evidence was in; that they were to decide only on the evidence presented in court, and that they were not to read, watch, or listen to media reports. They were to keep in mind two basic principles: the presumption of innocence and the requirement of proof beyond a reasonable doubt. And they were to always remember there was no onus on the accused to prove himself innocent.

Immediately after Judge Selbie finished his remarks to the jurors, Considine made his first move. Crown evidence included a book of 35 color photographs taken by forensic expert David Roberts at the scene of the crime. Some were of small details: the kitchen cupboard where some jewelry was found; the jewelry itself; the microwave oven with the door agape; and the four servings of lasagna. But at least half of them were of the victims: Doris lying on her back, her ankles crossed, her arms flung out, her head battered in; Sharon, also on her back, the upper portion of her body and the surrounding floor a pool of blood. There were pictures of a wide-blade kitchen knife, another of a bloodied knife in the kitchen drawer.

Considine, acutely aware that such evidence would arouse a strong reaction among the jurors, attempted to have the most damaging pictures weeded out.

"We have no objection to the photographs," he said quietly, "except those that show the deceased. There's no contest regarding the identity of the victims, or how they came to their deaths. The actual pictures serve no purpose other than to [distress] the jury."

Madigan leaped to his feet. The contested pictures were the core of his case, providing details of the crime that Amanda Cousins could have known only if she had been at the scene—or had been told by someone who had been there. Madigan was convinced that Huenemann had killed out of pure greed, and was determined to have every possible means available to ensure that the jury returned a first-degree conviction on both counts.

"*All* the pictures are very important re the jury and Amanda Cousins's evidence as to what it was like at the scene," he retorted. Leaning toward the judge, the book of photographs clutched in his up-raised arm, he stated the essence of his case: "These will help the jurors decide whether her account represents the true facts, and, if it does, where does she get the evidence from.''

"The enormity of these pictures is beyond question," Judge Selbie responded. "The defense says the evidence of the police is sufficient. I'm being asked to protect the jury, that these pictures would have a prejudicial effect on the jury. It is not an easy conclusion to come to." For about one minute he mulled over the problem. Then he said, ''The nature of the charge is such that I do not think I will exercise my discretion in keeping them out.''

Next Fran Maclean stood to give an outline of the Crown's case. Her presentation characterized the prosecution that she and Madigan would mount. In her typically calm voice, she gave a step-by-step account of the planned double homicide. "This case is all about greed," she said. The accused had arranged with two school chums to kill his mother and grandmother because he didn't want to wait for his inheritance. She spoke of Huenemann's earlier intentions of killing his stepfather, of his statements about killing his mother and grandmother while playing Dungeons and Dragons, of the rewards he promised Derik Lord and David Muir. Evidence would be presented, she said, that showed Sharon went over to Tsawwassen every two weeks, and that in August of 1990 Darren started working out the how and when aspect of the murders.

Maclean's focus on the August date had its intended effect. It left no doubt that the crime was premeditated. The Crown would call approximately 30 witnesses to show the truth of the facts it was presenting, Maclean said. They would include cabdrivers Parmjet Bhinder and Paul Martin, neighborhood children Daniel and Greg May, and pathologist Dr. Ruth Sellers.

"We will also hear from Amanda Cousins," Maclean said. For 45 minutes she had spoken without one second's hesitation as the jury tracked every word. "And from Amanda Cousins you will learn the who, the why, the how, and the when of the murders." This evidence would include the visit Muir and Lord made to Tsawwassen on September 21st with the intention of killing Doris Leatherbarrow and Sharon Huenemann on that date, and the rescheduling of the murders for two weeks later. Maclean then moved a short distance away from the jury box, paused, and concluded her case with a simple summation of its essence: "You will want to pay particular attention to the evidence of Amanda Cousins."

Constable Darwin Drader led off Crown counsel's examination in chief with a low-keyed, chilling description of the check he and his partner had made on Doris Leatherbarrow's home at 2:36 a.m. on October 6th. After failing to arouse anyone in the partly lit house, they had seen through a window two bloodied women lying on the kitchen floor. He had radioed immediately for assistance.

Special Constable David Roberts followed Drader on the stand, and described how, after arriving at the scene precisely one hour later, he had searched the house and noted the position of the bodies, the gas jets under the burned pots, the open microwave door, the four servings of lasagna, the chaos in the bedrooms, the hidden cash and jewelry.

As Roberts picked up the book with the photographs he had taken, he was interrupted by a clarification from the bench. The photos were not pleasant, Judge Selbie warned the jurors. But the reason for putting them into evidence would become clear as the trial continued. Meanwhile, jurors should guard against letting the photos cloud their judgment. "I trust you to judge on the facts, not on the emotions they arouse," he concluded.

After the luncheon recess, however, Judge Selbie told the court that he had decided to remove two of the photos, as their inflammatory nature outweighed their evidentiary value. If they became more relevant, he would revise his opinion. The decision sat badly with Madigan, who argued, ineffectively, that the two photos were the only ones of the kitchen knives that had been used to kill the women. Although he did not say so, they were important to his case because one of the handles had the bloody imprint of a marigold pattern made by a rubber glove. The only gloves in the house had a daisy pattern.

These arguments over the photo evidence should have had the effect of preparing the jurors for the hard realities of what they were about to study. This was not so. As specialist David Roberts presented his findings during the afternoon and the jurors were forced to pore over the corroborative pictorial evidence, several were visibly shaken. One of the male jurors looked down at the photos, then up at Darren Huenemann in something like amazement, before looking down at the photos again. One woman asked the sheriff for a glass of water.

One of Doris's employees, 57-year-old Mary Keighley, who managed the Surrey warehouse, then testified that when she left the warehouse on Friday, October 5th, at 5:15 p.m., Doris and Sharon were also leaving. Sharon was intending to catch the 7 p.m. ferry home.

While this was going on, members of Doris and Sharon's family who were sitting in the jammed courtroom studied the jurors' faces in intense and stony misery. As Keighley left the stand and Ralph Huenemann was sworn in, their expressions barely changed. Members of the Kryciak family had maintained a courteous, if distant, relationship with the economics scholar from Harvard during Sharon's marriage, but now that Doris and Sharon were dead little more than civilities appeared to remain. Ralph was accompanied by his own two adult children, and as they had all waited outside the courtroom, each side had given the other a wide berth. Ralph Huenemann seemed to be as convinced of Darren's innocence as the Kryciak family members were of his guilt. He was an important witness for Considine.

First Huenemann described how his long wait for Sharon on the night of October 5th ended with the arrival of two police officers with news of his wife's death early on the morning of October 6th. In response to Considine's questions, he then described Darren as a hard-working student who had always been stronger in English and social studies than in the maths and sciences. "I offered him tutoring [when at junior school but] by teenage years you don't intrude so much.

"The relationship between Sharon and Darren was very close and very, very friendly," Dr. Huenemann testified. "They spent a lot of time talking together. He spent a lot of time talking to me, but more to his mother. It was very obvious and strong. They had a very special relationship. Sharon was my best friend, but what she had with Darren..." He paused, then continued, "Darren was Doris's best buddy. When we were living in Tsawwassen we lived two blocks apart. We would see her Sunday and Darren was in and out of her house several times a week. On Sunday Darren would rake the leaves and do chores."

In reply to a question by Considine regarding Darren's "emotions and feelings" for his grandmother, Ralph Huenemann categorized them as "very special."

"Did he have knowledge of his grandmother's business affairs?" Considine asked.

"Doris talked about business all the time. Darren was around and heard that discussion. I had a strong sense that on Sundays she clearly told him a lot." Huenemann went on to say that Doris did not want to make a will and had resisted for many years. "Sharon and I both talked to her about it and finally she agreed and went to a lawyer and had a will made. It was a few years ago. [Actual date was May 25, 1989.] I knew in a general way what was in Doris's will. I knew, for example, that Mary Matheson was to be the executrix and we argued that that was unfair to Mary."

"In your discussions with Darren what were his goals and ambitions?" Considine asked.

"They changed," Huenemann replied. "He was going to university to get teacher's qualifications for history and drama at high-school level. He was working very hard."

"Did Doris try to get him to take over the business?" Considine asked.

"Doris talked about it," said Huenemann. "Darren was of two minds about it. He was aware that Doris wanted Sharon to take it over. Sharon wanted to wind down her involvement to a lower intensity. 'This is not what I want to do with my life,' she said. So the focus shifted to Darren, but Darren wanted to teach."

"Doris was always generous?" Considine wanted to know.

"She promised him [Darren] a car well before his sixteenth birthday. Later she said, 'I realized I overstepped the bounds— you should have had input. Is it okay?' We said that depends on what he is like at sixteen and whether he's a safe driver. Then Darren said, 'I'm not comfortable with that.' In point of fact it was a year later that he took his driver's test, and he and Sharon picked a car out then," Huenemann explained.

Considine then referred to the events of Saturday, October 6th. Ralph Huenemann said that after the two police officers had left his Gibson Court home, he and Darren had sat on the kitchen floor and cried. A few hours later they went to Tsawwassen to assist in the investigation as the police had told them the trail gets cold very quickly.

"Did you and Darren have a discussion re a reward?" Considine asked.

"Yes," Huenemann replied. "I posted $12,500 and Darren the same."

"Darren was in contact with Mary Matheson about the will," Considine stated.

"It seemed appropriate," Huenemann said. "Mary had had that dumped on her without warning. Darren knew the names of all the women in all the stores, as well as the names of the lawyers. We had lived that all the years. So it was perfectly appropriate for her to seek information and for Darren to provide it."

"You have attended the preliminary, followed closely, read all you can. Based on your knowledge, did this accused do it?" Considine innocently asked.

At this Madigan shot up. "You are not asking for character—you are asking for his opinion."

"It's up to the jury to make up their minds what his character is," Judge Selbie ruled.

Considine rephrased his question. "Based on your knowledge of Darren, does he have the type of character to do this crime? Is he a person likely to commit the charge he faces in this court?"

"I've known him for fifteen years and the character I know is incapable of doing it," Ralph Huenemann declared.

Short and stylish Mary Matheson followed lanky Ralph Huenemann on the stand. Facing her great-nephew, she painfully explained to assistant counsel Maclean that she'd known nothing about being the executor for Doris until four days after her sister's death. She had never seen the will. Since then she'd learned that Darren was the ultimate heir and would inherit everything at age 25. Until that time she would administer the trust. In the meantime, however, Darren would immediately receive Doris's house, car, household effects, jewelry, and a life-insurance policy valued at $20,000. Other incidental items amounted to $200,000.

"There were bequests made to the brothers and sisters?" Considine asked.

"Darren told me there would be bequests of $10,000. He talked about the jewelry, the house, the car. He said he'd want only one or two pieces of the jewelry—the rest was to go to the family. He wanted the house sold—some of the furniture could go to the family—and he wanted the car sold. He had his own little car at home that he wanted to sell, and would probably buy another." She added, "He seemed very excited."

Toby Hicks was far from excited when he got on the stand first thing next morning. The seventeen-year-old Saanich youth had the melancholy air of someone resigned to a sad duty as he took the oath, then told of attending family-management classes at Mount Doug High. In a low, crackling voice, he repeated Darren's assertions that "I'd get half the money if I killed my grandmother and the other half if I killed my mother."

Darren's old Dungeons and Dragons gang—Peter Tyrrell, Bjorn Friedmann, and Andy Thomas—told of similar statements by Darren as he both entertained and irritated them by disrupting their Friday-night game. Through all their testimony, Darren's talk of "snapping his grandmother's neck" ran like a theme song.

And then came the jewel in the prosecution's case, seventeen-year-old Amanda Cousins.

Amanda proved to be a prosecutor's dream. Clear, responsive, gifted with an intuitive sense of where the questioning was heading, she recounted step by step the development and content of her strange and enigmatic relationship with the accused. She told of her surprise when Darren had first phoned, spelled out the number of times he had called her before their first date—more than thirty—and the fact that in early July he'd told her he would like to get rid of his parents. She recalled his repeated references to his grandmother's wealth, and the fact that he would inherit some $4 to $6 million if his mother and grandmother both died.

For two full hours she spoke of the dates she'd had with Darren, starting with a shopping trip to the downtown malls on Thursday, August 23rd and a play the following night. On September 2nd she invited him and some other friends to her birthday, after which he drove her home and threatened to kill her, and her friends, if she talked. She next went out with him on Friday, September 21st, when Darren took her out to dinner, and then drove to the Swartz Bay ferry to pick up Derik Lord and David Muir returning from Tsawwassen. She recalled Darren's anger and his explanation that the boys were supposed to have killed his mother and grandmother that evening, but that "the idiots" could not find the house. In a clipped, clear voice she told the court that when she'd said that perhaps the boys hadn't wanted to find the house, they hadn't wanted to kill Sharon and Doris, Darren had replied, "They were very excited about it."

"Darren said his grandmother was going to Europe," she testified, "and was also signing over one and a half million dollars to a retirement complex, and he didn't want to have that out of his inheritance. So he said the next attempt would be made in two weeks. A few days later he told me it would be October 5th."

The most damning testimony was yet to come. After Amanda described going to the ferry with Darren on the night of October 5th and picking up Lord and Muir, Fran Maclean asked if there was any conversation in the car on the way back to Saanich. Amanda responded by giving an account of the murders that was so detailed, clear, and informed that it could only have come from the killers themselves. She told of the boys joking about the offer of lasagna and a ride to the ferry, of the crowbars used, the knives taken from the kitchen drawer, the dishcloths placed on the victims' faces, the upheaval created in an attempt to make the murder look like an interrupted break-and-enter. She told of the $1,580 in bills David and Derik split between them, and Derik

Lord's concern that if he burned his blood-splattered jacket, his mother would notice.

Faced with this testimony, Considine had only two options to salvage his case: one was to destroy Amanda's credibility, and the other was to hope that Darren Huenemann would deliver a straightforward, convincing account of events that would, at the very least, leave room for reasonable doubt in the minds of the jury. Whether it was Considine's decision to put Darren on the stand, or whether he was acting on his client's instructions, Considine later refused to reveal.

First Considine attempted to destroy Amanda's testimony by delivering a small, lethal blow on a critical but vulnerable target. He drew the court's attention to her original statement of October 6th, in which she had completely cleared Darren, and pointed out that since then Crown counsel and the police had reviewed her testimony several times. He tried to use the fact that her mother, Sara, and the wife of the chief investigating officer, Bill Jackson, were cousins. (Jackson had volunteered this information at the transfer hearing of Derik Lord, but it had not previously been mentioned at Darren Huenemann's trial, nor was it raised the following day when Detective Jackson appeared briefly as a witness.)

Considine then spoke of Amanda as "a teenager in turmoil" because of her parents' divorce, touched on the fact that her school attendance record was extremely poor, that she'd had great difficulty adjusting to Victoria, and had often lied to her mother.

"What were these problems adjusting?" Considine asked. "Wasn't your evidence at the preliminary hearing that you didn't think you liked the teachers?"

"More I didn't like the school system," Amanda calmly explained. "I figured out it was the school system that I didn't like. Teachers have to work within the system and it was the system I didn't like. In the fall of 1990, I liked all my teachers."

"You also believed certain rock crystals would give you powers and energies," Considine continued. "On September 21st you gave some crystals to Darren, and in that [your accompanying] letter you outlined your beliefs in the power of crystals."

Amanda shook her head firmly. "I told Darren some beliefs about it," she said. "But I didn't believe it. I know that I do not believe in crystals having power."

Referring to evidence in the preliminary hearing, Considine claimed that Darren was angry with Lord and Muir on the evening of September 21st not because they had failed to find Doris's house and kill her, but because "they were making remarks about ladies on the ferry that were inappropriate." In view of the vicious and powerful nature of the previous testimony, this explanation sounded quaint. Considine then fired other barbs from the small quiver fate and his client had provided him with—that when Amanda had had dinner with Darren three weeks after the murders, she'd drunk "half a bottle of champagne."

"You describe yourself as intelligent and capable..." Considine said.

"Capable—" Amanda began.

But Considine cut her off. "Quite capable of doing whatever is necessary to look after yourself and get your way. You said you went out to dinner three weeks after the murders, and you conveyed a certain sense [of celebration] with champagne, but why don't you tell the real truth? That it was Darren's father who suggested it would be a good idea for him to go out and relax. Why don't you tell the truth that after Darren broke off with you, you felt scorned, puzzled, and angry? And after discussions with the police, you made up your testimony, based on facts that Darren had recently learned and shared with you?"

"I am not lying," Amanda cried out. She brushed her eyes with one hand.

The jury listened impassively, but the resistance to Considine's line was palpable. Mystified though they might have been at Amanda's failure to inform authorities, still they believed her, liked her calmness, liked the fact that she couldn't stop a few tears from coming when she recounted Sharon's pitiful plea, "Why are you doing this?" A little while later, when Madigan snorted, "What teenager isn't in turmoil when her parents divorce, what teenage girl doesn't lie to her mother?'' several of the jury nodded in quiet agreement.

Pathologist Ruth Sellers followed Amanda on the stand, and again in her quiet, precise voice summarized the injuries inflicted on the victims. Next came Detective Ian Stabler, who described a photo lineup, which consists of a folder of eight numbered mug shots of people who look somewhat similar and is used at times instead of a physical lineup. Stabler described how Parmjet Bhinder, the 27-year-old Delta cabdriver, was shown two photo lineups and told that the person the police were looking for might or might not be there. Police had put Derik Lord's picture in slot eight, but Bhinder did not identify it. Stabler then showed Bhinder the second photo lineup, where David Muir's picture was in slot two. Bhinder looked at the pictures for fifteen seconds, then fingered slot two. ''That looks like one of them. Rings a bell,'' he said.

Parmjet Bhinder was then sworn in. He described picking up two youths at the Tsawwassen ferry at a quarter to five on October 5th and driving them to the Tsawwassen Mall. One was chubby, about 5 feet 8 inches, and he sat in the front seat, holding a map of Delta and making small talk about the weather. The skinny youth sat in the back and said nothing.

A brief sworn statement from cab phone messenger Kathy Toyne followed Bhinder's testimony, and the second day of the trial ended.


Wednesday morning opened with a string of witnesses: Doris's neighbor Charles Smith; Sharon's neighbor Geraldine MacKenzie; young Greg and Daniel May; University of British Columbia student Julie Anne McClung; Constable Scott Brandon; Detective Bill Jackson; Sergeant Hugh Davies; and bank manager Ken Terlesky.

Stanley Dick, Darren's confidant in C Unit of Wilkinson Road Jail, then took the stand. In a laconic voice Dick told of Darren's fears that Amanda would ''damage his case'' and of his fantasies of having Amanda shot by a contract killer, preferably gunned down on the courthouse steps.

Dick was followed by Randy Brown, another former C Unit inmate, who explained how a discussion of his own problems—he was being double-crossed by an accomplice—led Darren to talk about having Amanda "done." Brown said he'd checked into it. His girlfriend knew a hit man, but when she'd phoned him on his pager he'd turned her down. The hit man didn't fancy trying to wipe out someone under police guard 24 hours a day.

By mid-afternoon Wednesday, the case for the Crown was coming to a close. The final witness was dungeon master Colin Newall. As he concluded a detailed accounting of Darren's murderous remarks at the Friday-night games, Madigan produced the taped telephone conversation between Newall and Darren, recorded on December 30th while Darren was in the Wilkinson Road Jail. When Madigan attempted to play the tape, the recording machine broke down. Since the tone of the tape was critical to an understanding of its meaning, Madigan read a transcript of it aloud, faithfully rendering each sneer, giggle, and innuendo. His polished performance—this was the fiftieth murder case he'd prosecuted—caught the full attention of jury and spectators alike.

With the case for the Crown finished, Chris Considine rose to deliver the opening statement for the defense. Considine is reputed to be brilliant and thorough. He takes great pride in the fact that his maternal great-grandfather was Sir Joseph Pope, John A. Macdonald's private secretary and official biographer, and an organizer of the Charlottetown Conference of 1864. As Considine launched the defense's opening statement, police, press, and spectators braced themselves for a brilliant blast. "We were sitting on the edge of our seats," one police officer later said, "just waiting for the bomb to go off."

But no bomb went off. In fact, Considine hadn't been able to gather enough defensive powder to make a small firecracker.

He started gamely enough. "This is a case about the tragic death of two women, and whether or not Darren Huenemann had anything to do with it, whether he aided or assisted these deaths. The defense says that the Crown is wrong, and that Amanda

Cousins has woven a web of lies and deceit for her own peculiar purposes."

Considine indicated he would base his defense mainly on the character of Darren Huenemann himself, specifically that he'd had a loving relationship with both victims, and had had little to gain from the crime.

Three witnesses offering weak, almost irrelevant testimony followed. The first was Gus Paquette, a 39-year-old erstwhile miner, currently held on remand, who said he'd been in jail with Darren in the same block as Stanley Dick and Randy Brown, and at no time had ever heard Darren speak of murdering Amanda Cousins or attempting to escape.

"Do you suffer from a bad memory?" Madigan bluntly asked in cross-examination. "For instance, do you remember your criminal record?"

Considine sprang to his feet, the judge dismissed the jury, and for ten minutes Crown and defense argued before Judge Selbie on the issue of credibility, and whether Madigan could or could not mention Pacquette's record. Permission was refused. (Four months after the trial Paquette was sentenced to seven years in prison for setting his wife on fire after he'd gone on a drinking binge.)

This unimpressive witness was followed by real-estate agent Joyce Russell, who thought the Huenemanns were a model family, although, she said, she had met Darren only at his home and while showing him other possible houses for purchase. The third witness was Sean Campbell, an eighteen-year-old student at Mount Douglas, who attested to the love and respect between Darren and his mother, although he'd "only met Mrs. Huenemann once at an awards ceremony, and it's almost an unwritten teenage thing that you don't bring up your family and, when you do, it's a fleeting remark and you don't do anything negative."

As testament to Darren's character, these witnesses probably did more harm than good, conjuring up visions of Considine's having scoured Victoria in a futile effort to find people who knew Darren and had something positive to say about him.

By the time Darren himself took the stand on Thursday, it seemed as if nothing could add to the prosecution's case; no defense witness had offered the jury, already staggering under three solid days of stunning testimony of premeditated murder, any evidence that affected the credibility of this Crown counsel testimony.

After describing a happy childhood—good grades at school, Cubs, then Scouts, and swimming lessons—Darren launched into an account of his relationship with his grandmother. According to him, it was perfect. Love, respect, consideration one for the other—that's the way it was. No hint, no tinge, however faint, of anything amiss. His grandmother was proud of her business and he was proud of her. She was smart—"Always keep something hidden up your sleeve," she advised him. She put him on her payroll, told him about her will, and gave him all the money he needed. All he had to do was ask.

"Did you play the game Dungeons and Dragons?" Considine asked.

"Yes," Darren said, "[but] it's just a fantasy game, a time to get together, to talk and have fun."

Considine continued, "There's some testimony at Dungeons and Dragons that you talked about snapping necks, including your grandmother's."

"We would talk about that, but not in relation to Gran. At least, not me at least. Andy and I didn't like this character much and we'd make things up. I don't recall anything about snapping Gran's neck."

"Also talk of offering a player $10,000 to do it," Considine added.

"No, that is not true."

Considine again asked Huenemann about his feelings for his grandmother.

"I loved her," Darren answered fervently. "Always loved her. She's my grandma." He paused to look around the packed courtroom and then declared dramatically, "Do you know how hard it is not to see my mum and gran sitting there? They are the people I need most of all."

After establishing that Darren had no need for money, Considine moved on to Darren's association with Muir and Lord.

Darren said he had known Lord in Grade 10, and once or twice in Grade 11 had played Dungeons and Dragons with David Muir. Over the summer of 1990 he'd developed a slightly more intense friendship with the two and they had gone shopping and canoeing, and done other holiday-type things.

"Did you ever discuss your grandmother with them?" Considine asked.

"Yes, I told them what everybody asked me—a very nice car—what everyone asked. I told them she had stores. Everyone knew Gran's last name and that the family lived in Tsawwassen. But that's all."

Considine then asked Darren if he'd plotted or planned to kill his mother, grandmother, or Ralph Huenemann in the summer of 1990.

"No, no way, we loved each other," Darren responded.

"Did you meet Derik and David at the ferry terminal on the night of September 21st?" Considine asked.

"Derik and David wanted to go to Tsawwassen to get themselves a post-office box on the United States side. They didn't have people to drive them to the ferry, so I did it. So then I picked up Amanda and we came back to my house, basically sat around, watched television, and talked, and then we went and picked them up at the ferry."

"Amanda Cousins said you were angry," Considine stated.

"Yes, I was," Darren said. "Amanda Cousins was in the car and they were saying things I didn't think was [*sic*] proper to say in front of her, and I went inside and said it was entirely improper." He added that the boys had arranged for a post-office box because they wanted to ship in dirty movies.

"Had they told their parents where they were on September 21st?"

"David Muir did not tell his. Derik Lord told his. His [David's] were out and he was supposed to be baby-sitting," Darren said.

Considine then turned to the day of the murders. "What did you do on October 5th?"

"I went to school and in the afternoon took Derik Lord and David Muir and we drove to the Swartz Bay ferry terminal."

"Why did you not tell the police that?" Considine wanted to know.

"Because when [the boys] came back later they asked us not to say anything because, they said, David's parents would ground him. There was no alibi! Just a statement to keep two people from being grounded!"

Asked what happened after that, Darren said he waited at home with Amanda Cousins and then later picked the two boys up. He took them, then Amanda, home and went to bed because early in the morning real-estate agent Joyce Russell was bringing by a client who had expressed interest in buying the Gibson Court house.

When Considine pointed out that he'd misinformed the police regarding Muir and Lord, Darren said that he "felt there was nothing. It wasn't necessary for the police, knowing that." Indignantly he added, "Those people were my friends. Just to keep two people from being grounded!"

Daren then described the arrival of the police at 6 a.m. the following morning, his visit with Ralph Huenemann to the Delta police station, his offer of a reward, the advice he gave to the May boys to report anything they'd seen to the police, and, finally, his tour of Doris's house—"torn up and covered in black dust"— which the police had requested to determine what was missing. On Tuesday he returned to school because he wanted to be around his friends.

"Did anything occur that made you change your mind regarding the ferry trips [of Lord and Muir]?"

"Yes, the police wanted to know..." Darren replied.

"Why didn't you say they went over on the ferry?" Considine asked.

"Because Derik Lord at school said we couldn't do that, that [if I said nothing] the pressure would be off. And that's when Derik told me they'd been involved. Lord said he and David Muir had gone to Tsawwassen and had been at the house."

"Did they tell you why?" Considine asked.

"They said they went over to do a break-and-enter." At this point he sighed and said piously, "Dad always told me it wouldn't do any good to talk about money in front of people." Then he went on: "They said they'd gone over, they'd gotten into the house...I didn't want to know these things...they were in the house, they heard a car drive up, they hid, hoping to slide out of the doors without Mum and Grandma noticing. When they came out of hiding, they looked at them in recognition, and that's when Derik and David took two crowbars they had with them and they hit Mum and Grandma. Then Derik Lord said they stabbed them, and they managed to get only a few things that they had gone over for, and then they left the house."

"What was your reaction?" Considine asked.

"I thought he was joking," Darren answered. "But he told me it wasn't a joke. He told me that if I did say what I knew, both of them would make a statement that I'd wanted them to do this. I was frightened and agreed not to say anything."

"Why didn't you tell your father, Ralph?" Considine then asked.

In a voice thick with sincerity, Darren replied: "Do you know how hard it would be to tell him that two people I knew had done something like this? I loved my father and didn't want to hurt him at all." His voice started to rise. "Not only that! I didn't want them imprisoned! They had murdered my mother and my grandmother and 25 years was nothing! I wasn't there when Gran needed me most! And do you know how that hurt me? I wanted these people to pay and I still do!" Darren's voice rose even higher. "No! Not life in prison! *This* was a family affair! I wanted to kill them. So I agreed, I agreed to participate in helping them for a time."

"Why didn't you tell your lawyer?" Considine asked next.

"I didn't tell you, Mr. Considine, because I didn't want you to do anything. I could deal with it on my own. I owed it to Mother and Grandma to do it myself. I didn't tell anyone except Amanda Cousins. I *did* tell her! Amanda Cousins in the beginning didn't believe me. She said she wanted to talk to Dave and Derik."

"You continued over the next four weeks to see Derik Lord and David Muir," Considine stated.

"Because Lord said if I didn't do anything they wouldn't testify against me. It was wrong! I *know* it was wrong!"

When Considine concluded, Madigan moved in. He retraced the testimony that Darren had just delivered, eliciting the date of October 31st as the day on which Lord had informed Darren that he and Muir had committed the murders.

"You posted a reward?"

"Yes," Darren said.

"But you knew who committed the crime!" Madigan paused. "You were eager to find who the killers were?" He paused again. "But after October 31st your eagerness disappears. What were you frightened of?"

"Of Lord. Not of Lord, but of the statement."

"What? Of Lord? But he was only sixteen!" Madigan pointed out. "Both of them were going to write statements. You were not frightened of the people, but the lies they would write? According to you, you had done nothing. What were they going to do that made you so frightened?"

"Lord said he'd write a statement to the police if he was arrested, saying I'd planned the whole thing," Darren explained.

"Why didn't you make a call to the police without telling anyone?" Madigan wanted to know. "What did you care? You hadn't done anything."

"The police were getting very aggressive. They went to my father and did some bad things. They gave jewelry to my father marked Morgue B. I couldn't believe it!"

Madigan then asked, "What was your relationship with Muir and Lord after October 31st?"

"I wanted to convince everyone they were innocent. I didn't want to believe it. I was frightened."

"But they told you themselves they did it. And you went around saying Muir and Lord did nothing?" Madigan asked incredulously.

"They said if I didn't tell the police they wouldn't write the statements. I can't explain all my actions!" Darren shot back.

"Weren't you arranging lawyers for Muir and Lord? Why would you arrange a lawyer for the killers of your mother and grandmother?"

"I was protecting them," Darren explained. "I was helping them evade capture."

"All they asked was for you to shut your mouth. Did you want them to escape?"

"Can you imagine how I felt?" Darren asked. "I wanted to deal with it myself. I wanted these two people dead. I owed it to Mum and Grandma—to avoid capture—so I could do it."

Madigan then played the complete tape of the phone conversation that Colin Newall had recorded while Darren was in Wilkinson Road Jail, a transcript of which he had read in court the previous day.

"Colin Newall said these fellows were your 'hand,' " Madigan said. "Why didn't you tell Colin, your friend, 'Don't think badly of me. They did it. I didn't'?"

"Because I had not even told my legal counsel yet," Darren explained.

"This is December 30th. You talk about checking every bank account. This idea that Newall had—that you were behind the killings—was absolutely wrong. So why didn't you tell him?" Madigan persisted.

"I don't know," Darren replied.

"All you say is 'Check my bank account.' Then Colin says that he can't believe they weren't involved and you say, 'I know they are involved. If they have the same kind of evidence against them that they have against me, I know they are not guilty.' Now, that's a *complete* contradiction." Madigan paused. "You, the son, the heir, the only heir, had major evidence. Yet here you are, chatting on in a rather jovial fashion with a witness who may be testifying, and you never even hint to him that there is another story that will reveal all! All you say is 'I have stuff on everybody. Andy, too. I am an actor, so I'm not too concerned.' " Madigan paused once more. "So you engaged in this farce..."

"I was frightened...frightened about statements," Darren said.

"But you knew Muir and Lord were arrested! You regard them as killers—you knew how they killed. Lord told you on October 30th—and they were released on bail and you did nothing about it."

"What could I do?" Darren's tone was peevish. "I was in the middle of a court proceeding. You don't want to hear the truth from me!"

"Were you agreeable they should be released?"

"No," Darren shot back, "they should never have been released.

Madigan threw down his notes on the desk and asked one final question. "So you went on with this charade, this farce, for weeks so that you could kill both boys later?"

When Darren started up again that Lord and Muir had "killed my gran and mum, sir, and 25 years is not enough," Madigan cut him off with the words "This is the case for the defense."


There was little that Chris Considine could do to neutralize the overwhelming impression of lies and histrionics that Darren's testimony had created. There was almost a sense of sympathy for the hopeless task ahead of him as he rose to make his final arguments. The only possibility of acquittal lay in raising an element of reasonable doubt. In a low-keyed voice, Considine launched a step-by-step attack on the credibility of the evidence presented by the Crown.

He urged the jury to realize that all evidence can be interpreted differently. Evidence given by the Dungeons and Dragons players, for instance, merited no weight whatsoever. So Darren might have made comments about "snapping Gran's neck." But that didn't mean he was premeditating murder! These silly comments, made as a joke in the setting of a fantasy game, proved nothing.

As for Amanda Cousins—"the linchpin of the Crown's case"—what kind of seventeen-year-old girl, knowing that a murder was being planned, would not have sought to stop it?

"There are difficulties with Amanda Cousins's statement and they point to the fact she's not telling the truth," Considine said. The jury listened intently. They were mystified about Amanda's role and hoped Considine might provide an answer. ''Put yourself in the shoes of a girl, seventeen or eighteen. She tells of great and elaborate details of an aborted attempt at murder on September 21st, and is told in due course it would be done. She knows the persons to be murdered. Wouldn't you have sought protection [for them]? She did not go to the police. Her cousin is Detective Jackson. The reason she didn't go to the police was not fear of being stuffed. There was nothing to go to the police about.

''Why is Amanda Cousins not telling the truth?'' Considine asked. ''People lie for any variety of reasons. You can't put your finger on it.'' The face of every jury member was intense with concentration. Considine plunged ahead. ''Revenge! Revenge because the relationship was breaking up! Look at her background! Four years before, her home had broken up. The family moved around. Her school attendance was irregular. She admits lying to her mother. She was not straightforward. She admits the breakup in her relationship with Darren Huenemann. When you look at her background, odd schooling patterns, you can only conclude she was lying.''

The jurors moved in their seats, their eyes no longer on Considine's face. His scoffing at Amanda's background had lost them.

Considine labored on. His final arguments that Darren had no need for money, had no motive for the murders, weighed lightly in the face of Darren's theatrical plots for revenge. Even Considine's final words struck an ironic note. ''Adolescents are immature. They think they can be saviors of the world. While Darren Huenemann's actions were foolish and wrong, this does not constitute proof beyond a doubt that he was guilty of these murders.''

Madigan then began his closing remarks. ''In the past you've seen facts like this on TV. One of the benefits is that you are ordinary people who bring in common sense, knowledge of human nature, and a knowledge of life. Whether the evidence makes sense to you—that's all stuff that you have learned in your own life.

"The best plan is to look for motive. Who was going to benefit from the death of Sharon and Doris? Clearly, he [Darren Huenemann] is the one who is going to inherit all those millions. He's obviously been brought up that way—told about executors, told about stores, he is told everything. His father said it and he said it.

"The best way for you to start is away from all witnesses. In Exhibition One [the photo book] you find the real solution to this case. With your own eyes. Because in Exhibition One what do you see? You see two dead women. You know from Dr. Sellers their throats are cut. You know again from Sellers and from the pictures that each one has been savagely beaten on the head. Each has a dishcloth on the face. Two plates on the counter with food on them. Next to them two empty plates. A dish of lasagna with four pieces. A microwave with the door open. A drawer with knives with blood on the handle. You can see a key on the floor, an empty hiding place outside the building. You can see a sliding-door bolt on the floor inside. You can see the house is all messed up. The knife in Doris Leatherbarrow has markings of a marigold glove—and those gloves are not in the house.

"You don't have to be a film director to know these two women were preparing a meal. Two empty plates—two persons had arrived. The fact that they were known—invited. You don't leave a microwave door open all day. Then somebody, the visitors, struck these women on the head. And for some reason cut their throats. The pictures then show the effort at a phony robbery. Why did they kill them? They seemed to know them. Add to this the evidence of Mary Keighley that she saw them [Sharon and Doris] at five oclock and Sharon was getting the 7 p.m. ferry.

"When you stop at this particular time without any names and see these facts—then you think of Amanda Cousins and listen to her evidence as to what the plan was—that they were to go to Tsawwassen on the 3 p.m. ferry, take a cab, were to knock on the door, say they were visiting—that Sharon was friendly and would let them in. Then Lord and Muir were to hit them, use kitchen knives, leave the house messy, use gloves—remember the 'marigold' gloves? Where would Amanda Cousins get this information? No one has ever said Amanda Cousins was a killer, not the slightest hint. What is hinted is that she got it [this information] from Derik Lord. There is no evidence that Derik Lord knew the grandmother. According to the accused they went to Tsawwassen to do a break-and-enter. Imagine! With all the houses in Victoria they had to go to Tsawwassen to do a break-and-enter!''

At that point the emotionally wrung-out court rippled with laughter.

''This account is as phony as a $3 bill,'' Madigan said. ''This account of a break-and-enter could not have resulted in these pictures! You have been told that Darren Huenemann is bordering on a saint. You met one Darren Huenemann in this courtroom, and on the [Newall] tape you met another—a sneering, arrogant Darren Huenemann, a completely different fellow from the one crying in the witness stand. But he didn't realize anyone was listening to him—'We'll fry them in the witness stand. I've got dirt on you.' That's the man with the air-conditioned car, the man with lots of money, the man with a thirst for more money.''

Referring to Darren's testimony, Madigan went on, ''The accused tells us that he knows nothing about these things, that he found out about them on October 31st. 'I didn't tell anyone because Lord and Muir would put out a statement on me,' he said. 'I didn't tell a soul, didn't ask for help, but what I did do was get them lawyers. I was going to help them. Why? Because I was going to keep them alive so I could kill them.' This is a person who knows the killers of his own mother but because he's afraid for his own hide he tells nobody.

''All the evidence points in one direction. For pure greed and the hunger for money Darren Huenemann had his mother and grandmother killed so that he could inherit all the millions without sharing a cent.''

The jury agreed. Only three hours after retiring, the six men and six women filed back into the courtroom. Two women clutched handkerchiefs; one woman dabbed her eyes.

''Foreman of the jury, have you reached your verdict?'' clerk of the court Linda Russell asked.

"Yes, we have. On count one, we find Darren Charles Huene-mann guilty of the first-degree murder of Doris Leatherbarrow. On count two, we find Darren Charles Huenemann guilty of the first-degree murder of Sharon Huenemann.

A subdued but terrible sobbing broke out in court as a now-uncontrolled grief broke through the tough facade the Kryciak family had maintained throughout the ordeal.

Judge Selbie waited a moment and then quietly said, "Darren Huenemann, are you ready for sentence? Do you wish to say anything?"

Considine, who had gone to Darren as the jury filed back in, patted him on one hand, and said, "Be brave, good lad!" now turned to look again at his client.

Darren stood. "My Lord," he began, in a thin adolescent voice, "whatever this court, and whatever this jury may say, I am not guilty of the charges against me. I have no anger. All I find is a hurt, a deep scorn, that I could do such a thing. And even though they may take away my freedom, my liberties, my rights, and basically myself, I will always have memories of Mum and Gran to cherish. I thank you, my Lord, and this court, for a speedy verdict."

In a subdued voice Judge Selbie pronounced sentence. "Darren Huenemann, I sentence you to imprisonment for life without eligibility for parole for 25 years of your sentence. Court dismissed."

As the door to the side of the court closed on Darren, he dropped his mask. "Fuck this court!"

In two minutes the courtroom was empty; in five minutes the corridors were cleared; and in ten minutes Darren Huenemann was shackled in the back of a police van, en route to prison for life.

# Part IV

**Caligula:** How bitter it is to know all, and to have to go through to the consummation! Listen! That was the sound of weapons. Innocence arming for the fray—and innocence will triumph. Why am I not in their place, among them?

*Caligula*, Act 4

# REASONABLE DOUBT

## Monday, May 11, 1992

Nineteen months have passed since Doris Leatherbarrow and Sharon Huenemann were murdered, eleven months since Darren Gowan Huenemann was sentenced in this New Westminster courthouse to life imprisonment for organizing the killings. Justice has taken its time, but in an hour Darren's high-school hit men, David Muir and Derik Lord, will at last go on trial.

One hundred and forty citizens have been called for jury duty, twelve will be chosen. The candidates jam the hallway. A sheriff arrives and, unlocking the courtroom door, orders all potential jurors inside. Until selection is complete, there's no room for anyone else.

About forty people sit outside in groups and wait, glancing at one another with a tired, indifferent familiarity. There is the Leatherbarrow-Kriss group: Ralph Huenemann, looking aged and strained, with his daughter and son-in-law; the police investigating team; journalists; habitual court gawkers. The Lord family is out in full force—Derik's sisters and aunts and grandmothers and cousins occupy one corner. In the center of the group sits Elouise Lord, calmly knitting. Her hair is grayer, her face sallower. She has a grave manner and a sweet smile. "He had to work," she tells a reporter who enquires after her husband, David.

The Muirs are nowhere to be seen. Caught in a situation they can still only half believe in, they stay away until the last possible moment.

Two brutal murders have brought these groups together, but the atmosphere evokes a theater foyer before the last bell rings. Looking sober and preoccupied, Crown counsel Sean Madigan pushes through the crowd, as assistant Fran Maclean follows in his wake. White-haired Harold Rusk, who is replacing Malcolm Macaulay as Muir's defense, arrives with his assistant, Tom Morino, a former self-styled jack-of-all-trades and, for the last six years, a lawyer. Next comes Lord's counsel, Peter Firestone, his dignity undiminished by the folds of his shirt that hang out between his waistcoat and trousers. Beside him, in an ankle-length black skirt, is his assistant, Susan Beach, four days short of being called to the bar. Their gowns—black, full, medieval— are the stuff of theater.

This is the moment that Doris's family and friends have waited for. As the door of the courtroom closes and jury selection begins, John Kriss voices his outrage that Lord and Muir have been able to go on living "as if nothing had happened" while his family haven't been able to bury their dead and get on with their lives.

"Not that our lives will ever be the same," John's sister, Anne Ward, comments. Quietly, the Leatherbarrow-Kriss group swap stories of their changed lives, of newly acquired fears—noises in the house, strangers on the street, underground parking lots and basements, late-night telephone calls. Their anxiety for the physical safety of their children has doubled. The simplest things trigger unease: their sense of security has gone.

If Elouise Lord hears any of this she gives no sign. For relatives of the two accused, the wait has been just as endless. "It breaks your heart," whispers Marie Jacob, Derik's maternal grandmother, a sad-eyed slip of a woman, who, after all these months, still seems in shock. None of these people committed the crime but it taints every aspect of their lives. The financial cost has been the least of their problems. Still, the defense has taken everything. The Muirs emptied their bank account, then mortgaged their house to pay their legal costs. As all their savings have gone, David's counsel, Harold Rusk, will be paid by Legal Aid. The Lords also spent their savings, and then took out a first mortgage. When that was gone, they took out a second.

Nevertheless, Elouise Lord seems oddly upbeat. When a reporter remarks on her tranquillity, Elouise says that their nightmare will be over as soon as she tells "the truth." She smiles enigmatically and refuses to elaborate. She can only mean one thing—that she will testify under oath, as she did at her son's bail hearing eighteen months earlier, that Derik and David Muir were home with her on October 5th at 8:30 p.m. This being the case, it's clear that Firestone, known for his dedication to his clients, has geared up for a big fight. His weapons will be presumption of innocence and reasonable doubt.

Inside the courtroom Derik Christopher Lord and David Michael Muir sit side by side in the bullet-proof prisoner's dock, watching the jury selection. They face Justice Thomas Kemp Fisher, seated high on his bench and resplendent in the crimson and black robes of the Supreme Court of British Columbia. Justice Fisher is a meticulous jurist in his late fifties who hides a stern, austere temperament behind frequent tight smiles.

Both boys have grown into men since Judge Jack Varcoe ordered them, thirteen months ago, to be tried in adult court. David Muir has lost his baby fat: his chubby cheeks have gone, his shoulders have filled out, and his hips have slimmed down, although his full mouth has the same droop at the corners. In a gray tweed jacket and pressed jeans, David Muir looks like a conservative university undergraduate, which is what he is. He has made good use of his bail time to finish Grade 12 and complete first year at the University of Victoria.

Derik Lord has filled out slightly. The unflattering brush cut is gone and with it the lean, mean look. His thick, brown hair is combed back neatly from his face with its brown eyes, thick brows, and small, weak-looking mouth. He wears a dark-green knit jacket and cream-colored jeans. Derik did not finish Grade 12, but was accepted at Camosun College in Victoria. He dropped out when one teacher, aware of the charges against him, refused to accept him in her class. Since then he has spent his bail time working half-time at the Kmart, and keeping up his judo. He now has his green belt.

By 11:30 a.m. five women and seven men have been sworn in. The jury is young (the median age is about thirty-six) and predominately blue-collar—if wearing crew-neck cotton T-shirts in court signifies anything. The women appear to be in their mid- or late twenties and favor shoulder-length hair. There are two older men: one of them, strong-featured and serious, has been chosen by his colleagues to act as foreman.

Judge Fisher warns the jury that the trial will last about three weeks. If anyone has read or heard of anything related to the Huenemann trial, he or she must scour it from their minds. At that, press members sitting in the front row exchange dubious glances. The Huenemann murders and subsequent trial had led the nightly television news and press headlines for weeks. Does anyone really believe it's possible to find twelve people who have no opinions about this case?

"Come to court with a cleansed mind so afterwards you can say, 'I came to my decision on a level playing field,' " exhorts Judge Fisher. "I am the filter. If it sifts through me, it is material that is proper for you to hear. If I am satisfied you can hear it, you will hear it."

At once it's clear that all the legal players have differing opinions as to just what should be sifted through His Lordship's filter. These are so-called voir-dire issues—preliminary examinations concerning the competency of a prospective witness or admissibility of a certain line of testimony. These are held without the jury present, and the decision is made by the presiding judge.

There are seven issues in this case, two of them critical. Just before noon Judge Fisher sends the jury home, advising them to be prepared to return in three days, on Thursday, after these issues have been resolved.

### Thursday, May 14, 1992

The jury has not yet been called back. Despite days of argument, neither of the two major issues has been resolved.

Defense wants the evidence of Amanda Cousins excluded on the grounds that it was derived directly from a breach of Muir's Charter rights. (Police had read Muir his rights when he was arrested in Victoria but deliberately omitted to do so in Delta as they wanted Muir's statement to be inadmissible.) Firestone and

Rusk claim that the police were never interested in Muir as a Crown witness, nor did they want his statement so they could assess the value of his testimony.

In brief, declarative sentences, Firestone speaks his mind: Detectives Jackson and Tregear wanted a statement solely for information they could use to question Amanda Cousins, to get the facts they needed to arrest Darren Huenemann. Therefore, the information obtained from Amanda was derivative—"the fruit of the poisoned tree," he states with relish—and it should be excluded.

Detective Bill Jackson is called to the stand and endures a lengthy examination to establish that he took the statement of the "naïve, frightened, sixteen-year-old" Muir with one objective only—to nail Huenemann. In a calm voice Jackson reiterates that the police were interested only in whether Muir would be a Crown witness and what he would testify to.

Defense presents a second reason for excluding Amanda's testimony: the hearsay rule. "All Amanda Cousins's evidence relates to what Huenemann told her outside of the presence of the defendants," Rusk says. "As this relies on Amanda Cousins's filtering of Huenemann's statements, her testimony must be considered too unreliable to be admitted as evidence."

Defense also wants the taped telephone calls between Derik, David, and Darren kept out of court.

Madigan is prepared to protect these linchpins of his case.

"The Crown is required to put forward evidence of motive, of state of mind, and these have to be proven," he argues in the confident voice of a traveler who is on a familiar road and knows a sure way home. "There was a plot to kill but Muir and Lord are not charged with a conspiracy, but with murder. The agreement to commit a crime is the culmination of a conspiracy. But we had to prove that they killed, not that they conspired to kill. The plot included the fabrication of an alibi, and police need to show the continued cooperation of the accused after the crime. Crown doesn't allege that what was said on the phone was true—but simply that it showed an alibi existed, it showed a state of mind."

The legal wrangling goes on, day after day. Now and then Fisher cuts it short with an acerbic, "And what am I to draw from that?" Through it all David Muir sits like a statue, upright, unmoving, staring ahead. Lord glances around, occasionally yawns, fidgets.

Before and after the sessions the Lords walk past the cameras and a growing crowd of spectators. The Muirs attempt to avoid such exposure and run from their car to a back door. David sometimes holds a jacket over his head. At one point Vivien Muir, looking hollow-eyed and ill, bursts into tears when a camera is poked into her face. When the court finally recesses, she hides with her husband and son in the courthouse. Two and a half hours later, when the building and streets are deserted, they leave.

### Tuesday, May 19, 1992

Eight days ago Elouise Lord's optimism seemed irrational. The boys, after all, are guilty. There is Muir's confession to prove it. It doesn't matter that it's inadmissible: simply knowing that Muir has confessed—and that during his own trial Darren Huenemann described both boys as the killers—has made it hard to conceive that there could be a verdict other than guilty.

But what we're seeing, as the voir-dire arguments drag on, is the process of the law, and the law does not necessarily have anything to do with justice. Not one jury member knows that Muir has confessed, nor that he has described in detail the planning that preceded the killing of both women. The jury has no idea that if they acquit this pair, the decision will haunt them for the rest of their lives. Once the trial is over, Muir's confession will not remain a secret, known only to the police and a handful of others, for long.

### Friday, May 22, 1992

Judge Fisher has ruled against the defense on the two main voir-dire issues. The testimony of Amanda Cousins and the taped telephone conversations will be admitted. With two-thirds of the time alloted for this trial already consumed by legal pre-trial arguments, the jury is recalled and the real trial now begins.

Fran Maclean gets to her feet and skillfully lays out what the Crown intends to prove: that, while Darren Huenemann devised the plan, it was Derik Lord and David Muir who slit the throats of Sharon Huenemann and Doris Leatherbarrow. Their motives were money and property. She outlines the terms of the victims' wills and the discovery of the bodies by police. She names the witnesses that the Crown will call—Dungeons and Dragons players Peter Tyrrell and Andy Thomas, schoolmate Toby Hicks, Julie McClung, Amanda Cousins—twenty witnesses in all. The lineup makes it clear this will be a rerun of the Huenemann trial. The taped telephone conversations between the co-accused and Huenemann will be the only new Crown evidence.

By late afternoon Constable Darwin Drader and Special Constable David Roberts have finished their testimony. Six copies of Exhibit One—the book of photographs of the crime scene—have been examined by the jury. Once again Ralph Huenemann recounts his long, futile wait for his wife on the night of October 5th, 1990.

As Huenemann leaves the courtroom, prominent Vancouver lawyer Glen Orris stands up and leans across the aisle. He introduces himself, saying he is representing Darren in his appeal to the Supreme Court of Canada. Huenemann stops, briefly shakes his hand, and leaves. He says nothing to Orris.

## Monday, May 25, 1990

No sooner is His Lordship seated than Darren Huenemann, in dark jacket, open shirt, and jeans, arrives with a two-sheriff escort. Surprise ripples through the courtroom. Spectators in the back row lean forward and half stand to glimpse the mastermind behind the whole affair. They turn to each other in shock: he looks such a wimp! For six months before being transferred to Matsqui medium-security prison, Darren Huenemann was incarcerated in Kent, a super-maximum institution in the Fraser Valley. The experience tells. His face is pale and expressionless, his reddish-brown hair disheveled. He has a hang-dog air. The cockiness has gone.

Firestone leaps to his feet, furious, and asks that the jury be dismissed. In a low voice, he tells the judge that Glen Orris has already served notice that Darren Huenemann will not testify. When the judge dismisses both jury and Huenemann, Firestone argues forcefully that the prejudicial effect on the jury of this refusal would be overwhelming for his client, Lord.

Judge Fisher is unmoved, but promises to warn the jury about that aspect as the case progresses. But Firestone persists.

"I'll request a mistrial if he refuses to be sworn in in front of the jury," he fumes. "Throughout the first trial Crown designated his story as 'phony as a three-dollar bill.' It is therefore unfair for the Crown to recall him as a witness."

"Yes, I called him a liar and I will continue to call him a liar," Madigan snaps. "For the last year and a half it's been said that if Lord was downtown with his mother, he could not be on the ferry. Huenemann said he went to the ferry and picked them up. The Crown is *obligated* to call a witness who is essential to placing facts before the jury."

That being the case, retorts Firestone, Huenemann should be brought in, without the jury present, and asked if he'll be sworn. But Judge Fisher sees no basis for doing that and orders in both jury and witness.

The scene that follows fulfills defense counsel's fears. When the clerk of the court, Linda Russell, proffers the Bible and attempts to swear him in, Huenemann recites on cue. "My Lord, I am refusing to participate in this proceeding."

"For what reason?" Judge Fisher asks.

"My Lord, I am refusing to participate in this proceeding."

"For what reason are you refusing to be sworn?"

"My Lord, I am refusing to participate in this proceeding."

"Do you refuse to be sworn?"

"My Lord, I am—"

Madigan interrupts. "I won't call him, my Lord. It's useless to interrupt the trial because of this."

Firestone is almost beside himself as Huenemann is led out. Again he asks that the jury be dismissed. When the room is cleared he tells the court that nothing the bench can say will reduce the prejudicial effect of Huenemann's appearance. Therefore he is submitting an application for a mistrial.

Judge Fisher pauses long enough to scratch the side of his face: "Application dismissed. Bring in the jury."

When the jury returns, slightly mystified, the trial resumes. As Toby Hicks, Peter Tyrrell, and Andy Thomas give their evidence, Firestone tries to undermine the credibility of the testimony of the next witness, Amanda Cousins.

"Darren would speak in a high voice," Firestone says. "He would go on ad nauseam without saying anything. He was planning a world takeover. He was going to get together an army of 10,000 men in double-breasted silk suits and first take over Brunei."

A ripple of laughter runs through the courtroom. Tyrrell allows that nobody had real conversations with Darren. "It was Darren ranting and us listening." Tyrrell remembers other incidents: "Once when we were driving he jumped out at an elementary school and danced around, ranting and raving, screaming and laughing, for no reason."

Firestone looks smug. He has elicited a portrait of a man whose words mean nothing.

In mid-afternoon, eighteen-year-old Amanda Cousins is sworn in. "Angel face" is how one reporter aptly describes her. It's a look enhanced by an ankle-length, floral dress with a square neckline, flat shoes, and black stockings. In the last year her features have matured and softened; the trace of hardness has gone.

As Maclean smoothly questions her, Amanda repeats her story of the summer and fall of 1990 with the plots and murderous fantasies, the concoction of an alibi, the conversation with Muir and Lord on the night of October 5th. Her replies are clear and almost pat. Occasionally, Judge Fisher stops his note-taking to look down, mystified, at the witness. "Tarot cards? Could you spell that word, please? Did you say you *read* a tarot card?"

For 90 minutes Amanda talks, giving previously undisclosed details: how Darren said it would be neat if David and Derik shot her at the crosswalk; how Darren said it was a pity they hadn't eaten Sharon's lasagna as it was so good; how Derik said he'd had to kill Sharon quickly because she'd kept asking why they were doing it, and he didn't want the neighbors to hear her; how Darren thought knives were a fairer way to kill than guns, as they gave the victim a chance to fight back.

Firestone whispers to his assistant, Sue Beach. She starts searching through earlier transcripts.

Maclean has finished. In the morning, Firestone will cross-examine the "angel face" and he has every intention of making her out to be anything but.

## Tuesday, May 26, 1992

Overnight, a rope barrier has been set up to hold back the growing crowd of professional spectators. The sheriff at the door allows in journalists and the families of the victims and accused, identifying them from a list he carries. All briefcases and handbags are opened and searched. About 40 would-be spectators are told there's no more room; they wait anyway.

Firestone has decided to undermine Amanda's credibility in two ways: by showing that Darren Huenemann's statements to her were meaningless ravings, and by arguing that if Amanda had thought otherwise with any common sense she would have informed on him, or at the very least, have stopped seeing him.

Firestone has rich material to work with. He draws a picture of a certifiable lunatic—a rambling, ranting, dancing Darren talking about ruling in hell, being a demonic businessman one minute, the Duke of Borneo the next. He states that the murder plots were part of these ramblings, nothing more than "a great joking game." His next question is designed to plant the seed of reasonable doubt in the jury's minds: why would any rational person continue to date someone who planned to kill his mother and grandmother? The eyes of the entire jury now fix on Amanda's face. The question has hit home.

"Just what motivated you?" Firestone asks in an incredulous tone. "You found some intriguing aspects? A car, some means? Just what *did* attract you?"

Amanda calmly replies that Darren's tales of murder were at first "too absurd" to be believed. Then, by the time she believed him, she feared he would kill her if he suspected she wasn't "on side." So she continued her contact with him.

Firestone dismisses this out of hand. He asks how many acting classes she's taken at school, says that if she was scared she could have told Tregear everything when she was safe at home with him on October 6th. She could have told her mother. But she didn't, because the statement she gave that day—that she, Darren Huenemann, Lord, and Muir were all in Victoria on the night of October 5th—was the truth.

At the mention of her mother, Amanda bites her lip and fights for self-control. After all she's been through, it's a surprise that this reference to her mother provokes such emotion.

Firestone tracks the dates and facts of Amanda's statements. Yes, she admits, she lied to police on three separate occasions between October 6 and November 28, 1990.

"[But] when the police threatened you with being an accessory, you changed your story," Firestone charges. Pointing out that Amanda has been paid $800 a month since entering the Witness Protection Program, he concludes: "You were tired of all the police pressure, you were angry with Darren Huenemann, and you decided when confronted by Stabler and Beaudoin to pin this on Muir and Lord. And you were told by someone before then of the physical attributes of the crime scene in the Leatherbarrow house."

Rusk, on behalf of Muir, follows a similar line of attack, stating that Amanda's birthday invitation to Darren proved she wasn't afraid of him. Such an action would be something no one in her right mind would do.

"Then I suppose I'm crazy," Amanda says.

As soon as Rusk finishes, Madigan rises. He is red-faced with anger at Firestone's suggestion that "someone" told Amanda of the "physical attributes" of the crime scene in the Leatherbar-row house. The implication is that it was the police, not Lord and Muir, who gave her the details of the crime. Madigan's voice is shaking as he tells the court that "the normal thing is for the defense to respect the witness," and that he will call in witnesses to refute Firestone's allegation.

Dr. Ruth Sellers, who performed the autopsies on the victims, then gives her evidence. She's followed by Julie Ann McClung, who was a year ahead of Lord in junior and secondary schools for three years previously. McClung is a strong Crown witness. Firestone can't shake her conviction that she saw Lord on the ferry: she is emphatic that the date was October 5th.

Cabdriver Parmjet Bhinder takes the stand, and is followed by fellow cabbie Paul Martin, then cab employee Kathy Toyne, who again describes taking a call from a man named "Dave." Daniel and Greg May again describe the two young men seen near the Leatherbarrow house. Some details fit Muir and Lord, others do not. Second Officer Steve Lomax provides the hefty log books of the *Queen of Esquimalt* as proof that the ferry was running late that night.

Firestone is like a frisky terrier: he doesn't let one issue go by without sinking his teeth into it and giving it a good shake. The passage of time seems to have dimmed the memories of Bhinder and Martin. Their identification of the young men in their cabs is weak. They picked them up in Tsawwassen, but when it was exactly, they are not so sure.

### Thursday, May 28, 1992

The Crown spends part of the morning calling witnesses to rebut Firestone's allegation that the murder scene was described to Amanda before she made her final statement. Each witness denies it. Much of the evidence is repeated, and the crowd in the courtroom thins.

In the waiting room outside, Sara Cousins sits alone. Now that her daughter's testimony is over, Sara is free to speak. With little prompting, she explains why Amanda was so moved. She tells of living under police protection 24 hours a day, moving often, unable to have any normal home life, and becoming close to a teenager who is filled with anguish. Amanda, she says, has matured a great deal.

"She went through a very bad period, bitterly regretting not having said anything to me or the police," Sara says. She praises the police. "They were wonderful. They talked to her, and were able to help her. They really believed Darren would have tried to kill her, and perhaps me too. She had to work that out and come to terms with it. And I've had to come to terms with myself, for I've felt a lot of guilt."

Why guilt? Sara shakes her head. "I saw her behavior, and knew something was really bothering her, and I blamed myself for not trying hard enough to find out what it was. I saw that she'd almost stopped eating, and was depressed and nervous, and I should have tried to get to the bottom of it. I've always loved her, and always trusted her. I've great faith in both my daughters, and consider them very fine young women." She pauses. "I should have tried harder to get the truth."

Amanda's twenty-six-year-old sister, Tina, is down the hall. Told of her mother's remarks, Tina laughs and says that her mother is "up" today. She confides, "I'm not supposed to say anything because of security. But tomorrow she gets her degree at UVic." Her face beams with pride. "Despite everything, Mum's made it!"

Later in the day the court hears the tapes of the phone calls between Darren Huenemann, Lord, and Muir. Jury members pore over typed transcripts of the calls as they listen to Muir's voice telling of the police visit the previous day, and the need to change their alibis. They hear a hyperventilating Lord snap at Darren that the police are insinuating murder. They listen as Darren sneers and threatens to sue the "idiot" police. The word "alibi" keeps echoing in the courtroom along with Darren's high-pitched giggles.

The tapes having done their damage, the case for the Crown rests. Any loss the Crown might have suffered by the attacks on Amanda's credibility has been restored. Tomorrow the defense opens.

## Friday, May 29, 1992

After all the hours we've passed in this courtroom, growing daily more familiar with the ordinariness of their appearance, we still have no real knowledge of the two young men in the prisoner's box. Neatly dressed and silent—their bail conditions forbid them to speak to one another—Muir and Lord arrive with their parents beside them and their families around them. They stand respectfully, as required, as the jury or judge enters, their faces passive, their stance deferential. There's no sign these two could slit your throat for money.

Jury members have a hard task before them today as the defense opens. They know the facts of the crime, fleshed out by Crown with a multitude of details, but sooner or later they must make a decision. Making the right one will demand an immense leap in imagination. They will have to bring together the benign faces of the accused with the faces last seen by Sharon as the dishcloth descended. They will have to see—if only the possibility—black gloves on Muir's and Lord's arms and butcher knives in their hands. If their imaginations fail them—if they think criminals must look different from the rest of us—these boys will walk.

Firestone begins: "The key question is simply: Where was Derik Lord on the evening of October 5th? He was in Victoria, and I will present two witnesses to prove it. Mrs. Lord, my client's mother, will say he was home in Saanich at 8 or 8:30. The other witness is Derik Lord himself, who was in Tsawwassen two weeks earlier."

Lord, wearing an open-necked blue silk shirt, beige jeans, and white running shoes, takes the stand.

Speaking in a low monotone, Lord says that September 21st was a professional development day for the faculty, so he arranged to go to Vancouver with David Muir. His mother bought bus passes for them. Darren Huenemann, the only one of them with a car, drove them to the 1 p.m. ferry.

Lord said that en route to Tsawwassen, he and David decided there was not enough time to go into Vancouver, so they went to Tsawwassen mall instead to check out a sporting goods store there. They walked around the mall until 6 p.m. when they decided to go to Point Roberts to rent a post office-box. On the way, they realized they would miss the 7 p.m. ferry, so they called a cab and went back to the terminal. En route to Swartz Bay, they phoned Darren, who picked them up. Amanda Cousins, whom he did not know, was in the car.

As Lord tells his story the judge interrupts twice, ordering him to speak louder. Lord responds: "I'm speaking as loud as I can." It doesn't go over well.

Asked by Firestone whether he had ever talked to Darren Huenemann about killing Huenemann's mother and grandmother, Lord says no, never.

On October 5th, he says, "I got up at about 7 or 7:30. Dave rode his bike to our place and we put it in the basement as we planned to drive downtown with Darren straight from school. We stayed in Chinatown for a couple of hours window shopping. We went to a comic store on Market Street. Dave phoned Darren from a phone on Douglas Street and Darren and Amanda picked us up. I was back home at 8:30."

An exasperated Judge Fisher says: "Please speak up! I don't know how the jury is making out, and I'm only half the distance from you."

From the back of the court David Lord's voice comes loud and clear: "I can hear him back here!"

"Send that person out," snaps the judge. As David Lord leaves, he mutters "twit" under his breath.

Firestone continues, "And how were you able to say that it was 8:30?"

"The police visited me on October 16th and asked me what time I'd gotten home and I asked my mother," Derik responds. "She said around 8:30. At this time I was on a curfew set up by my mother, a 9 p.m. curfew." He went on to say that Dave took his bike from the basement and rode home, then Darren, Amanda, and he went for a drive. He returned home about 9:30.

"Why did you call Darren after police visited you at the Kmart?" Firestone asks.

Derik says he was keeping in contact with the investigation through Darren and his lawyer. That, he says, is also why he phoned Darren after Dave Muir had called him and suggested they change their story. "Darren wanted to be apprised of the investigation and I wanted to tell him the police had accused me of killing his mother and grandmother."

Firestone, in asking Lord why he had called Darren, has anticipated the Crown's cross-examination. Madigan's first question centers on the same call. Why call Darren Huenemann? Why go to a friend's home to make the call? Why not call his parents?

"By November 25th you had some idea police were interested in Darren Huenemann [as a suspect]. Why would you phone him?" Madigan asks.

"Because he wanted to know about the investigation."

Madigan asks sarcastically if Huenemann was paying him. "Why would you supply information to a person suspected of murdering his mother and grandmother?"

"Because I was with him that night. If he's a suspect, we thought we'd be suspected as we were part of the alibi."

Madigan keeps harping on the phone call. "Why tell him? You don't tell your mother or father."

"They weren't home."

"Where were they on November 25th?"

Lord says his mother is a teacher. Madigan suggests that maybe Lord phoned home and got a busy signal. Lord says no, he knew they were out.

"What time did the police come to your work?" Madigan asks.

Lord says he was working from eleven to five o'clock. Before he can stop himself, he says it was a Sunday. He backtracks in confusion: "I can't remember the exact time. I was working. I can't remember things. I don't have a good memory, I never have."

Madigan lets that sink in. Then he says: "On October 16th you weren't sure when you'd been in Tsawwassen."

"Well, I am now," says Lord. "I've gone over it with my mother."

"When you spoke to Officer Davies you didn't mention that you'd planned to go to Vancouver on September 21st, just that you'd gone to Tsawwassen."

Lord replies: "Sir, that was one year and a half ago." The reply sits ill with Judge Fisher, who glances at Lord with distaste.

"You told Officer Davies that Muir was dropped off at 9:30 and you yourself at 10:15 or 10:30."

"That's what he [Davies] put down," said Lord. "I didn't give an exact time. My mother told me [when it was]. It's my curfew."

"I don't care about your curfew," Madigan says curtly.

"Well, sir, people do. I wasn't wearing a watch and I don't care what time it is." The tone of Lord's reply isn't lost on the jury members, who are watching him intensely.

Madigan acts astounded: "This is a police officer investigating murder and you are doing everything in your power to help him and you're being accurate. So you said you dropped Muir off at 9:30 and then drove around with Darren and got home at 10:15 or 10:30. Now are you saying the 9:30 drop-off was wrong because your mother told you? Because she told you 8:30? You are unable to give an estimate of the time without your mother telling you?"

"She gave me the facts," says Lord.

The words hang in the air. Madigan then replays the part of the taped phone conversations where Muir tells Lord they have to change their story.

Madigan continues, "If, as you've told this jury, you had nothing to do with the deaths, why wouldn't you reject out of hand Muir's suggestion that the story be changed?"

Lord waffles, says he wanted to know what Muir was saying to his lawyer. He realized Muir was a suspect but he was also a friend.

As Derik Lord leaves the witness box his mother takes his place. Elouise Lord, simply dressed in a long white skirt and pink bouclé sweater, says she is a school teacher, has taught for twenty-two years, and has been married for as long. She describes buying a bus pass and a transit guide for her son and David Muir on September 21st. David Muir had heard of a sporting store in Tsawwassen which they wanted to check out.

On October 5th she was leaving for school when David Muir arrived with his bike. She returned home at 3:30 and saw Derik next at 8:30. Elouise Lord's words are clear and her tone confident as she says: "I checked my watch because he had a 9 p.m. curfew and I didn't expect to see him before then. Derik came into the house and asked if he and Darren could go driving for a while. I said yes, and he was back by 10 p.m."

Elouise says that after the police came on October 16th, Derik told her he couldn't remember when he'd gotten home. "I told him it was 8:30, and the next time 10 o'clock. I was asked about it for the first time at Derik's bail hearing."

The intent of Madigan's question is simple. "The truth is that after a police officer came to see your son, you weren't in what could be called a friendly mood with police and they were told they weren't to see him again. You really don't remember that particular day [October 5th], do you?"

Oh, yes, Mrs. Lord responds. She remembers both date and time.

Madigan then plays a tape of a brief phone call Darren Huenemann made to her at home on November 20th at 9 p.m.

"Oh Mrs. Lord," says Darren smoothly as she picks up the phone, "I have a slight question for you. All I'm wondering, on the night in question, October 5th, what time did you see him that night?"

"See him that night?" Mrs. Lord sounds bewildered.

"What time do you remember?"

There's a pause. Then: "Eight-thirty, I think. A quarter to nine. Somewhere in there."

"Okay, okay." Huenemann sounds brisk and satisfied. "That's no problem. That's all I need to know."

Madigan snaps off the machine and says he has no more questions. Grim-faced and confused, Elouise Lord steps from the box and walks out of the courtroom.

Lord's defense is finished. Now it is Muir's turn. But Rusk announces that he and Morino intend to call no witnesses on behalf of Muir. At that, the court is recessed.

As the jury files out, three of the jurors look quizzically at Muir.

Throughout the weeks of wrangling and arguments, Muir has given away nothing—he has not scratched his head, coughed, tugged his ear, or shuffled his feet. He has given no clue as to the person hidden inside the straight, rigid body, the expressionless face. Lord, with his insolent replies and smothered yawns of boredom, has at least given some sense of his humanity.

Now jury members learn that they will not get the chance to assess Muir on the stand, let alone hear his side of the story. What are they to make of Rusk's announcement? Are they wondering why Firestone has called Lord and Lord's mother as witnesses, yet Rusk has not called one witness to testify on his client's behalf? Are they wondering if it's just some legal maneuver? Or do they know that an accused who has confessed to the crime, inadmissibly or otherwise, is never called to testify?

## Monday, June 1, 1992

The trial was to have finished this morning. Crown and defense were to make their closing remarks, Justice Fisher was going to charge the jury, and the jury was going to start its deliberations.

But Crown and defense are both in this to win. From the very beginning, Madigan's feelings about this case have been powerful and apparent. A depth of response, rare in a prosecutor of his experience, has been stirred by this crime.

But if Madigan is determined to get convictions, Firestone is equally set on acquittals. He had had to battle with comparatively few weapons on a field that is generally conceded to be, at the least, uneven. Darren Huenemann's testimony at his own trial—naming Lord and Muir as the killers—has overshadowed the defense case from the start.

As the trial moves to a close, it is clear that Firestone is banking on the hope that law will make up for his poor arsenal. His only hope for his client lies in his ability to plant some doubt, however slim, in the minds of the jury.

The trial, therefore, will not wrap up this morning. Madigan is calling two rebuttal witnesses, Jacqueline MacIntyre and Danielle Protti. He isn't taking any chances that Elouise Lord's bold and public fight for her son will cost him victory.

The testimony of Danielle Protti is insignificant. She says that Elouise Lord—who gave extra tuition at a junior college that

Danielle attended—gave her a ride home in November 1990. During the ride, Mrs. Lord remarked that Derik "came and went as he pleased and was hard to keep track of."

The words bring Firestone to his feet, charging that this is not proper rebuttal evidence.

Judge Fisher agrees. In an irritated voice he snaps at Madigan: "How does *that* tie in with what happened on October 5th? Rebuttal evidence has to go to that issue!"

If Protti's words fail to advance Madigan's case, the testimony of MacIntyre is the stuff of a prosecutor's dream.

Jackie MacIntyre is a counselor on the faculty of St. Andrews High School, and Elouise Lord is one of her colleagues. In a soft, clear, authoritative voice, she tells of an incident in November 1990, following the arrest of Derik Lord.

"The school principal asked me to speak with Elouise and comfort her. When I got to her home, there were police officers there and they were searching the house. I hugged Elouise. She was very upset. We talked about many things, but I said to her at one point, 'Elouise, surely, Elouise, they have alibis?' And she said, 'No, they don't. They were all together that night and all of them are suspects.' "

During the days following the arrests Elouise visited Jackie, who lived a couple of blocks away, several times. On one visit, Elouise told Jackie that on October 5th she was with the boys all night.

Jackie tells the court that she remembers that conversation very clearly. It upset her so much she told her husband. "After that I said to quite a few people that 'Elouise is changing her story.' I was very worried, very scared for her. But I did not think it would go this far."

Firestone attempts to neutralize the damage. Why hasn't she come forward earlier with this information? Jackie explains that reading accounts of the trial [Elouise Lord's testimony] over the weekend convinced her she had to come forward.

Firestone suggests that any remarks Elouise Lord made following her son's arrest simply reflected her distraught state.

Jackie agrees that Elouise was distraught, almost hysterical. "But she was coherent enough that we discussed legal counsel,

VISA cards, and how to get money that was necessary, so she wasn't completely incoherent.'' Jackie pauses, then adds a devastating line, ''After I left the house that day, I knew that one of the boys was doing [had done] the planning, and two carried it out, but I wasn't sure who was to do what...'' Her voice trails off.

Firestone moves to get his defense back on track, regardless of the evidence that's just derailed it. No sooner has Jackie MacIntyre left the stand than he calls Elouise Lord back into the witness box on sur-rebuttal, a rare practice. He tries hard, but Elouise has little more to say. She recalls Jackie MacIntyre's visit on the day Derik was arrested, but cannot recall anything that was said.

''Did you ever tell her you were with the boys all night?'' Firestone asks.

''I remember telling her that the boys were all together and had gone out that night to visit comic stores and sporting goods stores.''

Madigan gets in the final word. ''You and Mrs. MacIntyre were friends. Do you know of any reason why Mrs. MacIntyre would be hostile to you, why she would not like you?'' As Elouise Lord sadly shakes her head and quietly says ''No,'' defense rests its case.

### Late afternoon, Monday, June 1, 1992

Judge Fisher instructs the jury that he will not consider second-degree murder or manslaugher. ''The sole issue in this case is who did it. Whoever did this heinous act committed first-degree murder.''

Firestone moves to the rostrum that has been set up by the side of the jury box, puts down some notes, and starts his closing remarks with a brief explanation of reasonable doubt, and the co-conspirator exception to the hearsay rule. Reasonable doubt is raised by the Crown's claim that Lord was in Tsawwassen on October 5th. The credibility of Amanda Cousins is the key issue in the question of the exception to the hearsay rule.

Firestone points out that much of what Amanda says relates to things that Darren said to her. He likens Darren to ''the ghost of

Christmas past, given to bizarre ramblings and fantasy,'' and asserts that there is no evidence that Lord was ever involved in planning anything. He depicts Amanda Cousins's testimony as ''a story that got larger in the telling, a story out of the movies, a bad book, gripping but without the ring of truth. She was over-prepared, too pat, like an actress. She sounded as if she were reading a grocery list.''

Firestone then harkens back to his theory regarding Amanda's knowledge of the crime scene. ''When I suggested someone told Amanda Cousins the attributes of the crime scene, someone did! This is where I come back to common sense. Her activity is inconsistent with her having had any prior knowledge of any murder. What this girl did all summer doesn't make sense! In almost every phone call Darren Huenemann talked about killing most of his family. She doesn't practice avoidance behavior. She goes out with him! They go shopping. They go to a play. She recounts—very pat—five plots. But she doesn't go to Lord and say: 'Is this true?' She invites Huenemann to her birthday party! She says that after this party her life, her sister's life, her friend Cynthia's life, are all put in danger. So does she avoid him? No. She goes out with him on September 21st!''

For 90 minutes Firestone attacks Amanda Cousins's credibility. He cites the lack of physical evidence at the crime scene—no prints, hair, fiber, or blood that could link Lord to the crime. There was so much blood at the scene, Firestone says, that there was no way ''those kids could have gone into that kitchen and not leave anything.''

Firestone describes Darren Huenemann's statements to Cousins as ''the unacceptable ramblings of a strange duck;'' scorns the Crown's restructuring of the accused's activities on the evening of October 5th as impossible within the time frame allotted; attacks the credibility of the May brothers; insists that a jury cannot convict because a face in a photo lineup ''rings a bell;'' and avows that Julie McClung had her dates mixed as to when she saw Lord on the ferry.

''Lord was unshaken under examination,'' Firestone claims. ''There's not one bit of credible evidence that he had any motive.

And, under oath, Elouise Lord has said her son was home in Saanich at 8:30 p.m. on October 5th. I'm not Perry Mason. I don't have to point fingers and say: 'He did it!' My job is simply to show reasonable doubt. If you have it, you must apply the law. You must acquit Mr. Lord.''

Firestone has spoken for more than two hours.

Rusk now moves forward to begin his closing remarks. Throughout the trial Rusk has seemed, in ways hard to define, ill at ease in his role as defense counsel. Now, in a strong voice that contrasts with his apparent discomfort, he homes in on the one possibility available to his circumscribed defense—the presumption of innocence.

"Dave Muir is entitled to presumption of innocence throughout his trial and continues to be presumed innocent throughout your deliberations. He is not obliged to prove he's not guilty. The burden of proof remains on the Crown.''

Rusk calls the Crown's theory of a murder conspiracy with Lord and Muir as the killers "a bizarre scenario.'' He travels over the ground just traversed by Firestone; points out that many people knew Doris hid her house keys; and dismisses the evidence of the Dungeons and Dragons group as irrelevant because none of the players knew the accused.

He concludes with a predictable attack on Amanda Cousins's credibility, and suggests that the question uppermost in the jury's minds should be: "Was it abandonment by Huenemann or police pressure that led to her final statement?''

Madigan begins the closing remarks for the Crown by commiserating with the jury over their tough job in having to decide "the fate of a fellow citizen,'' but assures them that their "common sense, ability to distinguish right from wrong, knowledge of human nature'' will see them through to the right decision.

He then leads the jury step by step through the Crown's case. He deftly skirts the weaker points, such as the tentative identification of Muir and Lord by the May brothers, and hammers at the strong ones. "You heard Julie McClung: 'I *was* on the October 5th ferry. It *was* the holiday weekend. And I *know* Derik Lord.' ''

Madigan then assaults the credibility of Elouise Lord. "I'm not going to tell you Mrs. Lord is a liar. *You* have to decide that.

We have Mrs. Lord in a number of disguises. 'I know he was home,' she said. Then, there is Mrs. Lord at her son's bail hearing: 'Oh, he was home at 8:30, give or take three minutes, because I looked at my watch.' But it's obvious from this [telephone call] transcript, that she doesn't know. She's trying to help. She...is...guessing. Then we have the Mrs. Lord who spoke to Mrs. MacIntyre. The Crown isn't saying Derik Lord was not in Victoria that night: we're saying he got there at 9:30 off the ferry.''

At this point Madigan produces the photographic evidence of the crime scene and, as he did at the Huenemann trial, he correlates the photographs with the evidence of Amanda Cousins. He describes Amanda Cousins as straightforward and honest, but ''a kid whose judgment was poor.''

Madigan continues: ''This wasn't a botched break-and-enter, because you know the guy who's going to benefit. He's the $4-million man. And who's fooling around with him? Muir and Lord. Why is Lord consorting with him after the police spoke to him? Because it's a gang making up stories to protect itself. Sharon Huenemann and Doris Leatherbarrow are dead. [Huenemann] didn't use his own hands but two other hands, one called Derik Lord and the other David Muir.''

As he concludes, Madigan returns to the testimony of Elouise Lord: ''One can feel sorry for Mrs. Lord. It is her son. But she is completely wrong. She's the one who told her son: 'That statement you gave Davies was wrong. You did not come in at 10, it was 8:30.' And suddenly her son develops a bad memory.'' Madigan sighs, his tone suddenly compassionate. ''The unfortunate Mrs. Lord!''

He turns to address the jury directly. ''But—what these boys did was first-degree murder. And the Crown would charge you, the jury, to convict them of these offenses.''

**Tuesday, June 2, 1992**

The time has come for the jury to assume the full burden of its responsibilities. The bizarre revelations and the fascinating legal fights are over. The realization that they now have to determine the lifelong fate of two young men is written on the face of every juror.

The hushed courtroom is jammed. Every principal player in the case is here to see the curtain fall on the biggest drama of their lives.Outside, some 50 disappointed spectators wait in the roped-off queue that trails down the hallway. There are sheriffs everywhere.

Judge Fisher's charge to the jury takes three hours. He painstakingly retraces every significant point of evidence and, whenever necessary, explains its relationship to the law. He pays particular attention to the questions of reasonable doubt and presumption of innocence. He explains the difference between direct and circumstantial evidence, and gives some general guidelines for resolving inconsistencies in statements.

As he concludes his instruction, he again states that there is only one charge open to the jury—murder in the first degree. It is a little before 3 p.m. when the jury retires and the wait begins.

## Wednesday, June 3, 1992

It's not unusual for a jury to go out for days, so this wait—it is now 10 a.m.—is nothing. But for those who know that David Muir has confessed it seems interminable. Nothing's a sure thing. The jury doesn't know about the confession; there was no physical evidence linking the co-accuseds to the crime; and Elouise Lord swore under oath that her son was home at 8:30 that night.

A sense of growing uncertainty can be heard in the words of BCTV reporter Stuart McNish as he stands before the camera on the courthouse steps doing an up-date for the noon news hour: "Yesterday Justice Fisher spent more than three hours charging the jury to find the co-accused either guilty beyond reasonable doubt, or to acquit them. For most of the more than 60 daily observers of the trial a quick decision was expected. That hasn't happened. The jury was sequestered in a local hotel last night and has been back deliberating since 9:30 this morning."

Hourly updates on radio and television have swelled the crowd of spectators vainly hoping to get inside. Amanda, still

under police protection, is here with Sara and Tina. Ralph Huenemann is here with his family, and Rene Leatherbarrow is with
Doris's. The police investigation team is here and the media are
out in force tapping away at their lap-top computers, writing their
stories in advance. They leave the lead and the first two para-
graphs blank, mindful not only of the specifics of this case but of
the old courthouse axiom that claims, heaven knows on what
basis, that the longer a jury is out the greater the chance of
acquittal.

Reasonable doubt: that's what might prevent justice from
evening the score. Can this jury—twelve ordinary citizens seemingly innocent of the extremities of either goodness or evil—
make the imaginative leap between the pictures of the murdered
women, and the faces of the healthy, well-loved young men
before them? Even the police—with all their experience and
gently jaundiced view of humanity—had trouble bridging that
gap. How could kids from good homes, without any record, do a
thing like that? Even if they wanted to kill for money, how could
they possibly overcome every inhibition, every trace of conscience, every lesson their mother and dad taught them, to
commit murder?

Firestone just might get them off.

That possibility has already crossed John Kriss's mind, who, in
an extraordinary coincidence, found a copy of Muir's confession
in an insurance file relating to Doris's death. (The confession was
placed in the file after the insurance company concluded an
unsuccessful attempt to determine whether Doris Leatherbarrow or Sharon Huenemann died first. The insurance payout of
nearly half a million dollars was paid into court.)

Now John Kriss is downstairs photocopying twelve copies of
the confession. He plans to hand one to each member of the jury
if Muir and Lord are acquitted.

Elouise Lord, sitting in the courthouse lounge surrounded by
her family, has taken up her knitting again. Derik lolls nearby.
Unlike Muir, whose burly figure appears and disappears on cue
as the trial starts and stops each day, Derik Lord has become a
familiar sight, popping down to the coffee shop, sitting on the

floor of the hall playing cards with friends, smooching with Shannon Erickson, his tall, chic girlfriend from Mount Douglas high, or sitting while she massages his neck.

Elouise looks remarkably relaxed. She smiles and mentions that ten of the family went to the Spaghetti Factory for dinner last night and they had a wonderful time. She muses that maybe they'll go back there tonight for a celebration, after the verdict is in.

John and Vivien Muir are nowhere to be seen. They have fought a daily battle for privacy. Two days ago Mrs. Muir—accidentally or otherwise—spilled hot coffee over the leg of a persistent cameraman. "If the Muirs had just given us one minute so we could do our job, we'd have left them alone," he grumbled.

Suddenly, there are three, four sheriffs in the hall. Firestone, shirt flopping out as usual around his waist, appears with Madigan behind him. Both walk toward the courtroom. The verdict is in. It is 11:15 a.m.

There is scarcely breathing room inside the courtroom. Every eye is on the jury as it enters. Their faces reveal nothing. Both Lord and Muir are now stock-still as two sheriffs take their places, one on each side of the prisoner's box, and face the spectators. Five other sheriffs are placed around the courtroom.

Clerk of the court Linda Russell turns to the jury: "Members of the jury. Have you reached a verdict as to the accused, Derik Lord?"

The foreman stands: "We have, my Lord."

"Do you find the accused as to count one, guilty or not guilty?"

"Guilty, my Lord."

"Do you find the accused as to count two, guilty or not guilty?"

"Guilty, my Lord."

"Members of the jury," Russell continues, "this is your verdict. So say you all?" Each member of the jury assents. She turns to Judge Fisher: "The verdict is unanimous, my Lord."

Russell repeats the procedure for David Muir. Guilty on both counts.

At first nothing happens. Nothing but a deep sigh of relief from the victims' families. Then they turn to each other, pressing hands, and reaching out to the police officers in gratitude and momentary affection. The accuseds' families sit still. Their grief is too heavy for words or gestures. Slowly the grandmothers physically bend, double up, beneath it. Elouise, weeping, puts her hand on her mother's shoulder, and whispers to Dawn, Derik's seventeen-year-old sister: "We must call Dad."

Briskly, Judge Fisher moves the process toward its conclusion. He informs the jury that three weeks earlier, on May 15th, there was a change made to the Young Offenders Act. A first-degree murder conviction in adult court, he explains, means an automatic life sentence of 25 years without the possibility of parole. However, if a young offender is raised to adult court and found guilty of first-degree murder, he can now become eligible for parole within five to ten years. The jury can make a recommendation to the judge as to parole eligibility. The jury is not obligated to do so, nor is the judge obligated to accept it.

The jury nods its understanding and retires. And while the courtroom waits, the spectators consider the implication of this change. Darren Huenemann was born on September 19, 1972. Had the long-planned murders been committed seventeen days earlier, Darren, too, would have had a parole eligibility set between five and ten years. Missing the new legislation by days will cost him years of his life. And at the end of it—not a penny of the longed-for fortune. For under the law, a convicted murderer is presumed to have "died" before the victim who wrote the will. The beneficiaries of Doris's estate will be her brothers and sisters.

Now the jury is back. Its recommendation is that both teenagers serve ten years before they become eligible for parole. A sheriff gestures to the accused, ordering them to stand for sentencing.

In the future, when the National Parole Board, or perhaps a new Sentencing Board, looks at the possibility of parole for these men, it will read these words of Judge Fisher and weigh them in its decision:

"A jury of your peers has found both of you guilty of first-degree murder. The circumstance of this heinous slaying is gross in the extreme. How two teenagers would enter into such a diabolical plan is beyond normal understanding.

"The viciousness of the slaying, the grotesqueness of the plunging of the knife in the throat to the spine of a defenseless and innocent person and, in the other case, the hacking in search of the jugular vein, significantly demonstrates the need for the protection of the public.

"The whole event occurred simply out of your lust and greed of material gain. For a mess of pottage, you were prepared to commit murder.

"The loss for the victims' loved ones, in some sense, equates with the tragic realization by your own family members of your participation in this crime."

Saying that he will make a decision on parole eligibility on June 30th, Judge Fisher now sentences both boys to life imprisonment. They step from the box, a sheriff on each side, and are immediately escorted to the door leading to the temporary holding cells. The crowd at the back of the courtroom is pushing out of the benches into the aisles and out the door. John and Vivien Muir hesitate a moment, as does Elouise Lord. Their sons turn, glance toward them, and then the door closes.


It's midday outside and the sun is clear and hot. The Fraser River is at the bottom of this sloping hill, no more than several hundred yards from the courthouse steps.

A log boom is moving downriver on the water's placid surface, pulled by a tugboat that has disappeared from sight. The mass of logs, drawn by an unseen force, easily overcomes the pull of nature.

Elouise Lord is standing nearby. Already, she looks more cheerful. Her eyes behind her round glasses are red but dry, and she is holding her head up. Her body is taut and poised, a little like a diver preparing to dive. All the cameras are on her as she says: "My son is innocent, the victim of a police conspiracy. He was railroaded. The police had to find someone. We will appeal..."

The last section of the log boom is beginning to disappear. The cables that pull it are not visible, being hidden beneath the surface. They must be extraordinarily thick and strong to cause such heavy timber to glide smoothly against the tide and out to sea.

### Monday, July 27, 1992

*Three months short of two years after the murders, the public show of justice has ended. This morning Justice Thomas Fisher ordered that both Muir and Lord serve ten years in a federal institution before becoming eligible for parole. Parliament had devised legislation that "protected, shaded, and sheltered" them because they had been raised from youth court, Justice Fisher said, but their acts were so cold-blooded, their attitudes so lacking in remorse, that no reason existed to give them the privilege of eligibility for early parole. Furthermore, Darren Huenemann was serving 25 years for the same act, and the public might well ask why his co-conspirators, younger by only a year, should be treated differently because of a new statute, "the logic of which rests with Parliament."*

*The decision comes as no surprise to the participants. In the eight weeks since they entered prison, Muir and Lord have changed once again. In green prison uniforms, they chat together in the prisoners' dock, laughing occasionally at some shared joke. Lord's hair is long, the restlessness is gone. Muir has grown a beard, titian and thick. Their manner is relaxed, almost brazen. The die has been cast and there's nothing to lose. As they walk out of the courtroom and disappear behind the door, it is clear the schoolboys have gone forever and hard-time inmates, the inhabitants of another world, are fast emerging.*